MILESTONES
IN A
MOTORING LIFE

MILESTONES
IN A
MOTORING LIFE

by Dudley Noble

With a Preliminary Chapter by
Alfred Pemberton

Foreword by His Grace
THE DUKE OF RICHMOND AND GORDON

Contributions by
Major Gordon McMinnies and
Group Captain Maurice Newnham, OBE, DFC
and H. G. Henly, Esq, CBE

THE QUEEN ANNE PRESS LTD
IN ASSOCIATION WITH
ADVANCED MILE-POSTS PUBLICATIONS LTD

First published 1969
Published by The Queen Anne Press Ltd
St Giles House, 49 Poland Street, London W1
in association with
Advanced Mile-posts Publications Ltd

Made and printed in Great Britain by
The Garden City Press Limited
Letchworth, Hertfordshire
SBN 362 00040 9

To

REGINALD KENNETH MUNDAY

without whose steadfast encouragement
this book would never have been written.

Acknowledgements

The author tenders his grateful thanks to the many friends who have helped him in the compilation of this book, and in particular the undermentioned:

Wilfrid Andrews Esq., Barry Appleby Esq., George Bell Esq., Reg. Bishop Esq., Herr Robert Braunschweig, Victor Bridgen Esq., Kin Burton Esq., Cecil Byford Esq., Laurence H. Cade Esq., The Marquess Camden, Basil Cardew Esq., Lord Chesham, Miss Helen Christie, Mrs. Josephine Curtis, Kenneth Davis Esq., O.B.E., S. C. H. Davis Esq., Courtenay Edwards Esq., George Eyles Esq., M.B.E., Eric D. Foster Esq., Sir George Harriman, C.B.E., Bill Hartley Esq., Walter Hayes Esq., S. A. C. Haynes Esq., Donald Healey Esq., H. G. Henly Esq., C.B.E., Sir Patrick Hennessy, Sidney Henschel Esq., Bernard Hopfinger Esq., Keith Hopkins Esq., Erik Johnson Esq., Dr. Evan Jones, Lord Kenilworth, Herr Artur Keser, M. Jacques Loste, Harry Louis Esq., Sir William Lyons, Mrs. "Bee" Masters, W. Martin-Hurst Esq., W. A. MacKenzie Esq., Dennis Miller-Williams Esq., Miss Denise McCann, M.I.M.I., Major W. G. McMinnies, Mrs. Valerie Munday, Group Captain Maurice Newnham, O.B.E., D.F.C., Charles Newsome Esq., John D. Noble Esq., Mrs. Margaret Noble, Harold Nockolds Esq., Robert Owen Esq., Miss Nellie Pamplin, Alfred Pemberton Esq., Robert B. Peters Esq., Mrs. Kay Petre, H. Sargent Pharaoh Esq., His Grace the Duke of Richmond and Gordon, Lord Rootes, Sir Reginald Rootes, Clive Scarff Esq., Cecilia Lady Sempill, Maurice Smith Esq., Sir Donald Stokes, Lord Strathcarron, Sir Miles Thomas, D.F.C., Brian Turner Esq., Harvey Warren Esq., Ian Webb Esq., F. A. Welch Esq., F.R.S.A., Lady George Wellesley, Spencer Wilks Esq., T. H. Wisdom Esq.

Contents

Foreword

BY HIS GRACE THE DUKE OF RICHMOND AND GORDON

In sixty years an awful lot can happen—and *has* happened in the world of motors. Not many people can claim, as can the author of this book, that they have been mixed up with it for that length of time.

I have personally known Dudley Noble for some considerable part of his career. He has always had a busy pen, and the recollections which he now collates into these pages do most certainly justify the title he has given to them.

Of many of the personalities mentioned in the earlier portion of this book I naturally have no direct knowledge, but it is very interesting to read about some of those who guided the motor industry in its formative years.

When he gets into more recent times, however, there are numerous friends and acquaintances who have contributed towards the promotion of motoring through the printed and spoken word, and by their illustrative art.

I was particularly interested in Dudley's record of the formation of the Guild of Motoring Writers, now practically twenty-five years ago. It has, I believe, helped the British motor industry quite a lot in its export drive, and I was happy to be associated with it during a period of years.

I do commend "Milestones in a Motoring Life" to all who like reading about the progress of what is today one of the principal industries concerned with our country's overseas trade.

Richmond

Goodwood　　　　　　　　　　　　　　　*September 1968*
Chichester

Author's Preface

During the past half century the world's inhabitants have become inured to new discoveries and inventions. It was not at all the same in the early years of this 20th century.

We who were youngsters at the time had parents born in the 1860s and '70s, and practically all the "modern" inventions they had seen make good were the steam engine and the electric telegraph.

Electricity was in an infantile stage. The carbon filament bulb was a poor and expensive rival to the gas mantle. Photography, too, was hardly to be taken seriously. When I got boyishly keen on a camera my father warned me that there was no future to a career with it. Cinematography was barely on the map, except in the most elementary state.

And horseless carriages were laughable things—so unreliable and such an impracticable alternative to the faithful equine that they might quite likely vanish without trace before long.

The penny-farthing bicycle was giving way to Starley's safety machine, which even ladies could ride if they were so lost to shame as to wear those shocking bloomers.

Roller skating was a rage for the "mods" of the period and rinks were built specially for its fans; and then it just went out of fashion utterly and completely. The same fate was predicted for many another invention. They would be a "flash in the pan" and die a natural death when their novelty was exhausted.

Everything would always be as it was and had been: the wind of change had not been heard of and could not even be imagined.

It was this attitude of mind that caused those in charge of our military forces to ignore the very idea that any form of transport save that pulled by horses could take part in a war. . . . Until Kaiser Wilhelm proved otherwise.

But in spite of my father's gloomy prognostications I chanced my arm in motors. I really believed they *had* come to stay.

Today I'm pretty sure they have, and in these pages I have set down my own personal experiences since I bought my first driving licence in 1906. Of the years before that I cannot myself speak with knowledge from ownership within my family of any sort of motor vehicle; my father was not in the slightest interested in things mechanical.

By good fortune, however, when I started to get the contents of this book down on to paper I discovered that my old friend Alfred Pemberton (almost exactly the same age as I am) had written some reminiscences of his own.

As the son of one who could justly be termed our earliest professional writer about motoring, he grew up in a petroliferous atmosphere. His father, Sir Max, tried and tested every car of note during the first years of this century and young Alfred rode with him on numerous occasions.

I am lucky to have been granted the use of Alfred's recollections and tender him my sincerest thanks. Several other "oldsters" have likewise collaborated and I similarly extend my gratitude to them.

Dudley Noble

Chiswick
London

December 1968

The Car as a Rich Man's Plaything

Alfred Pemberton RECALLS HOW, AT THE TENDER
AGE OF SIX, HE WAS IN CHARGE OF A "VEHICLE"
ON THE QUEEN'S HIGHWAY WHEN HE WAS
FORCIBLY INTRODUCED TO A HORSELESS CARRIAGE
DRIVEN BY HIS GODFATHER, ALFRED HARMSWORTH,
THE FUTURE LORD NORTHCLIFFE

I was weaned on motoring and motor cars a long, long time
ago. Indeed, in the Year of Grace 1898 I was in charge of
a vehicle on the broad highway, though admittedly it was
not self-propelled. The "vehicle" was a pedal tricycle; I was
aged nearly six and, in the high summer, happened to be
returning from the village shop in the hamlet then called
Ville de Sarre, near Canterbury. My mission had been to
acquire four ounces of "Ladies' Stockings", which were minty
sweets shaped like ladies' legs, with those bright red rings
round them such as you sometimes see in Victorian prints.

Anyway, I had nearly reached home, cracking along at
some two miles per hour—home being an old Elizabethan
mansion called "The Gore", on the outskirts of the village
of Moncton—when I saw a dust cloud approaching. The
cloud stopped and the dust drifted away to reveal a stationary
machine on four wheels, which was panting and shaking its
occupants as if they were jelly babies. I drew alongside, and
a figure in a fur coat with ferocious-looking goggles reached
down, picked me up by the scruff of my neck and landed me
beside him. I was to enjoy my very first ride in a motor car,
about 200 yards up the drive to our front door.

The car was a platinum-tube-ignited Canstatt Daimler
of about 6 h.p. with a wagonette body, and in it were two
ladies, also a chauffeur (a type of human I had never before
encountered) looking extremely smart in a green uniform
with peaked cap. The ladies wore long dustcoats with
balloon sleeves, flat hats and thick veils. The driver was my
godfather, then Mr. Alfred Harmsworth (later to become
Lord Northcliffe). He had, with the first fortune he made
(from *Answers*), bought "Elmwood", a dreamy old house set
in a belt of trees at St. Peters, near Broadstairs, only a few
miles from "The Gore". He was a great pioneer of the motor
car, and did much to popularise it.* A frequent visitor to
us, one of his favourite cars was a 6 h.p. Panhard.

Our transport, at "The Gore", consisted of a carriage and
pair, also a dogcart drawn by a pony called "Cabbages".
The gardener-cum-bailiff—known as "Dang-it"—used to
make shopping expeditions to Minster, and I would accompany him. On his way back, "Cabbages" would automatically stop at every pub along the road, and "Dang-it" would
pay each one a visit, reappearing duly refreshed. I reckon
that Minster must have been five pints away from our home!
Near by it, incidentally, was a chalkpit surrounded by
shrubs. My brothers and I used to hide in a haystack close
to it and let out moans and groans whenever travellers passed
on horseback, bicycle or foot—we did a good job in getting
the place reputed as being haunted.

During the summer there would be an occasional chara-
banc hauled by a four-horse team, full of holidaymakers
going to Margate or returning. Motor cars were a rare sight
and nearly every horse shied or bolted when one came along,

* Alfred Harmsworth was a keen protagonist of the motoring movement, and through his *Daily Mail* offered a special prize of £10 to every
competing vehicle in the great 1,000 Miles' Trial of 1900 which finished
the course and averaged 5 m.p.h. or more over every portion of the route.
He also invited all the competitors to breakfast on the first day at his
home.

their drivers hurling curses at the rich folk and their new-fangled locomotion. As that old ballad "Stone Cracker John" had it: "The rich go by in their wildcat machinery, and they kicks up a dust and they spoils all the greenery. So whack, fol-di-riddle-oh, if I had my way I'd whack 'em and crack 'em, if I had my way."

One day Alfred Harmsworth—Uncle Alf, as I used to call him—was brought to us in an ambulance, having been involved in a motor smash (probably one of the first ever) at Upstreet, not far away. He stayed a fortnight and, for a man of such drive and energy, showed considerable restraint while his broken arm and collarbone were setting. I can see him now, sitting in our garden swathed in bandages, a youngish man with a mane of golden hair and a face like a Greek statue, spotting me and calling out "Hello, Cockie!"

At the turn of the century my father took a house in Fitzjohn's Avenue, Hampstead. He was at the height of his popularity as a novelist, *The Iron Pirate* having brought him fame and fortune. Like Alfred Harmsworth, he had been a keen long-distance cyclist on a "penny-farthing"; consequently his first mechanically propelled vehicle was a motor-bike—a $1\frac{3}{4}$ h.p. Quadrant with a round belt for drive and a surface carburetter. The belt used to slip on any incline steeper than 1 in 15 when the road was dry, or all the time when wet. He soon got tired of this, and bought his first motor car, a 3-cylinder Brooke.

Mawdsley Brooke, builder of the car of that name, was mainly interested in fast motor boats, and won many international events. He had a 30 h.p. 6-cylinder car which was a real goer, and I shall never forget him taking me for a ride from Lowestoft to Gorleston, when we touched 60 m.p.h.—an unheard-of speed on the road in those days. It gave me the thrill of my young life. At about this time Father, in addition to being a novelist, became Editor of the top boys' paper of the time—*Chums*—and motoring correspondent of

The Field. As a result, we used to have new models of different makes calling at our house for him to test, much to my delight as I often got rides in them.

The Mercedes was now making its mark as the most advanced car of the day, with its smart honeycomb radiator and powerful engine. My godfather, who was never content with anything but the best, soon took them up and for years would have nothing else, touring thousands of miles on the Continent and throughout the British Isles. Tyres were the chief problem and a long journey was hardly ever made without a "flat" or two. Some tyres were plain rubber without treads, while others were leather covered and had steel studs protruding to grip the muddy road surfaces. When the two or three spares were used up, one had to be stuffed with straw to get the car to the nearest blacksmith-cum-garage, as they usually were.

One day a long silver-grey car arrived outside our house—it was the first Rolls-Royce Silver Ghost, and a small boy (me) was among the passengers on the trial run. After riding in most of the cars of the day this gliding machine was a revelation. It went along without a whisper and flew up hills—and remember, there were many cars which could not even get up Fitzjohn's Avenue without boiling. Frequently we took out cans of water to stranded motorists. Lord Northcliffe lost no time in owning a Silver Ghost, and thereafter was a confirmed Rolls-Roycer. He was a great friend of Claude Johnson, who had been the Hon. Charles Rolls's partner at the time he met Henry Royce; later, when Rolls-Royce was an established entity the slogan the firm adopted—"The Best Car in the World"—was given it by Northcliffe.

Father bought a Spyker after getting rid of the Brooke; this Dutch-made car looked very smart with its circular radiator, and went very silently. All but the cheapest cars in those days had anything from twenty to twenty-four coats of enamel on their bodywork, each coat rubbed down before the next was applied, achieving a lustre never seen today. Furthermore, highly polished brass lamps, etc., gave a finish totally different from the "tin toy" appearance of modern chromium plating, even if much elbow grease (which was cheap) was required to keep everything shining.

We used to go thirty or so miles out of London into the wide open country for picnics, and on one of these occasions lighting-up time overtook us on breezy Royston Heath. The acetylene headlamps and oil side and tail lamps had to be lit, for which purpose specially enormous matches called fusees were carried. My job was lamp-lighter, and I was very jealous of it. One day Father suddenly decided he would like a cigarette and asked me to hand him a fusee. At that time he had a long "handlebar" moustache—but when he struck the fusee there was a "poof" and half of it disappeared. I laughed, and got a thick ear as a result.

Even as now, the great racing drivers were schoolboys' heroes; two of the leading ones in 1907 were Charles Jarrott and S. F. Edge. You can imagine my delight when Father, having taken me to the opening of Brooklands Track, wangled me the supreme honour of sitting between the two of them at lunch. What they must have thought at having a grubby small boy sat next them goodness only knows, but they were both very kind and kept me entertained. After lunch there was a procession of cars round the brand new track in which, to my old man's dismay, his Spyker oiled up a plug and we had to run on three cylinders as we could not pull out of the procession to clean it. We were passed by the whole string of cars, one of which was a single-cylinder Oldsmobile whose exhaust note was a slow "toof-toof-toof". It particularly annoyed Father to think that his beloved Spyker should have to lose face to a "one-lunger".

Shortly after this we went to live in the country, at Troston Hall, a lovely Elizabethan manor near Bury St.

2—MIAML

Edmunds. Father bought a 12 h.p. Delahaye, in a very pretty green with green upholstery and large bucket seats. As we were seven miles from the station he needed a second car, and on hearing this his friend Harold Harmsworth, Northcliffe's brother and later Lord Rothermere, gave him a four-year-old Panhard limousine which had won a gold medal at the Paris show of 1904. The enclosed type of body was then a rarity, practically everything being open tourer or two-seater. One entered the limousine by a single door at the rear, and inside were two comfortable, well-padded leather seats with a third tip-up on the door. It was a wonderful old car, very reliable, and would crack along at 35 m.p.h. with its well-greased driving chains emitting a most pleasant swishing sound.

It was on this Panhard that I learnt to drive, secretly taught by Arthur Jaggard, our chauffeur, in a private park nearby. Two years later—1910—I was able to get my first motorbike licence, also a pretty little twin-cylinder "Moto-Reve" from Switzerland to go with it. But it had a dud Italian magneto, which was too much for a novice to cope with, so Dad had to fork out for a 3½ h.p. Bradbury, an excellent machine built like a battleship. This had a Bosch magneto, thoroughly reliable.

My brothers Max and Harold between them bought a tricar for a fiver. It had a thumping great 5 h.p. single-cylinder engine and seemed a bargain until they discovered it had a nasty habit of coming to a halt because of the engine shifting in the frame. Harold and I took this contraption across Hampstead Heath and down past the "Old Bull and Bush", where we came to open country. What is now Hampstead Garden Suburb was all fields and farmland, with the exception of a small group of yellow brick Victorian houses on the right-hand side of the lane before the Golders Green crossing. It was fields all the way to Hendon, our destination, which was at that time a small village. On the way back the inevitable happened and we had to push the outfit the whole way up to, and across, Hampstead Heath until we could freewheel down Fitzjohn's Avenue.

Back to Troston. Motoring was still a great adventure even in those not-so-early days. On a ride into London one would probably meet barely a dozen self-propelled vehicles. My Bradbury had only a single gear, but it did have a hand-operated clutch which enabled me to get under way on a down slope. On the level I had to lift the exhaust lever, run a few yards, let go the lever until the engine fired and then hop on. This was not particularly funny when riding through the City of London, which was just as busy round the Bank as it is today, although the type of traffic was different.

I went off to Canada in search of adventure at the age of eighteen in 1911, and brother Harold took on the Bradbury, to which I had fitted a sidecar of the flexible kind. Only a few were made, I believe, as it was not everybody's cup of tea because it was a tricky business keeping bike and sidecar vertical when stationary. When the bike heeled over the sidecar followed it, which made for great stability on the road. After I left for Canada, however, Harold and his fiancée travelled all over England in it without incident, so it couldn't have been too bad.

In Canada at that time, apart from the big cities like Toronto, Montreal and Winnipeg, there were virtually no roads outside city limits, merely tracks. I eventually found myself in Edmonton, Alberta, where I got my first situation driving a 40 h.p. Oldsmobile, a real blacksmith's job of a car. Driving it was like riding a rhinoceros. After that I drove a Tin Lizzie Model T Ford for some time—it was the only car that could go outside city limits without its chassis bumping on the potholes. For that reason it was universally used by country folk and farmers; it may have looked flimsy but it would stand up to anything.

The Stanley steamer was the most popular of all the steam

cars in the United States, with the White second. It is not generally realised that, between the years 1895 and 1930, some eighty different makes of steam car had been on sale there, or that a Stanley reached 127 m.p.h. on the Florida sands in 1906. I drove one—a most delightful car with terrific acceleration, and dead quiet. But it took twenty minutes to get up steam from cold, and if you accelerated too quickly the main fire was liable to blow out, which meant pressurised paraffin spraying all over the burners. If the main fire could be relighted quickly enough there was a loud plop and all was well—but you had to stand clear during the operation. One of my friends, who delighted in a very handsome moustache and beard, tried to perform this operation and lost a good part of his hirsute adornment in the process. He was in the police and had a remarkable flow of language, most of which would be unprintable even today.

When I returned to England in 1914, Harold was married and the proud possessor of a violet-coloured 10 h.p. Singer which had Sankey steel wheels, just in, so trouble with detachable rims and "Stepneys" was over. I went in for a twin Matchless bike, and followed it up with a 7–9 h.p. Indian and sidecar. While serving in the Tank Corps in World War I, I had a 3½ h.p. Triumph to ride, one of the very soundest and most reliable motorcycles ever to be made. I fell asleep on it after a strenuous argument with the Hun near Arras in 1918, and woke up to find I was heading straight for one of the poplars lining the road—in another split second I would have "had it". I also had to ride a 2¾ Douglas flat twin-cylinder bike, but it used to get tired on long journeys during the heat of the summer, enforcing a wait by the roadside for the engine to cool off. Next came a 4 h.p. water-cooled Douglas, sturdy and an excellent performer, which deserved more popular favour than it received; then a 3 h.p. twin Lea-Francis.

After the war I bought myself a 7–9 Harley-Davidson, an

American machine which sold well in Britain: with sidecar it set me back £155, which was a lot of money for a motor-bike in those days. Following it I acquired a three-wheeler, a Williamson with Douglas engine driving the back wheel by a single chain. I soon found out why it was so cheap—the chain used to come off every few miles. Anyhow, I thought I was making a good swop with this lot for a Daimler two-seater, pre-war and with sleeve-valve engine, enormous wheels and thin tyres. It consumed oil at an alarming rate, and was followed by an A.C. Sociable, another three-wheeler with tiller steering and two seats in front plus one behind, driven by a single-cylinder 5 h.p. engine—it amused my friends, who christened it "Tunk-Tunk-Too".

For a short time I was the proud possessor of a 1911 60 h.p. Mercedes with two enormous outside brass exhaust pipes protruding from the bonnet and cylinder pots like farm silos. On top gear, 1,100 engine revs. meant 62 m.p.h.—just ticking over. It was sprung like a farm wagon. At last I scraped up enough money to buy a new car (this was in 1923), and my choice fell on an 8 h.p. Talbot two-seater, a lively little bus with a sweet-running engine but alas no differential; the back wheels skidded round bends and tyres lasted no time at all. Later I had a 10 h.p. of the same make which did have a differential, and a superb motor car it was in every way. Then followed an 8 h.p. Eric Campbell, which looked just like a bathtub with a Rolls-Royce radiator. It was a rough job but quite speedy; would do 60 m.p.h. and 45 was quite enough to pass nearly everything on the road.

I had the good fortune to meet up with Vernon Balls in 1925, and bought an Amilcar from him—this would do 75 m.p.h., or 90 when tweaked up by V.B. for competitions. With it in the High Speed Trials run by the Junior Car Club at Brooklands, I even came in first in a race on one occasion, to my great surprise. Vernon Balls himself was a brilliant and spectacular driver, and always gave the crowd a thrill on the hairpins of the off-track circuit in the High Speed Trials and races run by the Junior Car Club at Brooklands.

Those Brooklands days were happy ones indeed. Among my friends I numbered Malcolm Campbell and Henry Segrave, and on several occasions occupied the mechanic's seat in Malcolm's cars—a great honour, for he was a past master at Brooklands. In the actual races he usually, of course, took his own splendid mechanic, Villa.

Malcolm was really a very highly-strung individual, meticulous about the smallest detail, but once a race had begun he became as cold as a block of ice. Segrave was also, by any standards in any era, one of the greatest racing drivers. He invited me to go over to Daytona Beach to act as manager on his world land speed record racing trips, but as I now had my own business I had, with a terrible wrench, to refuse. Incidentally, a year or so later Malcolm made me precisely the same proposal. I have never hated refusing such an opportunity so much.

My brother Harold ("Haj" to his intimates), became an apprentice at the Argyll Motor Company at Dumbarton about 1907. The journalistic life, however, attracted him more than did engineering or selling, and after completing his apprenticeship he came back to London and got on to the editorial staff of the *Daily Mail*. In due course he became motoring correspondent, but a rule of anonymity was in force for staff members then, so when the *Daily Express* invited him to write about motors under his own name he accepted and went across to the other side of Fleet Street. One of his lifelong friends was Dudley Noble, then of the Rover Company, and together they accomplished various motoring performances which attracted a great deal of public attention in the 'twenties and 'thirties. Dudley tells of them in following chapters of this book.

Harold's career ended when, on February 3rd, 1937, an

aeroplane chartered by the *Daily Express* to scout out domestic airline routes crashed over the Solway in foggy weather, failing to clear a hilltop by only about six feet. All aboard were killed. Few of Harold's friends knew much about his wartime exploits; that he was a D.S.O. and holder of the Croix de Guerre. He won both honours in the last week of the first war fighting on the Oise, when a vital bridge of boats was wrecked by enemy fire. The crossing seemed impossible until Haj, plunging into the river, swam across with a rope and enabled the bridge to be remade.

Just after the war, when he had returned to his paper, there was one occasion when his name literally went across the world. To demonstrate the possibility of the new wireless telephony he was equipped with a portable receiving set—a great novelty—and told to go anywhere he liked but to listen in at stated times for instructions from the office. The instructions were sent out by the News Editor on a special transmitting set and picked up in far corners of the earth by radio enthusiasts, by liners in mid-ocean and land stations everywhere, the message being preceded by the words "News Editor calling Harold Pemberton". So he became the first reporter in the world to receive instructions by radio telephony (he was actually in a London suburban train at the time). Haj was also one of the first journalists to deal with motoring from the human angle, and developed into an acknowledged expert on a subject which even then interested millions of people.

Just a few more experiences of the many and various cars I have owned, if I may. During the inter-war years I drove a clover-leaf-bodied Bugatti which cornered like a dream but did not like idling in traffic; it meant oiled-up plugs for certain. Also a three-litre Bentley, which was a fine old piece of ironmongery. Then there was a 20/98 Darracq, a tiger for speed with a really wonderful engine which used to have a disconcerting habit on occasion. The pressing of the starter might make the engine catch fire, but luckily this was easily extinguished by jamming down the accelerator, when the flames would be sucked into the induction pipe. This car had a Weymann flexible saloon body, with most comfortable seats, the front ones letting down to form a divan on which one could lie full length. Plus ça change! The Darracq was one of the fastest touring cars on the road then, but unfortunately it had very poor brakes and the gears seemed to be made of cheese.

I had a "Safety Stutz" after the Darracq, a powerful American saloon, extremely low-slung. In the heat of a Mediterranean summer a tyre burst one day, transforming the Safety Stutz into a wildly bucking broncho careering all over the road completely out of control. Luckily the traffic at the time was normal, i.e. there was nothing at all on the road. After this I went in for several Talbots, the best of which was a very nice "75" with a coupé body painted chocolate and fawn—very pleasing and unusual. Then I changed to a more spectacular vehicle, an Essex Terraplane —a real "shifter" with 8-cylinder 28 h.p. engine and open tourer body. But it was also delightfully smooth—the Hudson Essex people were very fussy about balancing their engines properly. Like most cars of the period, however, the brakes were not up to their job and so I had to drive accordingly.

I had never dreamed of owning a Rolls-Royce, as although I had a successful business, it seemed to me to be quite outside my budget. However, I had rendered a small service to R-R about which I had forgotten when, out of the blue, I was offered one of their experimental 25/30s in 1937. It was a close-coupled saloon with a 1937 engine and 1935 chassis, equipped with every modern device such as radio, heater and lights everywhere, to say nothing of jacks on all four wheels. I jumped at the offer and found myself the proud possessor of my first Rolls-Royce. To my lasting regret I foolishly sold it a few years after World War II.

We have come a long way since the days of which I have written. Later on in this book you will read about the founding of the Guild of Motoring Writers, which is today the largest and most successful body of professionals in that sphere. To me the fact that one of the principal awards it makes to its members is the "Harold Pemberton Memorial Trophy" is something of which I am tremendously proud, as also the fact that I number so many winners of the trophy among my friends, with a special thank you to Dudley Noble and Sidney Henschel, who first introduced me to the Guild.

The citation of Harold's Memorial Trophy is as follows: "Awarded to the journalist, artist or photographer, being a member or associate member of the Guild, who is considered to have made the most outstanding contribution to the cause of motoring during the year." Since its inception, the following have held it for the prescribed year:

1949	Basil Cardew	1959	Russell Brockbank
1950	Tom Wisdom	1960	W. F. ("Bill") Bradley
1951	Dudley Noble	1961	Harry Mundy
1952	Charles Faroux	1962	Jacques Ickx
1953	Sammy Davis	1963	Not Awarded
1954	Harold Nockolds	1964	Peter Garnier
1955	Laurie Cade	1965	Ami Guichard
1956	St. John C. Nixon	1966	Raymond Baxter
1957	Roy Nockolds	1967	Not Awarded
1958	Jacques Loste	1968	James Testridge

Long may the Guild flourish, and Harold's memory be kept green by this trophy. And now—over to Dudley Noble, a friend of over forty years, who has done me such honour in making me, an amateur, a sort of "avant garde" to an enthralling tale of pioneering by an expert.

ALFRED PEMBERTON

The Immediate Pre-War-One Years

I CHOOSE MY CAREER TO BE IN THE WORLD OF
MOTORING, ALLIED WITH WRITING ABOUT ITS
POTENTIALITIES OF SEEING COUNTRIES OVER-
SEAS AND TRAVELLING THEIR ROADS BY CAR

I suppose all of us have a first conscious memory, when in our very early days something happened that is for ever imprinted on our minds. In my case this was the night news came through that Mafeking had been relieved.

I didn't know who or what Mafeking was, but my father and mother were in a highly delighted state. On every house in our road in London's suburbs flags were hung out and red, white and blue fairy lamps, with candles inside, were festooned around the windows.

This was in May 1900, when I was just turned seven, and that evening my brother (who was three years older than me), with our bearded Dadda and graceful Mama, plus little "Callywonkas" (my brother's nickname for me), were taken to Piccadilly Circus to see the illuminations. How well I remember the gaslamp decorations everywhere, particularly on the pillared portico of the London Pavilion, then a "legitimate" theatre of some note.

This was the night when the patriotic crowds behaved with a fervour and abandon which was to coin a new word—"Mafficking".

How we got to Piccadilly, and home again, I just can't remember. We lived about four miles out, in Highgate almost exactly halfway up the famous hill of Dick Whittington fame.

There was only one means of reaching our road, other than on foot, and that was by the cable tram.

This started at the Archway Tavern, where the pair-horse trams from town terminated, and went to Highgate Village at the top of the hill. The fare to our intermediate stopping place was a ha'penny.

But it was the mechanism of the trams that fascinated me: there was a big wheel buried under the road just above Oliver Cromwell's house, near the summit, driven by a steam engine inside a building which has long since been turned into a garage. The "up" side of the cable took its drive from this wheel and presumably the descending tram lent a helping hand.

Between the tramlines was the same sort of slot we got to know later when London's horse trams were replaced by electric ones working on the conduit system. I used to spend a lot of my schoolboy leisure in the middle of the road, peering down through the slot at the big wheel going round with its peculiar sort of "trickling" sound. As there was no other traffic, the middle of the road was a perfectly safe place to lie.

The tram driver had a sort of grappling iron going down through this slot, and he twirled a brass wheel about a foot in diameter to hitch his vehicle on to the cable. Presumably they do the same thing to this present time in San Francisco, but I doubt if small boys can lie in the middle of the track to peer at *that* cable! I think there was a sprag at the back to hold the Highgate Hill tram at the stop by St. Joseph's church, halfway up, where we got off, but the whole contraption worked wonderfully well and I can't remember an accident ever occurring to these trams.

In our road traffic was also virtually nil. There would be the milkman in the morning, with his big, highly polished churn on a two-wheeled one-horse cart, and our parlourmaid would go out to him with a jug into which the day's supply was ladled—dust, flies and germs counting for naught.

The butcher's boy would come along with the family's meat on an open trug balanced on his head and the baker's man would wheel his handcart to the door. Every tradesman delivered his goods—to the servants' entrance, of course—while on the other side of the green baize door family prayers might be in session in the hall.

Each Tuesday evening a German band, in pseudo-military uniform, would take up station in the middle of the road, erect tripods for their music sheets and play for perhaps half an hour. Real good Wagner stuff, too. Three pennies would have been put out, and the parlourmaid on duty duly passed them over to the band's collector after the "recital".

On Thursdays a similar routine would be gone through when an Italian organ grinder with his wife or inamorata, also a dolled-up monkey, would give *their* performance (but I think one penny only was their reward). Never did any vehicular traffic interrupt these respective performances, but there were occasions when straw was spread over the roadway if some resident happened to be seriously ill, and that evening the music-makers were unlucky.

Life proceeded peacefully. The South African War was taking place a long, long way distant, and anyhow fighting was purely a matter for soldiers—what else did we pay them a shilling a day for?—so the average civilian was only raised to any enthusiasm when an outstanding victory like the relief of Baden-Powell after seven months' siege at Mafeking, or of General Redvers Buller after four months at Ladysmith, was reported. Britain was really Great Britain then, a power in the world as the red splotches on the map clearly showed.

With my brother I went to a school at Finsbury Park, which meant our having a season ticket on the G.N.R. from Highgate. The North London Railway had running powers over this section and its engines were finished in black enamel with a high gloss that never lost its lustre. But I liked to sit on the platform at Finsbury Park on the way home and wait for the Scotch Express to pull in, with its beautiful engine in the Great Northern Railway's green livery, polished in those greasy whorls that told of conscientious elbow grease, and glittering brass safety valve.

The train stopped at Finsbury Park for tickets to be collected, and I loved to watch the efforts of the engine's single 8 ft. 6 in. driving wheel to get the train going on the final stage of its journey to King's Cross, spinning furiously if the driver opened the throttle a shade too much.

It was at this Finsbury Park school that I acquired a taste for writing—I seem to remember that a comely young lady teacher took us in English and essays. At any rate, I was always top of the class in these subjects without much effort, whereas sums and algebra were literally my proverbial pain in the neck. Soon I was producing, on a jelly mimeograph, a school "magazine" (and it is a satisfaction to me to find that my grandson, Graham, in Canada, has done the same sixty years later at *his* school, whereas his father hasn't a clue in that direction, if he'll excuse me saying so).

The nineteenth century had turned into the twentieth, and every now and again my father would read out over the breakfast table some reference in his *Daily News* to those new-fangled horseless carriages. Once or twice I had actually seen one precariously chugging its way up Highgate Hill, sprag trailing in case of breakdown (but I never remember seeing one descend the hill, though). Now and again a motorcycle would tackle the climb, but frequently the rider had to leap off the saddle and run alongside on the steepest part near "Holy Joe's".

I became an avid reader of anything about motors that I could lay hands on. Stories in the *Strand Magazine*—all our family were keen devotees of Sherlock Holmes's adventures then appearing in it every month—now and again hinged around motorised carriages.

One tale that sent cold shivers down my back was about a

wicked squire who pursued a frightened female along a narrow, high-banked country lane from which she could not escape, his devilish engine belching forth fire and smoke, trying to cr-r-r-r-ush her into the muddy ground. He was foiled, of course, but I forget just how.

Then there was an absolutely fascinating book someone lent me (and I still have it!) called *The Lightning Conductor*, by a couple named C. N. and A. M. Williamson who were famous for their motoring novels.

This one, published in 1902, most alluringly described the adventures of a beautiful young American maiden who, with her dragon aunt as chaperone, came to Europe to finish her education, bought a car, engaged a chauffeur and, accompanied by the ubiquitous aunt, was driven to Newhaven (with various breakdowns en route) and arrived at Dieppe on the mail-boat, the car following on a cargo steamer.

On the road to Paris everything conceivable happened to the car: "Chains snapped or came off; if belts didn't break they were too short or too long. Mysterious squeaks made themselves heard; the crank-head got hot (what head wouldn't?) and we had to wait until it thought fit to cool."

Our innocent young American heiress began to think she had been sold a pup—the make of car is not specified beyond it being "of German origin"—and, when the final breakdown occurred before half the distance to Paris had been covered, miracle of miracles, "I heard a whirring sound and an automobile flew past us up the steep hill, going at fully 15 miles an hour.

"That did seem the last straw, and with hatred, malice and all uncharitableness in my breast I was shaking my fist after the thing, when it stopped politely." In it were two leather-capped-and-coated young men, one of whom was English and spoke nicely like a gentleman. The reader could then guess, after the first twenty or so pages, what the grand finale of the book would be.

Sure enough, when a further 300 pages of motoring adventure had drawn to their close, wedding bells rang out and the bridegroom was disclosed as the inevitable heir to a peerage. At any rate, our heroine bought herself a Napier instead of the "Brute Beast" on which the journey had been commenced, and thereafter a long trip to the Riviera through some beautifully-described French and Italian countryside went off so successfully that my imagination for motoring abroad was fired. By hook or by crook I was going to follow in her wheeltracks to that glorious sunny South.

One Whitsun—I think it was 1904—I learnt that a motorcycle trial was to start from the top of Highgate Hill, and to finish at Edinburgh. It seemed incredible—400 miles and throughout the night, too. I cajoled my father to come with me to see the procession depart, and there and then told him I had decided that my life was going to be lived among motors. He was less enthusiastic—thought they would prove to be a flash in the pan and fade out.

When my fourteenth birthday came along towards the end of 1906, however, I shook five shillings out of my money box, went to the local council office and asked for a motorcycle driving licence, please. With no more formality than buying one for a dog, "it" was handed across the counter and I was entitled to roam the roads of Britain, such as they then were, on any motorbike I chose and could lay hands on.

Before I could do this, though, I needed the bike, and had my eye on a $3\frac{1}{4}$ Rex, secondhand at a local cycle shop, price £8. Here a round of extra tough bargaining with Father was called for. Luckily, having made myself knowledgeable in electricity up to the standard of that era, I told him I could wire up his offices in London's Barbican and give him his lighting with freedom from those gas mantles that were always breaking. This I duly did, and it passed the City of London Electricity Co.'s inspector into the bargain, so he duly forked out eight golden sovereigns, and I became proud possessor of the 1904 model aforesaid.

This machine had the only engine I ever knew that was literally square—not in the modern sense of equal bore and stroke, but actually square in the finning of its air-cooled cylinder. Into one side of this the "silencer" (in name rather than deed) was fastened by four small grubscrews; it consisted of a mere perforated plate about three inches by two.

A surface carburetter was also a feature; a flat tray inside the tank proper from which the spirit evaporated, to pass in more or less gaseous form through a pipe with a throttle in it controlled by a little lever on top of the tank. There was a second little lever adjacent which opened a hole to the atmosphere, and one jiggled this to suit the gas supply and give the engine a combustible mixture.

The inlet valve was automatically worked by suction from the piston, and either its spring had to be weak enough to give easy starting or strong enough to allow the engine to get up a respectable rate of revolution, in which case herculean effort was needed to make it start. And if I could manage to get that wretched spring to the right intermediate strength I felt pretty proud of myself.

Petrol, the registered name for motor spirit thought up by Carless, Capel and Leonard, was pretty volatile stuff—it had to be to suit the primitive carburetters of the day. Pratts in the green cans and Shell in the red ones—everything came in two-gallon cans—were popular brands, and I bought my humble half gallons for 8d. as and when funds were available. I can't remember whether there was a carriage tax then—if there was I don't think I ever paid it.

What I *do* remember, and vividly, was the peculiar behaviour of that surface carburetter. On the smooth wood setts which covered the space between the tram-lines (and they were everywhere in the London suburbs), and a foot or so outside them, there would not be enough shaking on the part of the bike to cause much petrol vapour to be generated. The air control lever would have to be shut off tight to give the engine sufficient gas.

Immediately one was forced off the smooth setts and on to the rough macadam, however, there would be such a surplus of petrol vapour sent up that the engine choked and the air hole had to be flung wide open instantly to save the machine coming to a spluttering stop. Never a dull moment.

When winter came and the setts were too greasy to ride on, while the macadam was a sea of mud (crossing sweepers provided the local ladies with a reasonably clean path, saving them hitching their trailing skirts higher than to give the merest glimpse of an ankle, for which service they (the sweepers) gratefully received a ha'penny), I pulled the Rex to pieces in the street outside our house and carried the bits up to my little den on the third floor. Here I made glorious messes grinding in valves and decoking, out of sight of motherly eyes which would have been horrified at such goings-on.

My plans for attaching myself to the motor trade took a little step forward at the Cycle and Motorcycle Show in October—1910—when I answered an advertisement by some accessory firm or other for a temporary assistant to help on their stand at Olympia. I was duly taken on at the very reasonable wage of thirty shillings for the period, and got a free pass.

Every motorbike in the show I eagerly examined, particularly the new $3\frac{1}{2}$ h.p. Rover which seemed a close copy of the $3\frac{1}{2}$ Triumph that was currently a smash hit. To me it appeared the main difference was that the Rover had a red cross on its tank instead of the Triumph's green panels, and right away I decided that Rovers were going to have the privilege of my services in due course, even if they didn't then know it.

During the winter months there were, however, hardly any

3—MIAML

sales, hence no production, so I put my plans in cold storage until the spring. Meanwhile, a friend of my father's had opened a kinematograph theatre—they were starting up all over the place—and offered me the job of operator. This suited me down to the ground, so all through the winter I slaved away turning the handle from early afternoon to about 11 p.m., at first using limelight with oxygen and hydrogen cylinders and, later, an electric arc lamp when mains power was laid on.

Then, when Easter had come and gone and I had fifty pounds tucked away, I put the Rex together again—to my great surprise it ran quite well—"flogged" it for a fiver and blowed the whole £55 on a 3½ h.p. Rover.

Luckily, Father found he had a friend who knew someone who was acquainted with Harry Smith, then the big boss of the Rover Company at Coventry. I begged an introduction and first proceeded to enter my new bike for an A.C.U. Quarterly Trial, which took place regularly at about that time. Managing to make a pretty good showing in it, and being favourably mentioned in *The Motor Cycle*, I asked for an interview with Mr. Harry Smith. He graciously consented to see me, so off I hared to Coventry, was duly spoken to by the all-highest and referred to the foreman of the test shop, one Bob Whelan.

The upshot was that I got a job as a tester, at fivepence an hour. This was wonderful: here I was, doing exactly what I longed to do—ride new motorbikes all day—and getting paid for it into the bargain. At last I was "in" the motor trade. If I worked from 7 a.m. to 6 p.m. five days a week, and to one o'clock on Saturdays, I could earn 25s. a week—a golden sovereign and two silver half crowns—with no deductions for anything at all. Life had a more than rosy hue.

I found "digs" quite close to the works in Queen Victoria Road, where for 17s. 6d. a week I had a comfortable room to myself and all meals (no works canteens then). On the surplus of income over expenditure, maybe as much as 7s. 6d. a week, and no weekend expense as I went home to Highgate, life in Coventry could be very pleasant for a young chap. The place was a small country town at that period, with no more than about 80,000 inhabitants, and not a bit like the sprawling mass it has since become.

One could be right out in the leafy Warwickshire country inside a five minute ride. For one who, like myself, was almost completely disinterested in the other sex, evenings were usually spent meeting up with the local lads in the "back bar" of the old King's Head Hotel.

Coaches used to draw into this yard for night protection long ago—now in the bar one could linger over a tuppenny pint, or for a change take a circle seat at the Empire Theatre next door for threepence. Cigarettes cost 3d. for ten, tobacco ("Empire" from Rhodesia) 7½d. an ounce and I could live "en prince", or almost, on a bob a day over my cost for digs.

And, thank heaven, the demand for the Rover motorbike kept up, in spite of a nasty little habit which the early ones developed. This was for a tiny blowhole in the cylinder casting near the exhaust valve to enlarge itself and, before long, cause the complete top of the combustion chamber to part company with the lower portion of the cylinder with some force, the compression tap generally piercing the tank immediately above.

Co-testing bikes with me at Rover was one Charlie Newsome, who had been a pupil at Daimler and knew a thing or two which I gladly learnt from him. (Incidentally, he never left Rover except to go to World War I, and only retired from the firm about 1960.) His nickname, "Bush", stuck to him throughout his life, and I shall use it in all my references to him. He was a superb rider, with a built-in ability to cover more miles on a tankful than anyone I knew, including myself.

"Bush" and I were soon required by the management to

take part as official Rover riders in various trials and hill-climbs, which were as profuse then as rallies are today. This meant that, practically every weekend throughout the season, we would be riding in some event or other in company with a collection of chaps in similar jobs for a dozen or more motor-bike firms. One week we would be down in Devon; the next up in Wales, Derbyshire or the Lake District, Scotland and so on. I thought it splendid fun.

The hills were then pretty "hairy", inasmuch as they were in a primitive state so far as surface was concerned, compared with today. Porlock, for instance, is now a fine main road: in the days before the first war it was merely a track up the hillside which became a morass of red clay if the weather was wet, and in (I think) 1912 only about half a dozen out of some 100 competitors in the A.C.U. Six Days' Trial were credited with clean climbs. I was one, despite my handlebars having at one point touched the ground! (A motor road had been cut in easier stages up the hillside to make horsed transport, and the few motor chars-à-bancs then in service, practicable, but naturally for trials purposes the old road—now the one in general use—was the official route.)

One of the very best of the trials was definitely the Scottish Six Days, during which I saw more of the Highlands than ever I am likely to do again. Kenmore, Amulree, Mam Ratachan and so on were real teasers for our 3-speed hub-gear belt-driven bikes. The roads—well, they weren't roads for the most part (except the one General Wade had built to get his troops to grips with the turbulent Scots a century or so earlier)—were really severe tests, and to keep a clean sheet one had to check in on time everywhere. But the country was most lovely, and if the sun shone from a cloud-flecked blue sky (as it often did in late May when the trials were held), I thought there could be no more beautiful countryside than the Scottish Highlands.

I loved, too, the long-distance trials, the London to

Edinburgh at Whitsun, the London to Exeter at Christmas and the "Land's End" at Easter. On this last, a 300-odd mile jaunt, there was a rather dull and (if the weather was dry) very dusty section in Cornwall. In the village of Perranporth, on this stretch, there was a certain enterprising garage proprietor, by name Healey, whose son Donald was a keen young chap (weren't we all?). Outside their premises they put up a trestle table with a tea urn and dozens of cups —and never was a sight more welcome to we parched riders. It set us up for the remaining thirty or so miles to the End. Many a time have I reminded Donald Healey of what it meant to us on that dreary haul.

Rovers did very well out of us through these trials in the way of publicity, bringing prestige that led to sales. There were also the Tourist Trophy Races in the Isle of Man, in which a Rover team was entered in 1913 and 1914, winning the official team prize. Bush Newsome, A. J. Lindsay (he was with Rossleigh of Edinburgh, then as now the firm's agents in Scotland), and Duggie Brown, son of George Brown the owner of *The Isle of Man Times* and known locally as the King of the Island, constituted the team.

The T.T. course was in those days a collection of rough country roads and mountain tracks, very different from the speedway it has since become. Its condition—and the state of development of engines—can be gauged from the fact that Cyril Pullin won the Senior T.T. in 1914 on a 500 c.c. Rudge-Whitworth at 49 m.p.h.

Apart from motors, photography had been one of my great passions in boyhood days. Starting with a five-bob Brownie I worked up to a quarter-plate Cameo costing a guinea and using dark slides with glass plates. Their drawback was the amount of space they took up; in boxes of a dozen they lined the walls of my darkroom-cum-bedroom. When we came to move house, my mother grumbled about their bulk and I scrapped many a box of negatives taken in pre-first-war Belgium, where my father had sent me to school for a year or so in the hope of my learning to speak fluent French. This love for photography, coupled with things mechanical, was the reason I became so interested in kinematograph machines and moving pictures, then more or less in their infancy.

One day the thought struck me that it ought to be possible to film an interesting movie out of the various processes that went into the making of a motorcycle. So I got an interview with Mr. J. K. Starley, Rover's general manager, who combined with his main job the supervision of advertising and publicity. "Please, sir," I said, "couldn't we have a moving picture made in the works and get it shown in the bioscope theatres?" "Well, my boy," was his reply, "it would cost a lot of money."

"But please, sir," I went on, "if I could get it made for nothing would that be all right?" J.K. agreed that that *would* be O.K., so next time I was in London I went along Wardour Street and sought out the offices of Kineto Films, whose name I had seen on short pictures at the Coventry theatre, of the kind we would nowadays call documentary.

I somewhat nervously went in and asked to see the manager. Instead of being told to run away as the manager was busy, he, being an American, gave me an interview. I told him all about the way a motorcycle was made in the Rover works, starting with the molten metal running out of the cupola nearly white hot into the moulds to cast the cylinders; how the various bits and pieces were machined and fitted together, and the complete bike tested on the road, mentioning jumping over humpback bridges and so forth. He said it sounded "varry" interesting—he'd like to see it all himself and could he pay the works a visit?

Back I went to Mr. Starley and reported, and he said splendid—go and meet him at Rugby station with your side-car and take him to lunch, then bring him here. Thus was my initiation into expense account entertaining—the bill came to almost ten shillings, which was refunded to me by the cashier. Wonderful! I was getting to executive status, only we didn't call it that then.

And my Mr. Kineto came, saw and was convinced that there was picture material in those "woiks". He decided to go ahead, and in due course his camera crew arrived—it consisted of one young man who alighted at Coventry station with all his apparatus in his hands and under his arms—the camera, tripod, spare film—everything necessary, in fact.

Lighting was supplied by nature, aided by the glow of the molten metal in the foundry scene (printed on red-tinted stock this looked most effective). For other shots the cameraman chose a site near a door and the mercury vapour lamps which provided the normal shop lighting were turned on; alternatively, we dragged more or less mobile bits into the yard.

Finally came the testing; Bush and I went through all the stunts we could think of, leaping over the canal bridges near Leamington with the camera down in the ditch and winding up with a dash through the water splash at Kenilworth. I must have hit a brick under the water the second time through this, for my machine went into a sideways skid and performed a somersault right in front of the camera. Luckily, the young man kept turning the handle and so made a thrilling end to the film.

Back to London he went and only one or two shots needed re-taking. But the same young operator couldn't come again—he was away making a newsreel of the Greco-Turkish war. However, before long the picture was ready for its world première, which took place at the Empire Theatre, Coventry. We and all our pals crowded the threepenny seats, cheered like mad, and the film made its rounds of the kinemas with, I believe, some considerable success.

I begged a copy of it when its showings had been completed, and kept this by me until 1965, when the celluloid was found to have shrunk so much that the sprocket holes would not fit any 35 mm. projector. So I donated it to the National Film Archives, where it now rests; they have told me that it seems to be one of the first, if not *the* first, documentary concerned with motors, and a showable copy could be made if anyone wanted to put up £30 or so to make it.

Perhaps I should mention here that the J. K. Starley I have mentioned was the John Kemp II of that family, to which Coventry owes much of its rise to fame as the city that pioneered the bicycle and, later, the British motor car. Founder of this branch of the family was James Starley, fourth son of a struggling Sussex farmer who ran away from home in boyhood and landed up in Coventry when he was thirty-one. Young Starley introduced to the city of three spires the making of sewing machines at a time when the place was in dire need of a new trade to replace its collapsing ribbon- and watch-making activities, ruined by foreign competition and Britain's Free Trade policy plus, perhaps, Coventry's backward techniques.

During the ensuing twenty years, until he died in 1881, James Starley revived Coventry's industrial health by inaugurating cycle manufacturing as a sequel to the sewing machine enterprise. His cousin, John Kemp Starley the first, invented the safety cycle (with small wheels and chain drive to supersede the original "penny-farthing") in 1885, naming it the "Rover Safety Cycle". From this company evolved the Rover motorcycle- and car-making concern, whose first four-wheeled model appeared in 1904, but J.K. I did not live to see it, for he died in 1902.*

The general manager of whom I have spoken was the

* Hubert Starley, chief of Champion Spark Plug's organisation in Britain, has had a book written which describes the magnificent work his family did for Coventry in detail.

eldest son of J.K. I, born in 1877, and, at the period I am now writing about, *his* boss was Harry Smith, whose chief claim to fame seems to have been his forthright method of expressing himself. He was short, choleric, and could hardly say a dozen words without liberally sprinkling in what are today known as four-letter ones.

He was a dominating character, one that nobody crossed if they could help it, but what his qualifications were for running a motor works I never discovered. Certainly the firm was in a bad state financially at the time I joined it, making 8 h.p. and 12 h.p. cars with Knight sleeve-valve engines, but the combination was a decided flop. (The engine was used with some success in six-cylinder Daimlers, but it did not show up well in the Rover one- and two-cylinder cars.)

The motor trade—one could hardly call it an industry at this stage—had a sort of tacit headquarters at the Coventry and County Club, where a crowd of the top men would foregather for lunch. Birmingham seemed a long, long way away, and there was no love lost between the two cities, which were then infinitely self-contained. Wolverhampton was even further removed, and Coventry considered itself the hub of the motor world. Much of the business with suppliers was conducted at the club, mainly over the bar.

J. K. Starley, being sociable and holding so important a position with Rover, was naturally plied with hospitality, and no one had to ask him what he would have. It was always "a glass of fruit", consisting of a tot of whisky served in a tumbler with a slice of lemon. Each slice remained in the glass, and when there was no more room for any further liquid he reckoned he'd had enough. I always found him easy to get on with and he certainly was pleased with Kineto's film "How a Motorcycle is Made". My pay went up to 6d. an hour, and I moved into pricier digs, with high tea at 6 p.m.

At the beginning of 1913 I at long last realised my ambition to go motoring abroad. Bush and I were entered for the Paris–Nice trial, I on a solo machine and he on a sidecar outfit. We went over to Paris and there made the acquaintance of one Lucien Psalty, who ran a motorbike business and was the Rover agent for France. When we arrived it was raining hard, but Psalty reassured us about conditions in the South. "In Paris it always rain," he proclaimed dramatically, "but in Nice *toujours le soleil*—always, always the sun."

As passenger in his sidecar—a coffin-like affair specially built to save weight—Bush was to take a friend of Psalty's, a young French civil servant who was so junior that he had to take his summer holiday in mid-winter, and who thought this would be as cheap a way of getting to Nice as he was likely to find. So off we set in the gloom of an early morning from a starting point just outside the city walls (they still had the "octroi" then, and demanded local duty on the petrol a motorist brought into Paris in his tank).

Our first night's stopping place was to be Dijon, and all the way there the rain teemed down. The sidecar's mud-guard broke its stay en route and the wretched passenger had to sit holding it, the while a stream of liquid mud was thrown high into the air and descended heavily on his head. Worse was to come next day on the way to Lyons, when the stays holding the luggage grid broke on both our bikes more or less simultaneously. This was really serious, for the grids carried all our luggage and no makeshift repair was possible. Very regretfully, therefore, Bush and I had to find the nearest railway station, where we consigned both machines to Coventry, by "petite vitesse", and put ourselves on the train for Lyons.

The poor passenger just about possessed his fare back to Paris, so home he went, thoroughly disillusioned with these wonderful British motorcycles that Psalty had sold him on (we tried to make him believe it was the execrable French roads that were responsible). As for ourselves, well, we weren't going to be done out of our chance of visiting the Riviera, and anyhow we had our return tickets from Nice, so the firm's expense money was blown on getting us there. I should add that, when we did arrive, it was raining harder than ever (but in fairness I must say that we did have a fine day or two before entraining for home).

You have to bear in mind that, in those pre-first-war days, there were no real light cars with any pretensions to the same sort of sporty attributes as motorcycles. The "real" car was a heavy, clumsy, lethargic affair, too expensive for the younger generation to buy and run. There was the odd three-wheeler, like the Morgan on which its originator (H. F. S. Morgan) and his wife scored many a trials success.

It had a big V-twin cylinder engine—J.A.P. or Anzani—between the two front wheels (set to catch all the air possible), driving the back wheel through shaft and chains. Up the slippery tracks that figured in all the trials it was one of the sights to see the Morgan couple making their ascent bouncing in unison (quite a tricky art to master) in the hope, usually realised, of keeping the single driving wheel down to its job.

A move towards the cyclecar enjoyed a minor boom in 1910, and W. G. McMinnies, once editor of *Motor Cycling* and later of *The Light Car and Cyclecar*, says:

"We must have been pretty potty in the 1910–1914 period, for never before or since has there been such an extraordinary sprouting of weird ideas in the motoring world.

"It all started when Mr. Edmund Dangerfield, one time bicycle racer, and founder of Temple Press Ltd., publishers of motoring journals, conceived the idea of a single-seater monocar, more stable and cleaner and safer to ride than a motorcycle. Having been accustomed to the adventures of

T.T. racing on a $3\frac{1}{2}$ h.p. Triumph, I was keen to help to develop the idea and bought a single-cylinder, single-seater two-speed Morgan Runabout. Other motorcycling maniacs —among them Billy Rootes, then a youthful apprentice at Singers of Coventry, who was often the butt of more sophisticated trials riders who 'cooked' his machine by inserting bits of paper in the contact-breaker—were also attracted to what was to be called 'The New Motoring'.

"In those days we all thought Billy Rootes was a bit naïve—but how wrong we were! His engaging personality, which brought him fame and fortune, was evidenced by the fact that he never forgot his old friends of the pre-first-war days, for whom he always had a welcome. Success never spoilt him.

" 'The New Motoring' development, the birth of the light car movement in Britain, was sparked off by the secretly prepared first issue of *The Cyclecar* (spelt in one word), whilst our rivals at Iliffes—with whom we were not supposed to consort—insisted on spelling it with two. The prolific motoring writer A. C. Armstrong was appointed with me to run the T.P. venture. It sold 50,000–100,000 copies during Motor Show week and another edition was ordered.

"The results during the next few years were astonishing. From all over England weird designs of three- and four-wheelers appeared. Some were more cycle than car and others more car than cycle. The Morgan three-wheeler, with founder H. F. S. Morgan and his wife, was the most successful in trials, while I was fortunate enough to win the first Light Car and Cyclecar Grand Prix at Amiens in 1913 with Frank Thomas, the Hon. Secretary of the newly formed Cyclecar Club (afterwards the Junior Car Club), as my mechanic.

"Then there were such wonders as the friction-driven GWK, the belt-driven French Bedélia with yellow-bearded Robert Bourbeau sitting tandem with his passenger; the three-wheeled A.C., tiller-steered, in which a couple sat between the front wheels with a single-cylinder 5 h.p. air-cooled engine behind driving the single rear wheel.

Shooting stars of those days were Archie Frazer Nash and his partner Godfrey; J. F. Buckingham, who built his own engine and car in Coventry and afterwards invented the wartime tracer bullet; Carden, who produced a single-cylinder monocar with the engine at the back, verily the fore-runner of the modern Grand Prix car; the French Salmson and Violet-Bogey two-stroke; and the Duo-car, another belt-driven apparition favoured by my colleague on the by now titled *Light Car* Percy Bradley, later to be Secretary of Brooklands Track.

"But one of the greatest technical advances of those days was brought about by W. R. Morris: I knew him well when I was an undergraduate at Magdalen College, Oxford. He used to help me tune up my racing motorcycle 'Puffing Billy', and I actually took him for his first air flight in 1916 over Pool Meadow, Oxford. In return for this adventure he lent me one of the early Morris light cars for my honeymoon —I had had to sell my Grand Prix Morgan in order to get married!

"A year or two before that, Morris had invited me into his Longwall office to see the drawings for a new light car he was to market. His idea was to combine the best engine, gearbox and chassis of the time in one vehicle. He chose a White and Poppe water-cooled four-cylinder engine, a Wrigley gearbox and (I think) a Rubery Owen frame. The result was a first-class car in miniature. In those days the Longwall garage consisted of some one-time stables fitted with a few machine tools downstairs and the office, presided over by Morris's old father, upstairs. We, the customers, sat on apple-boxes in the open yard and tuned our various vehicles, William Morris 'junior' presiding.

"Every weekend in this period there were light car and

cyclecar trials and hill climbs all over the country. I remember one speed trial on the Brighton front where George Hands's Calthorpe was beaten by my Morgan, and a hill climb at Aston, near Tring, which was only open to passenger-carrying cars. I was nearly disqualified for going up solo on the single-seater—until I exposed a small boy hidden under the steering wheel between my knees.

"This single-seater water-cooled Morgan, called 'The Jabberwock', also made fastest time of the day at Doncaster in the A.C.U. Six Days' speed trials test, beating all the motorcycles. But sometimes the Jabberwock misbehaved itself, and when near the end of the Scottish Six Days' Trial, which I was reporting, the steering gear failed and it partially demolished a telegraph post and injured my passenger.

"One of the stunts we developed at Temple Press was the presenting of a cup for the holder of the Hour Record. H. F. S. Morgan achieved a 60-miles-in-the-hour record at Brooklands, watched by his top-hatted, frock-coated papa, the Rector of Stoke Lacey, near Malvern, where Morgan started his business in a single shed with the aid of one walrus-moustached, bowler-hatted works manager, by name Hales.

"These early competitions, when everyone knew everyone else, often ended hilariously with a sing-song and lots to drink: I suppose we were pretty wild. I mentioned the French Grand Prix at Amiens, but I did not refer to a then unusual outing which *The Light Car and Cyclecar* organised in the way of a supporters' tented camp alongside the circuit. There were about fifty of us, some ministered to by one fifteen-year-old plump Marie Thérèse from the local pub. For some years afterwards she used to write to me as 'Mr. MicMac'." [And many thanks for your interesting contribution, dear Gordon McMinnies.—D.N.]

Rovers did not go in for cyclecars, but were fortunate in

having engaged a clever young designer named Owen Clegg who, at about the time I joined the firm, was engaged on the production of a car that embodied so many *avant garde* features as to make it much sought-after on its first public appearance, at the Olympia Show of 1912. Christened the Rover Twelve, it had four cylinders cast monobloc, 75 mm. bore and, with a piston stroke of 120 mm., a capacity of just under two litres (even in those days metric measurements were employed in engine terminology, a tribute to the Continent's "fathering" of motor-making).

It was, for its time, a very good-looking car, but perhaps the Rover Twelve's greatest sales appeal was that, at its price of £350 it was not only extremely reasonable, but actually included such usual "extras" as windscreen, hood and (paraffin) side and tail lamps, also spare wheel and a bulb horn.

As electric lighting, let alone starting, was barely known on British cars before World War I, headlamps were bought independently from the maker of one's choice—acetylene, with the generator fixed on one or other running board (of which the spare wheel occupied the front end on the driver's side, usually). Dimming or dipping headlights was obviously impossible, but there were so few cars on the road that this was of little account. Joseph Lucas's famous "King of the Road" headlamps were *the* popular favourite.

Rover had almost an overwhelming success on its hands in this new Twelve, and the works, which then occupied a constricted site almost in the centre of Coventry, stretching from behind its showroom at the bottom of Hertford Street to the Queen Victoria Road, a mere few acres, had to keep going day and night to turn out even fifty cars a week. The foundry was part of these Meteor Works, and there was also a coachworks half a mile or so distant in Cheylesmore where all the bodies were made and painted—with many brushed-on coats finished with varnishing.

Incidentally, to help speed production, a somewhat similar dictum to Henry Ford's ("any colour so long as it's black") was laid down: Rover, however, adopted a decidedly attractive pastel green shade as standard, and stuck to it till World War I broke out and stopped the Twelve.

Rover's machine shop (like that of most other works) was a forest of belting, each tool being driven from an overhead shaft powered by a steam engine housed outside. The floor was of brick impregnated with the grease of years (yet another common machine shop feature).

Every engine, as soon as it was assembled, was wheeled along to the test shop to be run in; this happened to be the shop in which Bush Newsome and I had a corner for our motorbike testing. A petrol tank was fixed on the wall just above each test bed and it was no uncommon thing for a backfiring engine to set the whole caboodle ablaze.

When this happened, Bob Whelan, the foreman, would get casually off his high chair, unhook an extinguisher from nearby and stroll over to the sheet of flame. He was adept, from long practice, at putting it out in a few seconds, and I can never remember him getting the slightest bit rattled, no matter how ugly the fire seemed for a time.

It would have been unthinkable then for any car, or motorcycle, not to have a fairly lengthy testing, and even with our motorbikes a road test of up to fifty miles was the practice. As a matter of fact, Bush and I suited ourselves as to how far we went; if there weren't many bikes coming through from the assemblers we found it desirable to extend the distance, as otherwise we might have to clock off early and that meant losing the price of a pint or two.

Now and again under such circumstances I would decide to go and have a look at Oxford, which was fifty-odd miles each way. Once while there, and being uncertain if I could get back to Coventry on what was left in my tank, I decided to take on half a gallon at a convenient garage in Longwall

Street, which had the name Morris over it. The proprietor himself served me from a two-gallon can, which was the only way of tanking-up in those pre-pump days.

If I could have seen into the future I would no doubt have been more respectful to Mr. William Morris. He was just starting to market his bull-nosed Morris Oxford, but meanwhile was mainly a garage proprietor and cycle dealer. Gordon McMinnies has just told us his experience of Morris, and I was to learn about his humble beginnings in the car trade from one of my fellow subalterns during the war a year or two later.

Because of the time I was riding Rover motorcycles in trials I suppose my name became pretty well known to the "fans" who then, as now, devoured the appropriate papers reporting such events—I did, as a matter of fact, become known as "Rover" Noble. At any rate, I was paid visits by two persons in particular who were later to become rich and/or famous.

One was Billy Rootes, whose father had the Rover agency in Hawkhurst, Kent. Young Billy would ride his bike up to our works now and again, when he was about to go in for some trial down south, and I would always tune his engine up personally for him. We began a lasting friendship around 1912, the development of which played a big part in my life, as I shall presently describe.

The other visitor sought me out one evening in that "back bar" of the King's Head, where all we competition riders had the habit of meeting. He was a nice young fellow with a slight cast in one eye, and he came shyly up to me and enquired "Are you Mr. Noble?" When I admitted this, he told me his father had sent him specially to seek me out and arrange to buy a Rover motorcycle. He proved to be Stanley Gliksten, son of the man whose timber yard at Stratford, near London, was destined to capture most of the motor body-building trade in seasoned ash and unwarpable hardwood, an essential base then for every car's "composite" coachwork.

Stanley's grandfather had come from Poland as the proverbial poor immigrant, had started a small timber business and eventually bequeathed it to his son Reuben. In due course it was to make the latter's three sons, of whom Stanley was the middle one, all millionaires. The first war increased their business over and over again, but after it they developed into one of the biggest suppliers to the building trade, acquired forests in British Honduras and West Africa and turned their company into a highly prosperous public concern. Stanley rode his Rover motorbike with me on several of the London to Edinburgh and Land's End trials and we intended to join up in the Army together when war came, but his father refused to allow him to go.

In thinking of the motor trade of those pre-first-war days one has got to bear in mind that the public at large was not terribly interested in cars. Money had a totally different meaning: £100 was, for instance, an impossibly large sum to find for the average working man, and hire purchase was virtually unknown. Few could lay hands on the £500—or even half that—which cars cost, added to the mystery generally prevailing as to what made the things go. Also, there was a dearth of knowledge as to driving them, and no schools existed to teach that art—it was a matter of picking it up from a friend as best one could.

Realising that there might be a business in teaching driving, one Stanley Roberts, twenty-one years old in 1910 and already an enthusiastic motorist, had the urge to strike out on his own. Like me, he had made it clear to his father (a doctor in practice in South London) that he wanted to "go in" for motoring, and had got himself apprenticed to a garage in Fulham, of which Mr. T. O. M. Sopwith was a director. This was about 1906.

What put the idea of teaching driving into Stanley's head

was that he was asked by a coachman, whose master had bought a car, if he might pay to be initiated into the mysteries of chauffeuring. The idea appealed, and soon after the firm of S. Roberts came into being, located in the stables behind Father's house, with a staff—apart from Stanley—of one fully-fledged mechanic (£2 a week), another at 30s., two instructors (35s. a week each) and two boys (6s. 6d. and 5s.).

Prospects seemed good enough to justify the name of the firm soon being changed to the British School of Motoring, and the wages book a year or so later confirmed progress by revealing that ten times as much was being paid out every week to employees. The first instruction cars—a Spyker, a Richard Brazier and two Darracqs, plus a Milnes-Daimler for learner lorry drivers—were equipped with dual control.

One, however, was stripped down and could be built up by the pupils to give them a full understanding of what made the wheels go round. In 1913, when rumours of impending war were rife, Stanley Roberts took a stand at the Imperial Services Exhibition at Earls Court with the intention of bringing his school to the notice of the military authorities, among others. As must be said, the War Office had remained obstinately unconvinced that motor vehicles were essential to military requirements then any more than they were in the Crimean and South African wars; the generals were still horse-minded to a degree.

This was despite the efforts which both the Royal Automobile Club and the Automobile Association had made to demonstrate the motor's potentialities for the rapid movement of troops and supplies. On the other hand, the Germans had long been alive to motorised vehicles and were producing them in quantity; had built strategic roads along their frontiers as well.

Of course, there were many civilians needing instruction in driving; apart from the doctors, businessmen and landed gentry who were being weaned away from horse transport and wanted their old coachmen trained, there were taxicab, lorry and van drivers, also busmen, for the London General and Vanguard omnibus companies were using De Dion petrol-engined buses—there was no transport monopoly then. The Electrobus Co. had some quiet and fumeless vehicles which went very nicely but were awfully slow on hills with their great weight of batteries. Ludgate Hill almost defeated them, whereas the petrol buses snorted up it, their be-goggled drivers changing gear (usually) with no mean skill. I used to grab a seat right at the front inside to watch them perform on their various levers.

When the Kaiser set Europe, and the world, alight, there was certainly no lack of individual motor manufacturers in Britain, while across the Atlantic there was a still greater number. Henry Ford had introduced his famous five-dollar day in January 1914, and was the first American motor maker to open up a plant in Britain—in Cork at the outset and then at Trafford Park, Manchester.

He had won his case against the Selden patent holders: briefly, George B. Selden, born in 1846, had been impressed by the two-stroke Brayton engine exhibited at the Philadelphia Centennial Exposition in 1876. He improved on it and filed a patent application in 1879 broadly covering a road vehicle propelled by a liquid hydro-carbon engine of the compression type, and including a disconnecting device between the engine and the road wheels—in brief, the essential features of any motor car.

He kept his application alive but did not actually take out a patent (with a seventeen-year life) until November 1895. He did succeed in building a vehicle to the patent specification and it ran, but feebly. Nevertheless, he was able to sell his patent for ten thousand dollars (they were five to a pound sterling then) and out of this was born the American Association of Licensed Automobile Manufacturers. It extracted royalties from many firms in the U.S. industry—but not from Henry Ford.

When the Federal court upheld the Selden patent in 1909, the A.L.A.M. urged Ford to come into the fold of licensed makers but he refused, appealed against the court decision and, in 1911, won his case on the ground that only two-stroke engines were covered by the patent. In any event, there were no more than two years then left to the life of the patent, and the A.L.A.M. disbanded forthwith. Also at about this time General Motors was in process of stabilising itself after the haphazard collecting of companies by William C. Durant.

Passenger cars in the G.M. fold were pruned down to Buick, Cadillac, Oakland and Oldsmobile, and commercial vehicles to the General Motors Truck Co. Chevrolet, a company organised in 1911 to make cars designed by Louis Chevrolet, the French-Swiss mechanic who had been a racing driver for Buick (a Scot turned American), was added to the G.M. "portfolio" in 1915. Indeed, through the machinations of the U.S. bankers, whose activities largely governed the American motor industry, the Chevrolet Motor Co., of Delaware, in corporate terms owned General Motors for a time.

While in the U.S.A.—in spite of there being no proper road system, for the "Get America out of the Mud" campaign did not start before World War I—production was reckoned by the hundred thousand, British makers were still in the more or less spade-and-bucket era. Few firms could turn out above fifty or so cars a week, and that was probably more than Daimler, Humber, Siddeley-Deasy, Singer, Standard, Sunbeam or Swift was capable of—Rover, which was reckoned a big manufacturer, only made that number with an effort. The total number of cars recorded as being in use throughout the U.K. (which included the whole of Ireland) was about 100,000, but even so there were gloomy premonitions about saturation point being only just around the corner.

In the autumn of 1913 I was called to the Rover board-room and given a confidential job to do. It appeared that the firm had been in correspondence with Dr. Rudolf Diesel in Germany on the subject of his compression-ignition type of internal combustion engine. He had been facing problems in his own country and was paying England a visit to sound out possibilities here, Rover being one of them.

I was to take a Twelve to Harwich, meet him off the mail boat on arrival (the morning of September 30th), hand him a letter of invitation and, if he accepted, bring him to Coventry in the car. The ship duly berthed and I waited at the exit from the Customs for the person whose photograph had been several times published, to intercept him before he boarded the train.

But of Dr. Diesel there was no sign, although he was on the passenger list. His cabin had been found empty and the bed not slept in. There was no clue to what had happened and he was presumed lost overboard, complete with the dispatch case he was known to have had with him when he boarded the ship at Antwerp. Nor was any explanation of the worthy Herr Doctor's fate ever revealed; it was hinted that he might have known too much about U-boats to be allowed by the German government to make contact with, possibly, the British Admiralty. The question "did he fall or was he pushed?" has never been conclusively answered.

Hillman, Calcott and Singer were all turning over at this period to a small car, but a *real* car in miniature; they had eschewed the cyclecar rage. These were all four-cylinder, very pretty-looking jobs (for their time); the Humberette and Swift were rather less worthy of being termed scaled-down large cars but were more of the cyclecar type, or voiturette as the French had it. There was likewise the Calthorpe, from Birmingham, another genuine small car.

Of the rest of the producers, Austin and Wolseley (the latter then under the control of Vickers) were among the larger Birmingham manufacturers, but neither turned out any great volume. Lanchester, one of the very earliest English makes, and a really well-engineered car (as one would expect from the distinguished brothers who produced it) was well in the running with Sunbeam of Wolverhampton in the higher price bracket, while Rolls-Royce at Derby were, of course, in a class of their own with the Silver Ghost.

But there was quite stiff foreign competition from several *marques* which had been, and still were, very popular on the British market. Fiat and Renault had had their organisations here since very early days and were, as now, highly thought of. So, too, were Austro-Daimler, Bugatti, Delage, Mercedes (without the Benz), Metallurgique (from Belgium), Panhard-Levassor, Spyker (from Holland) and many another. The Liberal government under Herbert Asquith was a powerful political party then, with its Free Trade policy.

And so the months of 1914 wore on more or less normally until the fateful August Bank Holiday (the 4th of the month) came along. Kaiser Wilhelm had forced what he wanted on us, a war of aggression to make Germany the undisputed master of Europe. We light-heartedly laughed it off—it'll all be over by Christmas "when we've wound up the watch on the Rhine" was the popular feeling. So we young chaps were anxious to join up while there still *was* a war—never did we think it would take four years to "down" Kaiser Bill and his son Little Willy.

World War One "Blows Up" the Motor Car

WORLD WAR ONE FINDS BRITAIN IN NO SHAPE
TO WAGE A MECHANISED TRANSPORT STRUGGLE
WITH A MUCH MORE FAR-SIGHTED AND MODERNLY
EQUIPPED ARMY. BUT WE MUDDLE THROUGH AS
USUAL AND EMERGE WITH A NEW OUTLOOK ON
MOTOR CARS AND MUCH EXPANDED PRODUCTION
CAPACITY

Returning to the Rover works on August 5th, I found notices
had been placarded urging anyone who could drive a motor
vehicle to apply to join the "A.S.C. (M.T.)". It is curious
to recall how unknowledgable were we civilians then on the
subject of soldiering, in that neither Bush Newsome nor I
understood what A.S.C. stood for, although the M.T. was
clear enough. It was obviously the thing for us to join,
though, even more so than the dispatch rider section of the
Royal Engineers for which most of our friends in Coventry
seemed to be heading.

We were tipped off that we would get in quicker if we
went to Whitehall, so off to town we rushed, were interviewed
in due course (one almost had to have a personal introduction to be allowed to join up), pronounced fit medically,
signed on as full privates in the A.S.C. M.T. and a few days
later received orders to report to the Horse Lines at Aldershot.
No such thing as a mechanical transport depot existed in
1914, for the simple reason that there *was* no Army mechanical transport.

To the best of my knowledge the War Office did not own a solitary motorised vehicle, but had condescended to operate a "subsidy" scheme, whereby a commercial firm operating lorries received £50 per annum if it bought one of approved "Subsidy" type, on the undertaking to hand it over to the W.O. in case of national emergency. There were pitifully few of these, however, and so Government buyers were sent out to scour the country and commandeer anything that looked like a commercial vehicle and would run.

Meanwhile, we rookies had to live for a painful ten days in those squalid horse lines, sickened at mealtimes by the thick coating of dead flies caught in the dense spiders' webs spun over the years and allowed to remain. Heaven only knows what filthy conditions pertained in the cookhouse, but we soon began to realise that a bob-a-day soldier was regarded by the dandified horsey officer as so much scum. I would doubt whether any but the most newly joined subaltern was ever put on mess inspection, too scared of the fearsome sergeant majors to dare open his mouth about the pigsty conditions in which the men lived and fed.

We mechanical wallahs were drilled with dummy guns on the barrack square and gradually lorries began arriving—all sorts and sizes in a multitude of makes and models. Out of the fifty or so allocated to our unit—69 Company A.S.C. M.T.—there were no two alike. Parties of us were herded on to one of them for a test of driving; it was, I remember, a Straker-Squire, colloquially known as a Squeaker-Squag, and with the reputation of not being able to pull the skin off a rice pudding. Each in turn we were called upon to drive for a mile or two, and only a few seemed ever to have handled a lorry before.

One man tried to engage reverse instead of top while travelling forward in second and some pretty horrible noises occurred before the lorry came to rest and then started going backwards. Bush and I had taken the precaution before

leaving Coventry of chumming up with the foreman of the
test shop at Daimlers and had been able to "have a go" in
Warwickshire lanes on a 3-ton chassis, so we were not complete strangers to a heavy vehicle. Nobody was failed on his
driving, however, and the C.S.M.'s philosophy was "they'll
soon larn". They were able to have a little practice before,
in mid-August, our company was detailed to drive to Avon-
mouth, which, it is only fair to record, we reached without
accident other than mechanical failures.

Leading the way was our C.O., one Major Leland (nothing to do with Leyland), on a six-cylinder Wolseley which,
I recall, had a self-starter working off a cylinder of com-
pressed air fastened along one running board. Never did I
hear of this contraption actually working, and very soon the
cylinder had mysteriously disappeared. Second in command,
a captain, had a 16 h.p. Sunbeam and the two subalterns a
10 h.p. Singer apiece. This latter was a very nice little car,
but had one major fault—the gearbox was on the back axle
and, as chassis frames were then made of simple channel
girder which warped badly when on a steeply cambered road,
there was a tendency for either two gears to be engaged at
once or none at all.

I was allocated to a 5-ton British Berna which, having an
enclosed body (blazoned with Johnny Walker advertising
when delivered at Aldershot but laboriously painted khaki
while there), was designated the stores lorry. A very nice
chap by name Kenneth Hartridge, of the real "old school
tie" type, was designated my partner. His cultured accent—
which I must admit was rather affected—was mimicked by
the mainly rough characters in our unit, and particularly
the workshops. Kenneth was nevertheless a skilful mechanic
and fertile-minded to boot, and he had had a good deal more
experience of "roughing it" than I had, having been a
member of his school's Officers' Training Corps.

Our lorry had been fitted up with lots of little bins for

spare parts, nuts and bolts and so forth, and there was just a narrow passage running down the centre. This made conversion into a home for the two of us a rather baffling problem. It was eventually solved by getting the burly black-smith to forge eight sturdy brackets which, when fixed in position, made supports to carry suitably sized poles, between each pair of which a canvas stretcher-like bed could be slung.

Even if not the equivalent of a sprung mattress, they were at least more comfortable than sleeping on the road under the lorry, which we had to do at first. As to cuisine, we took over a section at the front end of the passage and installed there a Primus stove, together with a "sink" consisting of a large funnel with a length of rubber hose attached which passed through a hole bored in the floor.

We embarked on August 22nd in an ancient Cunarder, the *Ultonia*, overdue for the scrapyard and in a deplorably filthy condition—but reckoned good enough for soldiers even if she did swarm with rats and smelt like a sewer down below. Luckily the weather held good and in a couple of days we were in Le Havre. Disembarking, we were marched to the railway station and entrained in French cattle trucks ("Hommes 40, Chevaux 8") and proceeded to Rouen, where our lorries were waiting. My diary goes on to say that we covered forty miles that day and stayed at Evreux, then on to Versailles, being given by a hysterical populace showers of apples, pears, plums, peaches, bottles of wine, also bread, jam, cigarettes, chocolates and cakes. War fever was at its height in France.

Near Orléans we met up with the Indian troops to whom we were scheduled to act as supply column. That night a rumour went round that a body of Uhlans were wandering round our district and at about 2 a.m. there was a gun shot. It proved to be by a sentry who had tried to extricate a cartridge from the breech of his rifle and accidentally pulled the trigger. Came the dawn and an order to take a lorry, drive to Le Mans and pick up a couple of Rudge-Whitworth motorcycles which had been left in a cellar there by Cyril Pullin and his manager, Sidney Rowlandson, now of our unit, after practising for the Circuit de la Sarthe to await the actual race—since, of course, abandoned. We retrieved the machines and went back to our unit with them on the lorry.

From now on, Rowlandson and I were ordered to act as route finders for the lorry convoy, one of us going ahead to see it took the right road while the other leap-frogged to the next doubtful turn beyond. I rode Pullin's machine, which was a straight belt drive, while Rowlandson had his own Rudge Multi. At one town I stopped to consult the map and someone came up and asked if he could direct me—to my astonishment this proved to be Lucien Psalty, while a little further along our road I came across Duggie Brown, from the Isle of Man, actually on his T.T. Rover bike and now a dispatch rider. Eventually we reached our appointed base at Lillers, where Rowlandson and I were rewarded with a lance-corporal's stripe apiece (acting, unpaid).

Our Indians—the Lahore Division—had a wretched time during that cold, wet autumn. My unit's daily task was to go to railhead at Hazebrouck, pick up their rations of ghee, ghur, atta, etc., deliver them to where the Indians' mule transport awaited us and then go back to our billet, which was in the grounds of the Château de Chocques. Once this had probably been a seigneur's mansion, but now it was a distillery producing nothing more exciting than industrial alcohol. Made from locally grown beets (the "betteraves" of which motorists in France today are warned at harvesting time because they make a slippery mess when squashed on the road), the processing was going on that year just the same as if the Germans were hundreds of miles away instead of a bare dozen.

Carts laden with the beets conveyed them into the

distillery compound from where the local populace were digging in the fields, and tipped them into a pond through which ran a current of water. Cleaned of their coating of soil they were gently propelled down stream until, at the far end of the pool, a large Archimedian-screw type of lift carried them up to the top floor of the distillery building. Here they were mashed up, allowed to ferment and passed down to the stills. The end product held little appeal for us, but wine and spirits were still obtainable in the little town of Chocques.

We spent the first Christmas of the war in this distillery billet, and our four—Newsome, Rowlandson, Hartridge and I—applied through Colonel Leland for commissions. He promised to put us forward as workshops officers, a breed of which there was currently a marked shortage. But Christmas festivities were enhanced by a delivery of parcels from home— there was no such thing as N.A.A.F.I. at this stage of the war —and even the E.F.C. (Expeditionary Force Canteens) had not yet been thought up. Soldiers were soldiers in those days and not to be pampered, was the War Office's belief; there was plenty of cannon fodder to be had for the asking, or so the bumbles of Whitehall believed in those days when unemployment was rife.

Fowls were to be bought locally, and, believe it or not, Kenneth Hartridge and I cooked a chicken on our Primus stove and contributed it to the common feast. As I mentioned, Kenneth had a super-cultured accent and, as we bore our steaming hot bird into the mess, a chant went up "At Christmas we shall have a partridge—Hee-ah, hee-ah, says Corporal Hartridge". The part of that Christmas night which I remember most vividly was the rum punch session, ably presided over by Bush Newsome, when a most potent liquid was brewed up in a garret and by midnight I think that any roving Germans could have captured a certain A.S.C. unit with precious little resistance.

Shortly after New Year's Day Major Leland summoned Kenneth and myself to his billet and told us our commissions had come through. We were forthwith to proceed to England to buy officers' kit and, at the expiry of ten days, report to the War Office for orders. So we bade him a soldier's farewell (nothing derogatory, for he was a fine chap and an excellent C.O.), and caught the night train out of Béthune, which was under desultory shellfire from the German-held La Bassée region about seven miles to the east, bound for Boulogne.

The cross-Channel boats were still running, mainly for military personnel of course, and there was no enemy activity: aeroplanes were still hardly capable of flying the necessary distance and certainly not of carrying any more offensive weapon than a rifle, while the U-boats had not penetrated our naval defences. Dover was, in fact, still a harbour for warships, and the long-range gun "Big Bertha" was, according to rumour, being kept for use against Paris. Anyhow, it simply did not seem possible that any gun could fire a shell twenty miles, even if the Hun had a foothold on the coast of Northern France.

Having managed to scrounge an officer's star before departing—one for each shoulder—and ditched my lance-corporal's stripe, I took an undisputed seat in the first-class Pullman at Dover and we were soon at Charing Cross (Victoria was not used as the London terminus for leave trains until long afterwards).

Home leave for troops overseas had not, in fact, begun in January 1915, and anyone in uniform with French mud on his boots was automatically regarded as a hero. When I went to Coventry to look up friends there, Rovers were so carried away with enthusiasm for my imagined exploits that they lent me a Twelve on the spot to make my stay in England still happier. They were at the time building Sunbeam 16s, the War Office having decided that a Twelve was too small for Army service, even though the Rover was a two-litre.

While my second-lieutenant's kit was being made, I was notified that the War Office had posted me to the 4th G.H.Q. Ammunition Park and a travel warrant to St. Omer duly reached me. Meanwhile, I had paid a visit to an old acquaintance, a naturalised Austrian by the name of Kamm, who lived in a house my father owned in Highgate and ran a business making equipment for the electric palaces (cinemas) then proliferating. These were the days of Mary Pickford, Fatty Arbuckle, the Keystone Cops and other of the old original "flickers" favourites—but, up to the time I went to France, Charlie Chaplin had not come on to the silver screen. It was during the autumn of 1914 that he hit the headlines; before that I had been one of his fans in those music-hall shows (Fred Karno's, I think) in which he habitually appeared in minor parts.

To return to Herr Kamm; he was an actual manufacturer of film projectors with a small works in Goswell Road, London, and when I saw him that day he asked me, in his thick German accent, "And what do our brave boys do in the evenings? How do they amuse themselves?" I gave him a line on some of the more respectable of their activities, and he went on: "Why do not you take out a kinematograph machine and give them picture shows?" He offered to lend me one, and said that, if I went to see the Gaumont Company, he was sure they would send films out to me every week. I thanked him for his gesture, accepted the loan of the machine and next day went to interview Messrs. Gaumont. They were extremely co-operative and very kindly agreed that 5,000 feet of film would be dispatched to Boulogne each Saturday, to be collected there by me; the previous consignment to be returned on the first available boat.

Thus it came about that, when I went back to France from leave, I took with me as officer's baggage one Kamm bioscope, complete with arc lamp and tubular legs, the whole outfit contained in three not very large cases. I hoped that my C.O.-to-be would approve my little bit of unofficial daring. Luckily he did, being a youngish captain with an interest in his men. Even luckier, the little town in which my new unit was located (Arques, near St. Omer) boasted a glass works owned by a dignified, bearded Frenchman, who not only had a most beautiful daughter but a gas engine driving a dynamo to operate his machinery as well.

First I was accepted by Monsieur and Madame as a billettee in their very fine villa, and secondly he agreed to let our unit rent an unused part of his works, abutting on to the main street, for the men's recreation. Not only that: he offered to keep his gas engine and dynamo running an extra hour twice a week in order to give me the current I wanted for the kinematograph machine. Daughter, I am sorry to say, was packed off to finishing school in Paris almost as soon as I arrived.

On the strength of its luck the 4th G.H.Q. Ammo. Park Sports Club was founded, to which every man in the unit automatically belonged. There was no lack of volunteer helpers in getting the former workshop tarted up to look something like a club room. As I have made clear, the War Office had not got round to thinking about amenities from home for the troops, and so we ordered direct from Bass, Guinness, Worthington, Johnny Walker *et al.* quantities of their bottled liquids, likewise cigarettes and tobacco from Players and Wills—all of which came out duty free.

By charging our 6-bob a day men what they paid at home—3½d. for a bottle of beer or stout and 3d. for ten fags— we both covered the rent and put enough by to build a stage on which to give theatrical performances, boxing matches and the like. The worthy Gaumont firm continued to send out their batch of films every week, and I was able (and happy) to get away to Boulogne each Sunday to pick them up.

We certainly had to scratch around to form a concert party, but gradually some N.C.O.s and men confessed to being able to sing a bit or do some amateur acting. Every officer who went home (leave now having started) was expected to bring back a complete set of gramophone records of the latest musical comedy running in London. From these our eventually launched repertory company learnt the words and music, and scenery would be painted and props scrounged from here and there. The otherwise dreary lot of our men brightened as we waited and waited for the emergency calls for ammunition which hardly ever came.

The war was in a stalemate stage and our convoy of lorries, parked along the country lane that led to Blendecques, mainly moved its wheels on practice and training runs. Other companies in the more or less near vicinity paid us visits to see our twice weekly bioscope shows, but I never heard of any of them having a kinema of their own, so I think Herr Kamm's machine must have been the first of its kind used for our troops' entertainment in World War I.

We even started a monthly "Bulletin", with staff reporters in our unit whose contributions I carefully edited with a view to the preservation of not only good discipline but decorum. I found an imprimerie in Arques, where the wife and daughter of the proprietor (who was, of course, on active service with the French army) set up the type very creditably, even if they did not understand a word of what they were setting. They ran off about 500 copies, as most of the company liked to send one home (from "Somewhere in France") and the costs were paid, of course, out of sports club funds. Such illustrations as we used from time to time were with blocks ordered from London, and looking back on the complete set of issues, which luckily have survived, I can still chuckle at some of the thinly disguised lampoons of our officers, N.C.O.s and other ranks.

Thus 1915 drew wearily to its close in our little outpost,

5—MIAML

seemingly remote from yet actually close to the firing line. Bush Newsome was not far from us, or Rowlandson; they too had received their commissions from Major Leland's recommendation. Bush was second in command of an M.T. unit commanded by the former racing driver Hornsted, which specialised in unditching lorries that had gone off the pavé on to the soft shoulder—and it was *very* soft in winter on the average French by-road, often bordering canals into which many a vehicle found its unintentional way.

Night driving on these narrow roads without lights could be really dicey, especially when two lorries met going in opposite directions. Both Bush and Rowlandson paid me not infrequent visits, and on some Sundays we all went off to Boulogne together on the film lark. My unit was lucky by being billeted for messing purposes in a typical French château, where Madame la Marquise de Vilmarest continued to reside and had graciously presented us with a salon and a share of her cuisine, in which (I imagine) our mess cook learnt a thing or two, for the Army rations became distinctly palatable.

As 1916 wore on, though, it was evident that things were going to hot up in hostilities. In June I received orders to proceed ("forthwith", of course) to the 29th Division Supply Column at a place called Wormhoudt, not far from Dunkirk. This division had been badly mauled in the ill-fated Dardenelles expedition, and was now brought back to France for a "rest". I was obliged to leave all Herr Kamm's kinematograph equipment behind me at Arques (and he was duly paid by the sports club for it), but no sooner had I joined my new unit than an urgent circular arrived from Div. H.Q. demanding that any officer with a working knowledge of kinemas should send in his name "forthwith". Mine went in: I was summoned to D.H.Q., interviewed by some brasshat and departed with the title of Divisional Kinematograph Officer (acting, unpaid) and orders to get cracking.

A hall at the back of Poperinghe railway station, not far from Ypres, had been requisitioned as a social centre, and in it there was planned a continuous film show for every afternoon. My province was to be strictly the technical one; a "front of the house" manager had been detailed in the person of a young subaltern, who from somewhere or other procured seating—for officers in the gallery, other ranks in the pit. I told him what I needed in the way of a projecting booth and a screen, and then set about finding the equipment to show the films, which had been officially laid on with Gaumont— it would still be my job, however, to pick them up at Boulogne each Sunday and return the old lot.

I made out a list of the items required to produce the right current, turn it into arc light and project the films; sent this to Div. H.Q. and promptly received orders to acquire it "forthwith". Paris seemed to me to be the only place to obtain it, if it *could* all be got, so off I went on a 3-ton lorry with permission to spend ten days and whatever money was involved. On arrival (and Paris seemed to be reasonably normal even after eighteen months of war) I reported to the British Commandant and received some information as to likely sources of supply. Naturally, manufacture had practically ceased and there wasn't much choice, but I struck lucky with Pathé for the projector, arc lamp and ancillaries, and was recommended to try the well-known motor firm of Ballot for the generator.

Here, too, I was in luck's way, for they just happened to have one suitable unit left. It was a beautiful little job— a 10 h.p. 4-cylinder engine, identical with what they had been using on their immediate pre-war car. For this stationary purpose it was mounted on a girder chassis about five feet long, and through a flexible coupling drove a five kilowatt dynamo. This meant just on fifty ampères of direct current at 110 volts—exactly what I wanted, for the throw was longish. At one end of the chassis was radiator and cooling fan, while at the other was switchboard and rheostat. Fuel supply was by gravity, the silencing was effective and on trial the engine ran with delightful sweetness.

So back to Poperinghe I drove in triumph, my "loot" aboard the lorry and the bills left behind in Paris for the British Army to settle. Installation was soon completed with the aid of my M.T. workshop's electrician, and all went well. I taught my batman how to operate the projector, as the kinema was only to be a sideline for me.

My C.O. had given me charge of an advanced workshop located a mile or so outside Poperinghe—advanced in this case meaning nearer the enemy lines than Wormhoudt. Here I had a fleet of ambulances and a crew of artificers to do running repairs; more extensive work was for the main workshops or the base one to tackle. Every night these ambulances had to drive into Ypres, about eight miles to the east, and bring back the wounded from the dreaded salient where, almost surrounded by the Germans, the 29th Division was holding the remains of the town.

Of my ambulance fleet, more than half were Model T Fords, and wonderful service they gave, seldom calling for repairs unless they had got ditched on the moonless nights when there simply wasn't a glimmer to guide the drivers on their hazardous trip. The remainder were Siddeley-Deasys, which were continually in trouble with their worm-drive back axles. Defective wartime work by untrained female labour in the Coventry factory was probably the chief cause, but spare parts were almost unobtainable and so the gallant Tin Lizzies had to put in a lot of overtime.

The kinema carried on splendidly with its three to seven o'clock performance, and the front-of-the-house manager engaged local Belgian girls to act as waitresses and serve tea to the officers. Only once do I remember there being a "flap"—it would of course be on the very evening the Divisional General had announced his intention of "going to the

pictures". I received an S.O.S. that the engine was mysteriously slowing down and current inexplicably falling, so off I
hurried on my motorbike. The arc was certainly suffering
from malnutrition and the engine gradually dying on us—
but luckily, just in time, I discovered an obscure locknut on
the governor which had worked loose and was slowly but
surely closing down the throttle. A few moments' work
with a spanner and the Ballot regained its normally healthy
beat, while the ammeter needle climbed back across the
dial.

This rather agreeable routine was too good to last, and
one day I found myself with a badly upset tummy. My
"billet" was a hut in which gas masks had once been tested,
about nine by six feet; just about room to house my camp
bed and folding canvas washstand. The loo was in a far
corner of the field which was my "home ground", and soon
I was making almost continuous treks across the damp grass
throughout the night. As some home leave was almost due I
said nothing but went—and there became so ill that a
medical board assembled at my bedside. I was soon pushed
off to that grimmest of grim hospitals—the Royal Herbert at
Woolwich—and treated for dysentery.

So for an unconscionable time I was kept hanging around
that wretched place, filling in the time by writing articles
for motoring and motorcycling papers about an M.T.
officer's job at the front. When I was at last discharged I was
marked unfit for further service overseas and in due course
posted to Grove Park M.T. Depot, which, although an
ex-workhouse, had long since replaced Aldershot as the
home base for mechanical transport training.

First, however, I was given a spot of leave and during this
bought myself a motor car—a smart little four-seater, brand
new, which had only just arrived from America. It cost me
£120, was called an Argo (a name that does not appear in
any of my reference books except as regards an electrically-

driven vehicle, which mine certainly was not). Its water-cooled engine was of about one litre capacity and ran quite nicely—but the snag was in the gearbox, which had only two speeds—and not epicyclic like the Ford Model T. I soon tired of it, found a buyer in Birmingham, drove it there and got the money; then went into P. J. Evans and bought a 7–9 Red Indian motorcycle with torpedo shaped sidecar—a real honey. It cost just about the £125 I received for the Argo.

When at length I reported for duty at Grove Park I was allocated to the workshops, where to my great delight I found my old friend Freddie Dixon was staff-sergeant. We had ridden together in many a prewar trial—he was a great guy, a North countryman who called a spade a b— shovel and had a marked affinity for all fermented liquids. Half a century ago, of course, we were both comparative youngsters, but Freddie's ability to tune engines was as outstanding then as it was in later life (when, unluckily for him, his affinity referred to had brought him into almost continuous conflict with the law).

I next discovered that one of the second lieutenants in our outfit (I had by now two stars) was Tony Vandervell, son of the proprietor of the C.A.V. firm, which was then very much in the motoring world, making electrical equipment as a quite independent concern. Tony was a gay young spark, one of the brightest in the Grove Park officers' mess, which included a number of notabilities, present or to be. There was, for instance, O. E. Mocatta, a financial giant who dabbled in cars and had a good deal to do with Maserati; there was also the Earl of Macclesfield, who had been the "angel" behind William Morris in his attempt to break into the pre-war car market with the bull-nosed Oxford.

Lord Macclesfield, who sported a fearsome "Old Bill" moustache, and I had many a stroll up and down the work-shops' yard at Grove Park, for—except when a new intake of candidates for driving jobs in the M.T. was sent along for test, and at this stage of the war they were all C3 types, mainly elderly—we were not overburdened with work.

It has to be borne in mind that the Morris Oxford, as well as William Morris himself, was then hardly known in the motoring world, although at the 1913 Olympia motor show a new and cheaper model, the Morris Cowley, had been shown. This latter, Macclesfield told me, was built up from mainly American-made parts; an order for several thousand engines from the Continental Co. of Detroit had been placed with his (Macclesfield's) guarantee of payment when delivered.

Prior to the visit to the U.S. when Mr. Morris had given this order, he had been buying components from various British suppliers, as Gordon McMinnies has recounted earlier. During the war he had to switch to making mine sinkers for the Admiralty, but Macclesfield was confident that Morris would get down to his unrealised dream of a car for the masses when peace returned.

In his autobiography *Out on a Wing*, Sir Miles Thomas says that Morris sent Macclesfield a cheque for £25,000 after the war to clear his indebtedness—and incidentally to stop him from "interfering" in the works, when Morris Motors was becoming a biggish concern. When I again met Macclesfield, several years later, he was still incensed at this treatment by Morris, for his £25,000 would have been worth many times that sum if kept in the business until Morris Motors (1926) was formed as a public company.

Few car manufacturers, of course, were being allowed to keep on with their normal productions at this middle period of the war when I was at Grove Park. Daimlers went on making their limousines for the brasshats ("Kitchener's greenhouses", they were called by the irreverent soldiery); Vauxhall, Wolseley and Sunbeam were supplied to senior officers (the Sunbeam, as I have said, being made at the Rover works), while Singer 10 h.p. light cars went to lower-ranking ones. But a revolution was taking place in all the many and various plants where cars had formerly been the main, if limited, product.

Demands for war material of an engineering nature had caused Coventry to become a hive of industry. Every vacant building was taken over by one firm or another; the population shot up to far above the 100,000 mark and, from being (as I described it earlier) a small countrified town, the place had begun the sprawl which has swallowed up acres upon acres of the pleasant green field I used to know, and the lanes where those who wished could "court" in peace in the evenings.

Getting Back to Peacetime Business

THE CESSATION OF WORLD WAR I FINDS BRITAIN'S
ESTABLISHED MOTOR MAKERS WITH GREATLY
EXPANDED PRODUCTION FACILITIES TO TURN TO
PEACETIME USE—AND ALSO A GREAT DEAL OF
COMPETITION TO MEET FROM FIRMS NOW ATTEMPT-
ING TO ENTER THE INDUSTRY FROM SCRATCH

When, at eleven o'clock on the morning of November 11th, 1918, the Armistice was declared, the United Kingdom had lost close on three-quarters of a million dead out of her peak force of nearly four million mobilised (Germany's equivalent figures were two million and eleven million respectively). Gradually Britain's land, sea and air forces were demobilised and their constituent units faced with the problem of returning to civilian employment and endeavouring to resume careers abruptly broken off up to four and more years previously.

We at Grove Park, now all Home Service types, were in the main discharged early on. For the last year or so there had been precious little to do in the workshops there, and my 7–9 Indian and sidecar had benefited from some sub rosa efforts on the part of Freddie Dixon. Tony Vandervell had presented me with one of the car lighting dynamos with which his father's firm was experimenting, and Freddie fixed this up most ingeniously on the bike's nearside footplate, driving it by a Whittle belt from a pulley fitted on the engine shaft chain sprocket and projecting through the chain cover. Electric head- and tail-lamp were already on the machine, powered by a battery, so the dynamo was wired into circuit through a neat little switchbox which attached to the top of the tank and exactly matched up with its curve.

Freddie Dixon was certainly a splendid craftsman: he also made for my sidecar the attachments and connections to the Indian's engine for a gasbag, which was necessary in those days of extreme petrol rationing if one wanted to do any joyriding. I did, in order to get away from the drinking and gambling that went on at Grove Park depot every night, in which Tony Vandervell was one of the prime movers, seemingly with a bottomless purse. Evidently *he* didn't exist on a second lieutenant's pay—but I never discovered what physical disability caused so many of the Grove Park "permanents" to be marked down for home service only!

Demobilised early in 1919 I found myself unwilling to go back to Coventry to live, and being now nearly twenty-seven had got to set about finding the right niche in life without too much delay. The various wartime articles I had written for motoring and motorcycling papers had put me on good terms with both Iliffe's and Temple Press, but, as the former then had their headquarters in Coventry, it was to Rosebery Avenue, London, I turned my attention. From here *The Motor* and *Motor Cycling* were published, together with *The Cyclecar* and *Commercial Motor*. I duly approached them through their formidable general manager, one Ernest Perman, and after being vetted by him was taken on at a £400 p.a. salary—which sounds precious little now, but would probably be the equivalent of at least a thousand today. Young Roland Dangerfield, son of the firm's founder, Edmund, came out of the Royal Flying Corps and joined a short while after; so, too, did W. M. W. Thomas who, much later and after a spell as Chairman of B.O.A.C., was knighted and became Sir Miles.

The British motor industry—I could say the whole European one—was in a pretty chaotic state. My old firm

Rover had acquired a very useful design and prototype for an 8 h.p. two-cylinder air-cooled light car from "young" Jack Sangster, whose family owned the Swift concern. It had made motorcycles and a light car prior to 1914, but this new model was entirely novel and not so much a cyclecar as a genuine light car.

The Rover Eight proved a best seller for several years after the firm marketed it in late 1919: they also revived their Twelve, renaming it the Fourteen but leaving it otherwise unchanged except for fitting a self-starter. Bush Newsome had returned to the company, and I remember him demonstrating the new starter to me in London one day. He proudly pressed the button; there was a loud cracking sound and some bits fell from under the car on to the road. Then silence. More development work was evidently needed.

Most of the established motor manufacturers returned to their immediate pre-war productions, but many new names appeared. One that looked like making good—and, had it done so, might have been a serious competitor to Morris— was Clyno of Wolverhampton. Up to the war they had concentrated on motorcycle and sidecar outfits, and during it had supplied many thousands to the War Office, with machine guns mounted on the sidecar. Now they set about making a light car, almost the same size as the Morris Cowley but a lot more peppy with its overhead valve engine.

Frank Smith, son of the proprietor of Clynos, had been a successful competitor in numerous pre-war motorcycle trials and they certainly had much technical knowhow. They also secured the Rootes as their world exporters, and seemed all set for big business with a good product, but they were obliged to fold up after a few years of producing a very promising product.*

* *Note by Alfred Pemberton:* Clyno Cars went bust in 1927, at a time when their sales were going up. I know, as it cost my agency £6,000! We were then advertising agents doing a successful job.

My first big assignment for Temple Press was to cover the Paris–Nice trial in January 1920, for which a number of British competitors were entered. There was the usual post-war dearth of cars, but nevertheless Ernest Perman instructed me to go over to Paris and "borrow a car from one of the French manufacturers". This of course proved completely impossible, and so I perforce fell back on a plan of travelling from one overnight stopping place of the trial to the next by train. I had one of the firm's photographers with me, but could only take over his equipment, let him go thankfully back home and hope there would be some chance of getting a few pictures.

The start took place at a squalid suburb of Paris called Montgéron at some unearthly hour on a January morning, when about a hundred competitors, including a number of old British stalwarts, set off on the first leg of the journey with Dijon as the overnight stop. When they had left I hurried back in my taxi to the Gare de Lyon, took train to Dijon and arrived at about the same time as the leaders.

Here I was given a résumé of the day's doings by Rex Mundy, who was competing on I forget what but had had a clean run. Dr. A. M. Low was acting as British representative official, and I made my first acquaintance with him on this trial; he amplified my collection of news, which was duly written up at the hotel. Similarly on the second day I entrained for Lyons, and the same routine applied.

But on the third morning I was stymied over catching my train because, unknown to me, French daylight-saving time had come into operation at midnight and it had already left when I reached the station. The afternoon train got me into Cannes too late to meet the competitors as they came in, but my informants genned me up, and the trial finished at Nice next day.

There was then a decrepit tram which ran along the corniche road from Cannes to Nice, and I took it in preference to the train. I have vivid memories still of the way in which the body of this tram weaved as it went round the innumerable bends: one had to sit well clear of the corners. Otherwise a vulnerable portion of one's anatomy underwent the treatment which (they tell me) pretty girls are none too averse from accepting from young men in Italy today. However, the tram got me to Nice, where I finished my story and sent it to the office on Press telegram forms (there was no telephone through to London at that time).

Now came the problem of getting back to England. The French railwaymen were on the eve of one of their periodical strikes, and any north-bound train was crowded to the gunwales. Dr. Low (whose official transport was remaining at Nice) and I decided to get away as quickly as ever possible and did get aboard a train eventually, but had to stand in the corridor all night, the whole way to Paris. During that time I got to know him better, and found him a very likeable man, gifted with a quick brain and an extensive knowledge of science.

I was to become still more friendly with "Archie" Low as time went on, and do not subscribe to the belief apparently held by some people that he was a charlatan. He possessed the knack of making a scientific problem seem clear, which (apparently) a "real" scientist must not do without risk to his reputation. He was, also, certainly the wittiest after-dinner speaker I have ever heard.

One of Low's specialities was an audiometer, his early attempt to measure noise in a comparative manner. He had used this in the one and only silencer trial ever held for motorcycles, conducted by the Auto-Cycle Union on Brooklands track before the war. Now he was commissioned by London's Underground railways to get readings with this instrument of the improvement effected by adopting double-skinned (with cork interlay) coaches in place of the wartime, and terribly noisy, single-sheet-steel-skinned ones.

I went with Dr. Low on a trip the length of the Central London line, first on one type of coach and then on the other. The apparatus certainly indicated a big difference between them in favour of the double-skinned one. And this outing gave me the opportunity of asking Archie Low whether he would act as my best man in a certain function due to take place very soon.

This he very kindly did, when I was married to Pat Dunham at the Chapel Royal, Savoy, on July 31st, 1920. He kept everyone in fits of laughter at the reception in the Hotel Cecil afterwards. Then, when my bride and I were seen off to Paris from Victoria he caused so much hilarity that I clean forgot to pick up my briefcase, containing our passports, at the barrier. I discovered its absence in the train en route for Dover, and the Pullman conductor obligingly threw a note out of the window at one of the stations through which the trained whistled. But that didn't solve the problem of how to get out of England and into France, and at that early stage after World War I officialdom was just as suspicious of everyone as it is now.

It seemed such nonsense in the first place to have to *have* a passport just to go to France—before the war no country but Russia demanded such a thing of any travelling Englishman, and his golden sovereigns were welcomed by one and all. Now (1920) we had dirty paper pounds to change into even dirtier pieces of paper instead of louis d'or and whacking great silver five-franc coins. I don't think we had descended so low as having limited travel allowances just then, though.

When we arrived at Dover I told the passport official of our plight, and he said that, although he would let us go on the boat, there was no guarantee that the French at Calais would be equally accommodating in reverse. So, as the boat steamed into its berth alongside the Gare Maritime, I spoke earnestly to one of the ship's officers who happened to be leaning over the rail. He pointed out a man in leggings on the quayside and told me that he was chief of the Sécurité who vetted arrivals.

I sought this official out when we had disembarked and explained that we had been married that morning and were on our way to Paris for the honeymoon. He beamed, all but said "Vive le Sport", and told me, when I got to the guichet where passports were examined, to look out for him. I did so, and he very graciously saw us on to the train and gave us, so to speak, his benediction. Next morning, or it may have been the one after that, our passports arrived in a registered letter from my father, who had collected our forgotten case from the lost property office.

Motoring journalists are no modern invention. Before and during my time there were such early stalwarts as Max Pemberton, Gerald Biss, John Phillimore, Massac Buist, Thornton Rutter, John Prioleau, Edgar de Normanville and Wilfred Gordon Aston, to name a few outside of the staff of the actual motoring journals, among whom W. F. (Bill) Bradley is perhaps the best remembered because he lived on into the 1960s, even though he reported the disastrous Paris to Madrid race of 1903.

Most of the national daily papers and glossy weeklies had a motoring correspondent, despite the fact that the public's interest in cars was but a tithe of what it is today. But a new model did not necessarily cause a real splash in the dailies, probably because motor manufacturers on the whole were not then big spenders in the advertisement columns.

An advertising manager handled publicity as a side line; the term Public Relations Officer had not been heard of, or Press Officer either. The advertising-cum-publicity manager looked after everything to do with that aspect of the firm, and was usually subservient to the sales manager. Professional P.R. firms I never imagined any need for, although advertising agents did exist, but on a rather smallish scale. Catalogues, instruction manuals and often spare parts lists—

all had to be looked after by the advertising/publicity manager in the 'twenties. I think the first British concern to separate the two branches was the Rootes, of whom more anon.

Certainly the most successful publicist of immediate post-first-war days was John Prioleau, who had been personal assistant to Lord Northcliffe for a long and exhausting spell. His chief, who, as we have seen, was a keen protagonist of motoring, told him after the Armistice to take a working holiday. Prioleau was himself an enthusiast for cars and what they were made for—travel—and he went off "into the blue" with a British, but anonymous, motor car. Every week he turned in two or three instalments of his romantically thrilling adventures in exotic-sounding North African towns. Little was known in Britain of this part of the world (except that the films were glorifying the desert sheik, but few people knew in those days just where Morocco, the Sahara, or Rudolf Valentino's stamping ground lay). At any rate, Prioleau's stories kept on appearing in the *Daily Mail*, which then had by far the largest circulation of any national daily paper, and were followed with the keenest interest by hundreds of thousands of readers, motorists and non-motorists alike.

More and more people kept asking what make of car was Prioleau's "Imshi", the only name by which he ever referred to it. But he kept his secret until the very last line of his final story—" 'Imshi' was a Morris Oxford". I have always believed that it was this journalistic enterprise which caused the public at large really to be aware that Mr. W. R. Morris did make cars.

Whether Lord Northcliffe considered that W. R. M. got too much for too little I don't know; but I do know that Prioleau left the *Daily Mail* very soon afterwards and joined Morris as advertising/publicity manager. He remained in that job until Mr. Morris, with his hiring and firing mentality, took on W. M. W. Thomas to replace Prioleau. Thomas stayed the course until November 1947 when he, too, went out of Morris Motors at more or less a moment's notice.

In view of my now being a married man, Temple Press had graciously—I nearly said grudgingly—raised my stipend to £500 p.a., and we were just about managing on this. Early in 1923, however, I received a long-winded telegram from J. K. Starley at Rovers, asking me to call in and see him "when I was next in Coventry".

The very next day I certainly *was* in Coventry, and J. K. told me that, as Harry Smith would shortly retire, and the directors had designated him (J. K.) to take over, he would no longer be able to handle advertising and publicity— would I care to come and take it on? This sounded a wonderful chance, especially when he asked me to name the salary I should want. With forced bravado I said £800 and, as this left him apparently unshaken, the deal was concluded there and then.

With as little delay as possible I removed myself from the purlieu of Ernest Perman and transferred my wife and self to Coventry; we went at the outset to the old King's Head hotel. Memories came back of my first stay there in 1911 when, as a callow youth of eighteen, I had joined the Rover Company. Then, I had been allocated a little bedroom, candle-lit, with a corner cupboard which, when opened, revealed the body of a man.

After my initial shock, I noticed that "he" was dressed in a curious, old-fashioned style, with a three-cornered hat. I realised then that this was Peeping Tom, looking out over Broadgate in perpetual penance for having disobeyed orders and spied on the beauteous Lady Godiva when she rode, according to legend, naked through the city of Coventry centuries ago. (I believe this same figure is now in the Leofric Hotel in Broadgate, the King's Head having been destroyed by the German air raids in World War II.)

6—MIAML

But next we had to find a desirable residence where an £800 a year executive might have the amenities compatible with his status. Bush Newsome, back again at Rovers, told me he had heard of a furnished cottage to let in Bridge End, Warwick, a part of the ancient town which, in spite of my pre-war familiarity with it, I had never seen. Bridge End is a tiny lane lying on the south side of the River Avon, facing across it to the castle and hard by the bridge over which the road from Banbury enters Warwick.

We duly went along one evening and found the most picturesque row of cottages it is possible to imagine, their gardens at the back running down to the river's edge. Knocking at the door of an ivy-covered one called "The Nook", as directed, we waited for quite a while before there was any response and, when at last there was, a dignified gent carrying a black bag emerged, an elderly woman in the background.

It appeared that her husband, tenant of the cottage, had passed away only minutes previously, and the doctor had just signed the death certificate. Yes, she said, she did now want to let the cottage and we could have first refusal. We expressed our condolences and left, returning next day, when matters had a satisfactory conclusion and shortly after we entered into possession.

"The Nook" consisted of two adjoining cottages converted into one and although it was not, perhaps, perfection—the bathroom was in an outhouse, for instance—the place was so delightfully olde worlde and conveniently situated that we enjoyed every day we lived there, once I had learnt to duck and avoid the beams. After our flat in a busy part of London, the peace and quiet of Warwick seemed almost oppressive at first, especially at night. And, in the following year we were blessed with a son, whom we christened John Dudley. Life seemed idyllic.

Back in the 'twenties traffic on the main roads around

Coventry was comparatively light, and I could easily make the ten miles from Warwick to the works in a bare twenty minutes on my Rover Eight. But great though the success which had attended its introduction had been, sales were falling off as new models came on the market from other firms, notably the Austin Seven. This, with four-cylinder water-cooled engine was, according to Rover dealers, something the public thought much superior to a twin-cylinder.

Air-cooling, too, was suspect, and I was called on to devise demonstrations of its reliability and economy of running. One such was to make a non-engine-stop trip from Land's End to John o' Groats under R.A.C. observation, which duly took place and would have been a complete success had not one of the drivers (there were six altogether, taking over at different points along the route) inadvertently stalled his engine in Bristol traffic.

It became clear, however, that the Rover Eight was moribund, so hastily a four-cylinder model called the 9/20 was produced, with the required four-cylinder water-cooled engine, and the poor old Eight departed this life. Now I had to convince the public that the 9/20 was as economical to run as the Eight had been, so this time I arranged that the R.A.C. should take any one they chose off the showroom floor and, with two girls driving it, see how far it would run for a fiver.

In fact it covered 2,147 miles, the plan being that what was paid for out of the £5 should be the petrol, oil and cost of replacing any damaged or broken parts—labour charge only should the part be covered by guarantee. The trial proved a great success, especially as the route took in most of the Rover dealers up and down the country, who naturally made the most they could out of it publicity-wise in their local Press.

Soon afterwards, however, a letter was published in one of the motoring journals from the Hon. Victor Bruce, claiming that our good average of fuel consumption was obtained simply and solely because of the British 20 m.p.h. speed limit. Had it been conducted on the Continent, where more realistic ideas on the subject of speed applied, the consumption, he claimed, would have been much greater.

We could not let this pass unchallenged, so I asked J. K. to approve a trial from Calais to Monte Carlo at a "normal" touring speed, once again under R.A.C. observation. He did, and across the Channel from Dover we went with an open four-seater 9/20, a cheerful little party comprising Bush Newsome, Jack Starley (son of J. K.), R. W. Sprague, the R.A.C. observer, and myself. This was in August 1923, and the weather was superb. Beaucoup of M. Psalty's soleil, in fact.

Such accompanied-car traffic as there then was to the Continent was easily handled by a solitary Southern Railways' freighter, which could take up to a dozen cars and made a single round trip daily. Or one could, with the captain's permission, have one's car craned aboard the mail boat, which cost more and meant that the tank must be drained completely dry. If luck were in, a man with a push cart containing a few bidons of *essence* might be discovered on the quay at Calais: on the freighter, however, could be left enough juice in the tank to get into the town. We therefore chose this route, which deposited us at Boulogne, the one and only car aboard—and in August, too! I mention this to indicate that very few people took their cars with them to the Continent, even in 1923.

From Boulogne we drove down the R.N.1, not very different then from now, to Beauvais, took the diversion to avoid Paris by way of Pontoise and Versailles and rejoined the main road south near where Orly Airport is today. We stopped at Fontainebleau the first night and here, in the absence of a secure lock-up garage, the car was packaged in a waterproof "bag" made specially to be sealed by a rope passing through cleats with an R.A.C. padlock at its ends.

On, next day, through Auxerre and Avallon—no bypasses
to the numerous villages then—and an overnight stay at
Orange, where the same procedure was gone through with
the car.

The following, and final, day saw us driving along the
Riviera coast, and my most interesting recollection is that,
in this glorious mid-summer weather, there just wasn't any
holiday traffic—a general belief was held that the South of
France was unhealthily hot in summer; all the big hotels
were closed. We drove along the deserted Promenade des
Anglais at Nice, stopped the car by the kerb, went down to
the beach and bathed with hardly another soul in sight.
Arrived at Monte Carlo, our goal, we drove right slap up
to the front door of the Casino, placed the car in front of it
and took all the photographs I wanted with never an interfering official to say us nay. Just fancy trying to do that
nowadays!

The results of this trial of the 9/20 Rover, as certified by
the Royal Automobile Club, were satisfactory to our firm,
because average speed worked out at 30 m.p.h. and fuel
consumption about the same as on the 20 m.p.h. effort. I
drafted up some advertisements for our quarter pages in the
weekly illustrated papers—*Bystander*, *Sketch*, *Tatler*, *Field* and
Country Life were about all we could afford to go into with the
budget then in operation of £5,000 for the whole year. (I
should add that I had a very serious talk with J. K. about
this parsimony, by reason of him wanting me to squeeze
catalogues out of it too, and the outcome was that the
directors agreed to quadruple it the following year.)

Very soon after the Monte Carlo trip I was called to
a meeting in the boardroom attended by the heads of works
and sales departments and presided over by the managing
director. I should mention that Owen Clegg was no longer
with the company—he had left long before to take up a
better-paid position with Darracq in France—and there was

in fact no really competent designer at Rovers. The meeting had as its object the remedying of this deficiency, and, after J.K. had outlined the sad lack of orders for the Fourteen—which, as I have said, was the resurrected Twelve of pre-war days—he told us a replacement on thoroughly modern lines was an urgent necessity.

Rovers had, continued J. K., no less than £150,000 cash lying at the bank, which should be fully enough to buy the best talent in the international motor engineering field and, not only that, but also to put the new car into production. It must, however, be in the firm's tradition of appealing to the middle-class buyer who appreciated quality and wanted reliability. So the search for *the* designer was on; it was to last for quite some while—and in the end to yield results very far from what had been hoped for. Nearly, in fact, to bankrupt the old company, and to sound the death knell of J. K. Starley into the bargain.

Meanwhile, however, I learnt that a mechanic was to be sent out to Budapest, where the Rover dealer was in dire trouble with the worm drive back axles of the 9/20. He was one of only a very few European motor agents daring enough to import an English-made product which, although well enough suited to the good roads (comparatively speaking) of its home country, was quite frankly incapable of standing up to Continental conditions.

Exports were not favourably regarded by the British industry; selling abroad was a damned nuisance and not particularly necessary as, even after the first war, the country was in no great need of foreign currency. We still had an Empire and owned railways, tramways and public utility companies all over the world which had not yet encountered nationalistic difficulties—nor had British prestige so far been dragged down by the politicians.

It seemed to me that some useful publicity could be obtained by making the journey to Hungary on a car instead of sending the mechanic out in the train, and the project was agreed. A Fourteen with Weymann saloon body was made ready for the trip—then considered somewhat adventurous—and so once again I soon found myself on the other side of the Channel. The car had been transformed into an "export" model by fitting it with larger wheels and a lower ratio back axle, as was done with those sent to Australia, New Zealand and South Africa, each of which countries did import a certain number of British cars.

Roads were very bad nearly everywhere abroad, however, and our cars simply were not made to cope with conditions overseas like the Americans were. The campaign to "Get America out of the Mud" was only just starting to take effect; it was still a sheer impossibility to motor from coast to coast of the U.S.A. with any degree of comfort.

My co-driver on the Budapest trip was a mechanic, Gethin by name, well versed in the vagaries of worm-driven back axles. Our Weymann body was the current "rage"—a flexible skeleton of hard wood uprights, with thin steel jointing plates, supporting a fabric covering. The basic idea was that, as the simple girder used for chassis construction left it so whippy, a coachbuilt saloon body creaked as it weaved, whereas with the Weymann system it silently followed suit. Although quite effective, it naturally had to have severely square-ish lines—which came to be regarded as fashionable.

We headed east from Ostend, having reached there in the mailboat from Dover, and bumped our way over the Belgian pavé to Aachen, then across Germany and into Austria. In Vienna we were met by our man from Budapest, a dignified bearded gent who looked like nothing to do with selling motor cars. I don't know what his nationality was—his name was Saile, pronounced Zyler—and he was the very soul of courtesy.

While we were in Hungary we were his personal guests;

he took us out to every meal and, just before its conclusion, would ask to be excused, disappear for a few moments and come back having settled the bill, so that we should not even glimpse such a sordid thing. In the end we had to lay plans to evade him, so we could do a little sight-seeing on our own, but he certainly was a very kind man and I did hope he wouldn't have any more trouble with his worms.

I do recall, however, what a heartrending performance it was when departing from a hotel in Austria or Hungary at this era, when a service percentage on the bill was unknown. As one passed along the corridor to the front door there would be a long line of mainly elderly women, whom one had not previously seen, but who obviously expected the English milords to distribute largesse with a lavish hand. One had to (well, *I* did) hurry along the ranks with head averted, feeling like a cad to let the British Raj down, and very likely the old ladies had to pay the hotel management to take up their stations in the corridor.

But what beautiful cities Budapest and Vienna were in the 'twenties, with little cafés out in the woods from which my beloved tzigane music poured forth in a continuous soothing stream. The violins of the gipsies throbbed and moaned the night through, and I would not have missed this glimpse of near-eastern Europe at that time for anything.

Home again, I found plenty of outlets for stories about our adventurous trip "across Europe". It has to be remembered that only very few British motorists—or even non-motorists for that matter—took their holidays abroad at a time when travel agents (apart from Thos. Cook) hardly existed, and the belief was widely held that "wogs begin at Calais" and all sorts of unknown hazards lay in wait for travellers abroad.

Cars were not yet noted for their reliability and there were no service stations on the Continent capable of coping with the British product (except for Rolls-Royce, whose owners always were ably catered for, being rich and noted for their wanderlust). The formalities also were daunting: one had to carry a triptyque, a separate one for every country to be visited, and an International Driving Permit, for which one had to pass a driving test conducted by the R.A.C. in London. Frontier formalities were generally time-consuming, and if one got through a pair of customs posts within half an hour one was lucky. Finally, our British railways did all they could to dissuade cross-Channel traffic with cars.

Back at the Rover I found that two designers were on the short list for the job: one was Major H. E. Barker, whose simple, straightforward H.E. car had recently been well received by the knowledgable motoring world, but who was definitely not of international stature. The other was P. A. Poppe, a Norwegian who had achieved distinction by his work for Dennis Motors, the commercial vehicle manufacturers, and for his engine and carburetter firm of White and Poppe. He already had a design on paper for a car which certainly seemed fully modern in that its four-cylinder engine had hemispherical combustion chambers, an overhead camshaft, valves set at 45 degree angle, a four-speed gearbox and spiral bevel back axle. It looked as if it filled the directors' requirements exactly, and it was not long before they signed up Mr. Poppe to produce a prototype.

Now, there is no doubt at all that P. A. Poppe was a clever engineer; he had, however, an inability to express himself clearly in English, and when a technical question was put to him he would reply in somewhat un-understandable language, producing a slide rule to give the impression that critics were talking without any genuine knowledge. He also had the habit, which I came up against time and time again, of starting to reply to a question as he filled his over-sized pipe.

He would then apply a long wood match to it and let the match burn down as he endeavoured to find the words he wanted. Finally the flame would get too close to his fingers for comfort; he would shake it out and restart another match. Eventually, one left him without ever quite getting any answer to what one wanted to know. Since none of the Rover directors was a very technical man, they had to take him on his reputation to a considerable extent.

At any rate (and I was at the meeting in the boardroom when he did so), Mr. Poppe guaranteed that his new car would (a) weigh 25 cwt., (b) cover 25 miles on a gallon of petrol, (c) sell profitably for £450 as an open four-seater, and (d) have a top speed of 65 m.p.h. All of which was just what the old firm called for, and everyone brightened up on the decision to go ahead at full speed.

Alas, there's many a slip . . . and this brave new 14/45 Rover did not measure up to its creator's no doubt genuine beliefs, or the directors' sanguine hopes. Whether it was the design itself or the way it was put into effect I don't know, but I do know that, when the works director (Mark Wild) saw the first cylinder head he walked out, never to return.

It was a huge affair, weighing best part of a hundredweight, the operation of the valves being that the inlets were actuated directly off a single camshaft in the head, and the exhausts by long pushrods running horizontally across the wide head. Drive to the camshaft was by a massive shaft rising vertically from the centre of the crankshaft, with skew gears at each end.

When a complete car came through for its testing it was found (a) that it weighed far more than 25 cwt., (b) that it would not do 25 miles to a gallon, (c) that it could not be made to sell for £450, and (d) it would only get the speedometer even to 60 m.p.h. under favourable conditions. But the great snag was that the camshaft driving gears set up a loud clickety-clack if there was the least little bit of backlash in them—the engine sounded as if a big-end had gone. It had to be priced at £550 as an open four-seater and even then was hardly a viable proposition.

Exhibited at the 1924 Olympia show it certainly attracted plenty of attention, though rather overshadowed by the 14 h.p. Hillman, which was a plain, no-frills four-cylinder car not very dissimilar from the H.E. of Major Barker. However, the 14/45 Rover duly went into production, but it gave the Service department one long nightmare trying to cure the gear noise from the engine. I must say, however, that if you could disregard this the car was quite comfortable to ride in, as I found on a publicity run from Land's End to John o' Groats. It was very obviously underpowered, however, with a mere two-litre engine, so it was upgraded to a 16/50 by boring out the cylinders.

I did my best to think up stunts to popularise it, and the only one that really paid off was to make fifty consecutive climbs of the North Wales test hill—Bwlch-y-Groes, between Dinas Mawddwy and Bala—in a day. The hill was much used at this period for proving new models (it was said that, if you camped out at the top for a week or so in September, you would see every new model to be launched by the motor industry at Olympia the following month). At any rate, Rover was awarded the Dewar Trophy for this effort, which gave me something to advertise.

Sales lagged badly, however, and the financial position of the company degenerated until, in 1928, it became desperate. Suddenly one morning there arrived in the boardroom a Colonel Frank Searle, and he began decimating the office and works staff. J. K. Starley he packed off on a world sales tour, and, when he reached New Zealand, the furthest point away, was sent a cable telling him he was sacked. (When he did get back to England, J.K. started a one-man insurance broking business without any great success, and did not live very much longer.) The stock of cars was jobbed off to David Rosenfield, a Manchester dealer, for much-needed cash, and the works were readied for a complete change of product.

In this the resilient P. A. Poppe regained his reputation, for he came up with a plain, straightforward six-cylinder-engined car of the popular two-litre size, with pushrod valves and no nonsense. The Weymann saloon body was retained and, with it, this new Light Six Rover, designated 16 h.p. for taxation purposes, sold for £395 complete, or £425 with a very smart Sportsman's Coupé body.

The first cars were handed out to motoring journalists on which to cover the International Six Days motorcycle trials in the Lake District, and the general verdict was extremely favourable. Production soon got under way and, at the 1928 motor show, the Rover stand was besieged and the orders placed astonished even Colonel Searle, who saw that his surgeon's work was almost at an end. But he also had done what proved to be the best thing that could have happened to the old firm during this trying period—he had persuaded Mr. Spencer Wilks to become general manager.

"Spen" Wilks had, until shortly before this, been a joint managing director of the Hillman Motor Car Company, his co-m.d. being brother-in-law Captain John Black, and the reason for their relinquishing these positions will be explained later. To return to the Rover Company, however, things were starting to look a lot brighter and we were able to "push the boat out" in the advertising sense, after severe cutting back during the previous critical period.

Col. Searle laid down a policy whereby our entire advertising appropriation was concentrated in a whole page once a month in three daily newspapers. The *Daily Mail*, then on the crest of the wave with the largest circulation (topping two million), charged £900 — £1,200 if one took the front page—the *Daily Express*, with around 1½ million, charged £750, and the *Daily Dispatch* of Manchester £350. It was my job to fill the space, and I would rough out a design and get it drawn up by a Coventry studio. We put a coupon in every one, and they brought in hundreds of applications for catalogues. Sales went up and up and dealers began to have faith in the old firm once again.

One day our commissionaire, who inhabited the ground floor front room in a house adjoining the Meteor Works entrance, telephoned up to my office to say that "a Mr. Sidney Henschel from the *Yorkshire Post* would like to see you". This gentleman had a novel proposition to put forward: if Rover would take half a page, the paper would get advertisements from dealers throughout Yorkshire, also from component suppliers, and there would be editorial space to fill altogether two pages into the bargain. To the best of my knowledge, this was the first "composite" page to be published in connection with the motor industry, and it was to become so much copied that its very popularity brought it into disrepute in due course.

But this proved the start of a firm friendship between Sidney Henschel and myself, which endured and strengthened over the years. He moved on to the *Financial News* and, later, to the Advertisement Directorship of the *Financial Times* when the two papers merged sixteen years after.

For the 1930 season a new version of the Rover Six was to be launched, priced at only £325, plus £7 extra for a four-speed gearbox. One day Col. Searle and Spencer Wilks called me into the boardroom and said they wanted something done for it in the nature of an announcement demonstration that would put the new model over to the public in a big way. "I want to see it splashed in a national daily paper," said the Colonel, "something that will make people really talk."

I unfolded a scheme which had, as they say, been burgeoning in my mind for some time past. It was that a car should race, and beat, the famous "Blue Train", which (in those days long before air travel) conveyed the wealthy and/or high-born away from the chill winter of England to the sunnier clime of the French and Italian Riviera.

Consisting entirely of blue-painted luxury wagons-lits coaches and restaurant cars, the Blue Train departed from Calais quay on the arrival of the 11 a.m. service from Victoria to Dover, which connected with the Southern Railway's crack mailboat across the Channel; this would be about 2.30 p.m., as soon as the nobility and gentry had settled down in their Pullmans. It was the quintessence of gracious travel in an era when the French Riviera and Monte Carlo were the winter-time goal of all those in the social swim, and wanted to be seen to be so.

The Blue Train took close on twenty-four hours to get right through to its terminus at Vintimille, just over the Italian border from Menton, and most people imagined that it travelled all the way at fully a mile a minute. So did I, until careful investigation of the timetable revealed that in fact its average speed from start to finish was some 40 m.p.h. This was because its passage around Paris on the Ceinture railway, from the Gare du Nord to the Gare de Lyon, wasted nearly three-quarters of an hour; it also stopped at Dijon for a change of locomotive and, at Marseilles, went into a dead-end and had to come out, with a fresh engine, in the reverse direction. To beat it on its trip to the glamorous Riviera would—I was sure—make a popular news story.

The idea found favour in the boardroom and an estimate of expense was called for—I still have a copy of my costings—and, allowing for three persons' expenses for a week, plus petrol and cross-Channel fares, it came to just under £100. Yes, the firm could stand this, and so off I went to see Harold Pemberton at the *Daily Express* and put the project to him; would his paper let him come? He was as "sold" on the scheme as much as I was, and we both went along to see his Editor (then Beverley Baxter), who also was favourable. Next I had to convince "Bill" Needham, the advertising director, that his paper's advertising columns would not lose anything over it, and he too agreed. Finally, we went together to see "Robbie" (E. J. Robertson), then general manager, and got *his* approval.

But I was in dire trouble at home, for Pat, my wife, had been seriously ill during a long time with lung trouble, and the doctor had warned me recently that the end could not be long delayed. Poor Pat actually passed away on January 10th, 1930, at the early age of twenty-eight. Everything that could be done had been, including a stay at a Swiss clinic, but T.B. treatment then was not nearly so efficacious as it is today. John, our son, was nearly six years old, and I installed him and his nannie in a comfortable hotel. It was a sad time for me but, as I have said, not unexpected over a period of fully a year.

So Harold Pemberton and I, accompanied by one Bennett, a tester from the factory, now fixed our departure date for January 20th, went across to Calais and stayed the night there. Next day we stationed ourselves alongside the Blue Train's locomotive on the side of the level crossing where we could get clear away into the town and thence on to R.N.1. The mailboat duly arrived to time, and the usual flurry of passengers and porters streamed along the platform. Gradually things quietened down and before long whistles shrilled and a hoarse blast from the engine's siren indicated impending departure.

At the first puff from the smoke stack we, aboard the car with engine running and first gear engaged, made our way at all speed out of the dock area, through the town and on to the main road *vers* Boulogne, Abbeville and Beauvais. Clear of this last, we bore right to avoid Paris, as on the Monte Carlo trip already described, hit the main road to the south at La Belle Épine and so into the wooded country preceding Fontainebleau forest.

The wintry daylight had faded by this time and we noted

with some dismay that cars coming towards us had a corona of mist around their headlamps. Fog ahoy, we told one another, and sure enough down it came and the further we went the worse it got. By eight o'clock we still had an hour in hand over the train, but we were driving without headlamps and keeping up any real speed was out of the question.

When we eventually reached the Saône river at Châlon it was three in the morning and the street lamps could only be faintly glimpsed when right under them. There was no alternative but to call it a day; we groped our way to an hotel which luckily had a night porter on duty and put up there for the rest of the night. We had only covered 300 miles in twelve hours' running.

With morning the fog disappeared and we held a confab, the outcome of which was that the Blue Train both went to the Riviera and came back therefrom—so let us wend our way to the Mediterranean and have another go from the southern end. This settled, we covered the remainder of the run to Nice with just one stop, at a rather delightful country house type of hotel at Brignôles. It was an unintentionally lucky choice, as we were to discover a night or two later. For, having once again set off in company with the train, this time on Sunday evening from St. Raphaël, the first (or last) stop on the Riviera coast, we had only covered some thirty miles when Bennett, who was driving, misjudged a sharp bend in the teeming rain—and over the edge we went for, as they say, a burton.

Exactly what sort of a burton was unknown to us as, for what seemed an age, we sat in the car, airborne and with the headlamps pointing towards the sky. Would it be six feet—or sixty? Luckily it was no more than about eight, but we came down with a horrid-sounding crash and tinkle of broken glass. Luckily, too, the headlamps continued to function and showed us we were in a sodden field.

Pem, who was in the back, was knocked out by a cross-beam in the roof, but not for long. I tried my door, found it would open, and got out: Haj followed suit, and temporarily disappeared, having stepped down into a gully running with water between the front and back wheels. Now we saw that what we had "flown" over was the banking of the curve where the road modernisers had graded it to prevent just this kind of thing happening—but not at fifty miles an hour.

So there we were, at ten o'clock at night on a deserted road (the R.N.7, as a matter of fact) with the rain pouring down and already soaked to the skin. For all that it was a main road, it might have been a byway on the Yorkshire moors for any sign of life that was apparent. Not a lone cottage, not a wayside telephone . . . but stay, a feeble flicker appeared away down in the valley and got gradually brighter—a car, and coming towards us. It started to breast the hill with our curve at the top; we shouted and waved and the driver pulled up, thank heaven. A small Citroen it was, carrying four young Frenchmen in an advanced state of merriment—evidently returning from a wedding party or something of the kind.

They all got out, looked over the edge of the curve at our ditched Rover and, to our astonishment and some chagrin, burst out laughing more heartily than ever. It was the funniest thing they had seen, apparently—but it was our turn to laugh as their Citroen was found to be making its own way back down the hill, the handbrake not being man enough to hold it. They had to sprint to save it being scraped along the rocky roadside, and this sobered them up a bit. At any rate, they promised on leaving to alert the first garage they came to, but it was best part of an hour before a breakdown lorry arrived from Le Luc, a few miles back along the road we had come.

From the manner in which the *mécanicien* set to work it seemed as if our incident was a not uncommon one. He

quickly had a chain from his winch fixed to the Rover's
tail end and we all heaved until the two back wheels were
once again on the road. Chocking these, the chain was now
transferred to the front end of our car and before long it was
standing normally with all four wheels on *terra* wet but *firma*,
at a safe distance from the edge.

Fearfully we examined it; little damage was apparent and
the engine started up, but when we gave a trial run there
was such a nasty grating from the region of the back axle that
it seemed as if something was seriously amiss there. It proved,
however, to be nothing more than the valance of the nearside wing, which had been bent so that it fouled the tyre
tread, and Bennett pronounced the car runnable.

We gave thanks to our saviour from Le Luc, together with
generous remuneration—and then remembered that hotel at
Brignôles, not very far distant. So, with infinite caution, we
made our way to it. By the time we got there it was well
after midnight on this miserable Sunday and, with so little
traffic on the road, we feared the hotel would be shut up
tight. But a French hôtelier doesn't lie down on his job; as
we turned from the road into the drive, festoons of lights
shone out from the trees, the front door opened to let out a
flood of welcoming light and we were given a warm reception.

In no time at all we were in comfortable beds, in three
rooms which opened off one another; our soaking clothes
were down in the boiler house and we ourselves were sipping
hot grog preparatory to eating a miraculously produced
meal. Always do I think with pleasure of this occasion
whenever I pass through Brignôles, but alas the hotel is no
more. Sometimes I wonder if it actually existed at all, or
whether it was a phantom place dropped where we found it by
our guardian angel or an equally well-disposed good fairy.

Next morning Bennett gave the car a thorough going over
and the report was that all he could find wrong was a broken

silencer. This hardly seemed a matter for concern in the France of those days, and so we set off back to St. Raphaël and made a second start on the same lines as before. The weather had cleared and nothing at all untoward occurred on this effort. We rolled up to the Gare Maritime at Calais with twenty minutes to spare before the Blue Train puffed in.

Pem's resultant story hit the front page of the *Daily Express*, with photograph by a local operator whom I laid on by telegram, and was better than I had dared hope for. With newspaper publicity as profuse as it is today where car "stunts" are concerned, it may be difficult to realise how great was the influence wielded by a national newspaper in 1930. Here is how Harold Pemberton wrote the story, datelined Calais January 28th:

When the Blue Train from the Riviera, one of the most famous of Continental expresses, drew up dead on time this afternoon here at Calais, a British motor-car, all plastered in mud, was parked alongside the platform.

Two young Englishmen, unshaven, with red-rimmed eyes and almost as dirty as the car itself, stood by and greeted the train with cheers. They had raced the express right from St. Raphaël, on the Mediterranean, and they had won by twenty minutes! The heroes of this episode were Mr. Dudley Noble and Mr. F. Bennett, who had been paying a visit to the Riviera.

For twenty hours on end, through all the night and half the day, these two adventurers raced the Blue Train in their gallant little car, from sea to sea, across 750 miles of France.

They were at times slightly ahead of the express on schedule, and well behind it at others.

While the lordly Blue Train roared along on its metals, secure from trouble, the two travellers in their motor-car were handicapped by fog, level crossings, and deep water-courses, in addition to the normal obstacles on the great highway.

The Blue Train left St. Raphaël at 6.30 p.m. yesterday. The motor-car, a two-litre Light Six Rover, was set in motion at the same time.

Between St. Raphaël and Brignôles, where road and rail run parallel, there was an actual neck-and-neck race between the car and the train.

The road ahead was straight and clear, and the travellers had the satisfaction of seeing their modest vehicle take the lead—but their luck was out. A level crossing was ahead, and the gates were closed to let the Blue Train pass. It faded into the landscape, and was seen no more until it arrived twenty minutes after the car at Calais.

Between Macon and Avallon, just before dawn, the task seemed hopeless. Wisps of mist kept floating across the road, obstructing the driver's vision, and the speed dropped to 28 m.p.h.—the lowest recorded. The average during the run was 48 m.p.h.

When dawn broke a puff of wind suddenly dispersed the fog and the way lay clear ahead. A dead straight tree-lined road stretched as far as the eye could see.

Rovers were delighted, and so were their dealers. One at least wrote in to say that he had clinched three sales as a direct result. Another, in Manchester, sent a letter to the managing director saying "Your consistent and extensive advertising has been of an unusual quality, and in particular yesterday's announcement regarding the 'Defeat of the Blue Train by a Rover Light Six' has brought us a number of enquirers—Stanley B. Reece." Naturally, therefore, I was as pleased with the results as were the Colonel and Spencer Wilks—the latter took over from hatchet man Frank Searle, whose job was done, and he retired leaving S. W. to carry on with unequalled ability in the m.d.'s chair.

As was, of course, to be expected, many and various people emulated this racing of the Blue Train, and in one case there was a claim (uncorroborated) to have beaten it by several hours. It gave rise to protests from the French authorities to the R.A.C., who issued a stern warning that disciplinary action would be taken against future "offenders" contravening international competition rules.

In his weekly "Motorist's Logbook" soon afterwards, Pem gave an insight into our tribulations in his own inimitable style. He wrote:

It is always good to have as a passenger in the car someone to whom you can show new sights. I have just paid my annual visit to the South of France. One of the party was a veteran in Continental touring. The other had never set foot out of England.

When we left Calais under grey skies we were able to describe to the novice the joys ahead, how he would see butterflies fluttering against the windscreen at Avignon, women in sun bonnets gathering in the olive harvest in Provence, and the sun dancing on the blue Mediterranean along the Corniche . . .

Our novice laughed sardonically. We said it was a mistral or something and that these local storms disappeared as quickly as they came, to be followed by hot sunshine. We splashed along the Corniche to Nice. At Beaulieu the rain became torrential.

We went to bed that night, having returned to Nice, cheering our novice up by telling him he would see the sun shining through his bedroom window in the morning.

It rained all that day and the next, and on the following evening we had to leave for the return journey.

"If this is the Côte d'Azur," said our novice, "give me Warrington." . . .

Shortly before leaving the South the driver mistook his

road in a blinding storm. Instead of negotiating a sharp bend he went straight on. I suppose we were doing about 50 m.p.h. The car jumped over a wall and came down plop into a shallow ravine.

In a long career of motoring in all parts of Europe I have been off the road on sundry occasions. But I have never jumped the road clean into a ravine. I must say, however, that the car did the jump most gracefully. It landed astride a rock, which kept it from running down to the bottom of the declivity . . .

After a general survey it was found that neither car nor its occupants were seriously damaged. This was really rather remarkable. Two thermos flasks went west, a suit-case inside the car was bent in two, the floor by the driver was full of glass from a broken window, and a small bottle of cognac made of thick glass was shattered. A box of fragile peaches was intact.

The exhaust pipe of the car was bent, the engine sump dented, and it was battered in other places, but received no vital injuries. Congratulations to the Rover Company. It must be a sturdy chassis to withstand such a shock.

During the period covered by the foregoing account of the decline and resurrection of the Rover Company, many developments had been taking place in the British motor industry. But imports of American cars selling at prices no British maker could emulate were proving serious in the home market, and we had still comparatively little export in motors. Britain was a free trade country, but, bowing to the serious situation in our motor industry, the Chancellor of the Exchequer—Reginald McKenna—introduced the import duty on cars which made his name famous, and the flow of imports was stemmed. From this began the trend towards modernisation which now started to build up production volume in Birmingham, Coventry and Oxford.

The Years Between the Wars

DURING THE INTER-WAR YEARS, AND IN SPITE OF
THE GREAT DEPRESSION OF THE 'THIRTIES,
BRITAIN'S MOTOR MAKERS FORGED STEADILY
AHEAD WITH THE PRODUCTION OF CARS WHICH
APPEALED TO THE MAN-IN-THE-STREET WHO HAD
NEVER IMAGINED HIMSELF AS A MOTORIST

Morris "went public" in 1926, taking no cash for his business but only shares—which grew in value so much as the company prospered that he became the many-times-over millionaire who gave his name to such a multitude of laudable objects. Herbert Austin got his firm out of the red, with the skilful help of both Payton and Engelbach, largely through the success of his Austin Seven. Singers came to the fore under the dictatorial guidance of William Bullock, whose methods were in keeping with his name. Hillman's made good going with what could well have been the first sports model along lines with which we are familiar today. William Hillman, at the time an elderly man, was one of the pioneers of cycle making in Coventry along with the Starleys: he had two very capable henchmen in his sons-in-law. One, as I have mentioned, was Spencer Wilks; the other was Captain (later Sir John) Black, destined to become the saviour of the Standard Motor Company.

Now, the cause of these two leaving Hillman's was the entry into the motor manufacturing jousts of the brothers Rootes—William and Reginald—young in years but already highly experienced in the art of selling cars, and knowledgable into the bargain about what motorists wanted—overseas as well as at home. Their father, in business at Hawkhurst, Kent, mainly and for a long time a cycle dealer, had commenced dealing in cars as far back as 1900. Billy, the elder son, was not a shining success with school books, and so, at the age of fifteen, he went off to Coventry as an apprentice to Singers.

He did not stay long there, and in 1912, when he was eighteen, went back home to the parental business, having induced his father to take the agency for Singer, whose completely new 10 h.p. model was about the first real light car to be made in quantity. Almost immediately afterwards he went to Maidstone to start a branch of his father's business, but when the 1914 war broke out it was virtually closed down because Billy joined the Royal Naval Air Service.

Four or so years later, and with a vastly increased enthusiasm for motors, Billy returned to civilian life, convinced that fortune was knocking at his door. He persuaded his younger brother Reggie to throw up his post in the Civil Service and join him in the great adventure. Their father contributed the capital—£1,200 to each son—to start up their own business in Maidstone.

Here they concentrated on new cars, even though the secondhand trade in those early post-war days was booming, because they considered this was the only right way to lay the foundations for the future they contemplated. They took as colleague a local friend, Joe Chaldecott, and the trio soon made the firm of Rootes Ltd. famous in Kent's county town for its enterprise and fair dealing.

"W. E.", as Billy was known to most people, was no uncertain leader of the team, and spoke his mind (as was always his wont) when his colleagues, in his opinion, fell short of the Rootes' self-set standard of one hundred per cent efficiency. Maidstone soon proved too small for their energies; this was a period when it was practicable for car dealers to operate a number of agencies. Therefore they took premises in London's West End—Long Acre, then Bond Street—and won the distributorship for the Austin Motor Company. They had already opened certain local depots in Kent, and had also acquired car businesses in Birmingham and Manchester.

Next, when the high wall surrounding the Duke of Devonshire's estate in Piccadilly, at its junction with Berkeley Street, was torn down and the new Devonshire House built, the Rootes plunged in and leased an extensive section of its ground and mezzanine floors at a reputed rent of £10,000 per annum. The motor trade shook its collective head and predicted an early downfall for these daring young men who had "gone west"—too far west, many thought—for this end of Piccadilly was then almost out in the "long grass" so far as the West End was concerned.

But the Rootes had their sights set high. It was all part of their promotional plan, and nothing was going to stop them. In 1928, after the death of old Mr. William Hillman, there were difficulties among the various members of his family, and as a result of them the Rootes agreed to purchase the whole of their interests.

Subsequently they acquired the assets of Humber Ltd., next door, and helpful to this end was Sir George May of the Prudential, to whom their plan for acquiring both the Hillman and Humber companies, modernising and rationalising their products and suiting them to export markets, appealed strongly. As I have said, export business was none too popular at that time with British motor manufacturers: why should they go to the trouble when our foreign currency position was still strong?

We still had an "All-Red" route through Africa, from Egypt in the north to the Cape in the south. Perhaps the Rootes were more farseeing than others, but, with the backing

of the "Pru" and its enormous influence, they secured
control of both Hillman and Humber, whose factories in
Coventry adjoined. Colonel J. A. Cole, the elderly and
esteemed Chairman of Humber, found the prospect of
working with the young Rootes agreeable; the brothers paid
him the greatest respect and he acquired new importance,
becoming Chairman of what became known as the Humber-
Hillman-Commer combine, for Commer Cars of Luton had
been a commercial vehicle subsidiary of Humbers for some
little while.

First outcome of the new planning spirit at Hillman and
Humber was the three-litre Humber Snipe, considered well
suited to countries like Australia and South Africa, where
antipathy to current British cars existed on account of their
low ground clearance and inadequate engine power.

"W. E." had had considerable contact with American
manufacturers and was well posted with the progress they
had made in production methods and automation. He had
seen how General Motors, by gathering together a bunch of
likely winners among the less financially stable firms in the
U.S. motor industry and rationalising their products, were
building up an organisation rivalling that of Henry Ford.

Also, Billy Rootes had greatly helped H. O. D. (later Sir
Henry) Segrave to produce his Golden Arrow world land
speed record-breaking car. The Rootes brothers had
acquired the Cricklewood coachbuilding firm of Thrupp
and Maberly, founded in 1760; there was built Segrave's
car's body to the design of Captain J. S. Irving. This mag-
nificent-looking vehicle was powered by a Schneider Trophy
Napier Lion aeroplane engine developing 930 b.h.p. at
3,250 r.p.m. and driving the back wheels through a three-
speed gearbox.

Twin propeller shafts allowed Segrave to have a low
seating position between them inside the beautifully stream-
lined coachwork, which featured a vertical stabilising fin at

the tail of the 27-feet long body. It weighed no less than 3·6 tons and on it deHane Segrave put the world land speed record up to 231·44 m.p.h. at Daytona on March 11th, 1929. Billy Rootes went over with Segrave, and shared to some considerable degree in his success and the jubilation attending it.

When the Rootes surveyed their acquisitions at Stoke, Coventry, they found plenty of scope for their new broom. The 14 h.p. Hillman which had been such a big hit on its introduction in 1924 was losing its steam, while a straight eight model had proved a flop—the remaining stock of it was sold off under the name of Vortic. On the drawing boards immediately went the design for a new six-cylinder car by Capt. J. S. Irving which was to be suitable for the roads of the world.

It was to feature alternative engine sizes—15·72 h.p. mainly for the home market, where the £1 per R.A.C. h.p. tax was now in force, and 20·9 h.p. for overseas and for those in Britain who did not mind paying £21 p.a. tax. One had a 65 mm. bore, the other 75 mm., and these were to be the model designations of this new Hillman "Wizard"; both otherwise identical and with four-speed gearbox of which a feature was a silent third ratio to be known as the "traffic top".

For its time a novelty of the Wizard was to be its pressed steel body, manufactured at Cowley close to the Morris factory in a new plant only just put up by the Pressed Steel Co., a subsidiary of the American parent. The Rootes were quick to seize on this method of body construction, already widely employed in the U.S.A. but as yet almost unknown and certainly untried here.

During the period of gestation, while the prototype Wizard was under way and being tested, the Humber-Hillman works were being modernised. Manufacturing processes were being rationalised to make best use of the total space available at both factories, and Reginald Rootes moved in as managing director. Harold Heath, son of the veteran George Heath whose car dealing business in Birmingham had been acquired by the Rootes, was appointed works director.

One evening in June 1930 I happened to go over to Birmingham to have dinner with a certain newspaper man— Ted Sherren of the *Daily Mail*—at the old Queen's Hotel over New Street station. As I pushed round the revolving door so someone was making his exit. It was Billy Rootes and, with mutual recognition, he made a gesture that he wanted to speak to me.

"Hi," he jerked out in that abrupt style of his, "I like that publicity stuff you're doing for Rovers—how are you getting along with them?" As a matter of fact, the old firm was still in the process of recovering from its setback and I was not over-happy with prospects. Billy and I chatted for a few minutes, and parted with an invitation from him to call in at Devonshire House some time "and meet my brother Reggie".

I see from my diary that it was on June 30th that I complied with the invitation and had the pleasure of meeting Reginald (now, of course, Sir Reginald) Rootes for the first time. Utterly different in looks and temperament from his elder brother, they were a perfect pair in the business sense— Billy seeing the visions on the horizon and striding towards it with, so to speak, seven league boots; Reggie surveying the intervening ground with his keen and calculating eye and making sure that no loose ends in whatever project was afoot were left untied.

They were exactly complementary one to the other and I never saw Reggie lose his perfect composure, even when Billy would dash into his office during a meeting and, in his impetuous way, demand to know why this, that or the other thing had (or had not) been done. Had Reggie stayed on in the Civil Service instead of obeying Billy's call to join him at the end of World War I, I feel quite sure that he would have risen to some very important position, with wall-to-wall office carpeting and a knighthood after the routine period of unblemished career.

The upshot of my interview with him on that last day of June was that I joined the Humber-Hillman-Commer combine on August 1st, 1930, after a very friendly leave-taking with Rovers, and in particular with Spencer Wilks. He asked me to recommend a successor and I suggested Sid Phillips (familiarly known as "Swilloughby" because his middle name was Willoughby and not through any undue addiction to the bottle). At that very moment the firm he was with—Lanchester—was closing down; Phillips had been its advertising and publicity manager, but the days of the Great Depression were disastrous for cars of Lanchester quality and price. He was therefore delighted to accept Rover's offer, and filled my old position with distinction for some thirty years after I left it.

As for myself, I was happy to move back to London, and at Devonshire House the first job given me was to organise the Rootes' magazine—*Modern Motoring*—along regular monthly lines. There had previously been a couple of issues of a publication of that name produced by Capt. Wilfred Gordon Aston, on a freelance basis; now the plan was to bring it out regularly.

The new version was to start coincidentally with the announcement of the Hillman Wizard, planned for January 1931. This would, naturally, call for a big story—and not only for *Modern Motoring* but for the Press of the world in view of the model's potentialities in export markets. I was therefore bidden to think up some demonstration which would drive home its capabilities for coping with as many climates and road conditions as could conveniently be covered in the somewhat brief period between a car being available and its public announcement.

Harold Pemberton and I went into a huddle on the subject, and evolved a scheme frankly based on John Prioleau's
stout "Imshi" effort of ten years previously. Not only,
however, would we go into the heat and sand of the North
African desert but we would follow this up immediately
with a trip through the Alps in mid-winter. Discussed with
Billy and Reggie the idea was approved and all arrangements made, but the identity of the car itself was to be kept
strictly secret until (we hoped) the name would be disclosed
in the final article the day before the announcement. There
would be no time to lose once we started, however, since the
earliest an actual Wizard could be made ready for the trip
was the latter part of December 1930.

Meanwhile I had been busy making the preliminary plans
for the production of *Modern Motoring* in its new format.
Printing had been arranged for with a firm at Letchworth in
whom I had great confidence; potential advertisers had been
notified and canvassed and I had engaged an editor. This
was Tom Mulcaster, who had been editing the *Auto, yellow
cover journal* and also the *Motor Owner*, a monthly glossy
magazine owned by Capt. de Normanville. Unfortunately,
the depression was hitting motoring journals as well as the
trade, and both these publications were closing down at the
end of the year. Mulcaster was therefore as pleased as Sid
Phillips had been to have a new job awaiting him, and he
took on as editor of *Modern Motoring* on January 1st.

Just before that, on Boxing Day, 1930, Pem and I crossed
the Channel from Southampton to Le Havre, and aboard
also was the one and only Wizard, plus a Vortic to act as
tender. With us as technician was George Bedford, who had
done some notable things with the Hillman sports car in
speed events prior to the change of ownership of the company.

The fourth member of our little crew was a man from a
photographic news agency who brought a ciné camera and

was to make a film which, it was intended, would be shown at the announcement party. He would also take still pictures for general publicity purposes. We had orders from Billy Rootes to be back not later than January 20th, so in the ensuing three weeks we looked like having a pretty hectic time, with short daylight hours for photography.

Arrived in France, Pem soon started sending stories back to the *Daily Express*. His first one, reporting our run from Le Havre to Bordeaux, he titled "A Lover's Lane 400 Miles Long", from the prevalence of mistletoe in the trees all along the road. "Mistletoe," he said, "the French government regards as a parasite, and has dealt a blow to lovers by issuing an edict that it must no longer be cultivated." He christened our Wizard "Cosmop", mentioned that it was a new British car being taken on test and said we were bound for the Sahara. He reported that "The Owner" (me) was asking if the Bay of Biscay was living up to its reputation; and went on:

> They told him it was more turbulent than it had been for years . . . He has bought a wonderful remedy against sea-sickness from a local chemist. Even if the remedy is not good it has a marvellous publicity agent. The descriptive matter that goes with it is most reassuring. It specifically mentions that it will stop sea-sickness in the Bay of Biscay. Tomorrow will tell.

Next day's story began "We are steaming pleasantly down the River Gironde, but there is trouble looming ahead. We shall shortly pick up our pilot to conduct us across the bar. This innocent-looking stream has one of the worst bars in the world. At least, so the purser has just told us. He has explained that the waves entering from the Bay of Biscay are so immense and the channel is so shallow that there is danger of our 9,000-ton boat being lifted up and dashed against the bottom of the river . . . The Owner (of Cosmop that is, not the boat) has just taken his first 'No-Sik' capsule. It is called the warning or preliminary dose." To quote further;

> Everything the purser said is right. I have crossed many bars, but this bar of the River Gironde takes first prize for wickedness. They are not waves that come rolling in, but Everests of the seas.
>
> The man I am sorry for is the pilot. He joined us from a motor boat. His job is only to see us over the bar. Once outside the river he cannot go back because the seas are so rough. So he has to come all the way to Casablanca with us. He is rather a sad little man, with an erratic home life. A short while ago he crossed the bar and had to go all the way to Cardiff . . . The next three days must remain blank. There is nothing to report. Life, in fact, since we entered the angriest sea in the world has remained blank for nearly everybody except the crew. The Owner is too ill even to write asking for his money back in accordance with the guarantee on his seasick cure. The crew of Cosmop, except for The Interpreter [Harold Pemberton himself] are completely laid out . . .
>
> The boat awakened again on the fourth morning. Instead of clouds a ribbon of silver showed on the horizon. It was the dawn coming up on the African coast. Within an hour or so we sailed into summer. The Owner appeared and explained that he had not come on deck because he had felt tired. Three days is a long fatigue . . .
>
> The most beautiful girl on the ship, looking pale but interesting, also appeared and stood leaning against the deck rail gazing soulfully toward the great white city of Casablanca. Alas, it is too late now for romance. Land once more! A new land of motoring adventure.

None of us, I believe, had been on the "Dark Continent" before. A good part of Morocco, and all of Algeria, was then under French rule and so the roads were quite good.

Casablanca proved a big, bustling modern port which we would have liked to explore, but time was pressing. So off we set with hardly a pause, and now Pem's story carries on:

This afternoon we left Casablanca, the Alice in Wonderland port of Northern Africa, and this evening arrived at Marrakesh, an oasis city of almost incredible beauty that lies at the foot of the Grand Atlas . . . Roads are the life stream of a country that is being civilised. Marshal Lyautey, the Allenby of France, realised this. Here, where houses are growing as quickly as flowers in an oasis—even more quickly, in fact—roads are keeping pace.

Before the war motor cars were a rarity. Now in Morocco there are 16,000. The number is increasing daily. Yet I am told you can count the number of British cars in the country on the fingers of one hand. This is all wrong. You see, they believe that in Britain we build either baby cars or ones that only millionaires can buy. Cosmop is here as an advance guard and her presence has already attracted widespread interest . . .

Our highway has a separate track for camels, donkeys and other desert craft. In the darkness we passed camels loping along and strange, ghost-like figures of Arabs leading their heavily-laden donkeys. Modern and ancient are thoroughly intermingled. In Marrakesh pictures that might have come straight out of the Bible are staged next to scenes from Hollywood. The hotel we stayed at could not be improved in a film of a resort for millionaires. Yet close by in the market place a descendant of a long line of snake charmers performs to an admiring crowd of Moors. A woman modestly veiled does the tummy dance and beggars with maimed limbs appeal for alms. The whole place is a fascinating medley.

Marrakesh hasn't changed much to this day: Winston Churchill was to put it, and its luxurious Mamounia hotel, on the British tourist's map. But at the time of which I write the Atlas Mountains, so plainly visible from the hotel, capped with snow, were out of bounds to tourists because they were inhabited by tribesmen who had not up to then been "subdued" by the French. We had intended to follow the piste, or track, via Boujad and Khenifra to Meknès. But a European friend who knew the country informed us that it ran very close to the unsubdued area. The possibility of meeting brigands if we wandered from the road could not be overlooked.

He informed The Owner [Pem wrote] that the custom is to send an ear home to relatives with the suggestion that more important accessories would follow in due course unless many bags of gold were forwarded. The Owner said that an ear arriving in a small wooden box at his office, duly opened by the customs and marked duty-free, would probably cause merriment more than anything else.

Let me say at once that it was not the possibility of losing an ear that made The Owner take the straight path to Meknès. It was the likelihood, he said, that the piste would almost certainly have been washed away by the recent heavy rains.

Before departing from Marrakesh we inspected the souk or native market, where everyone haggles and haggles over even a cup of water out of a goatskin. The water seller keeps a dirty thumb over a hole in it until the customer comes to terms. Then the thumb is removed, filling his cup by the law of gravity.

Here is a fashion note by The Map Reader of our party [George Bedford]: "I cannot say whether or not the native women are beautiful. They wear the purdah to cover their faces—that is, the good ones. The naughty ones have no purdah and wear stockings. They would look better with the purdah. The latest fashion seems to be a bath robe made of bedroom sheets. Skirts or bath robes are definitely long. Feet in most cases are bare, but some of the girls prefer a pair of men's bedroom slippers."

We took Cosmop through a hole in the wall and it was good to get out in the sunshine again, where even the smell of garlic seemed sweet. Marrakesh we left in hot sunshine and plodded along the highway until, in the distance, we saw an immense cloud and prepared for the rain which descends without warning in these parts. The cloud approached. As it got nearer we heard a soft singing sound. Suddenly we were in it, a cloud of insects about twice the size of grasshoppers. Locusts! They blotted out the sun, they hit the windscreen like pellets—there were millions and millions of them—and we soon had to bring Cosmop to a stop.

Not only was it impossible to see the road ahead, but the thermometer was rising rapidly, showing that the radiator was choked with the pests. We could not give Cosmop a black mark for this. For some time the cloud passed us. When we stepped out of the car to de-locust the radiator we had to walk over a carpet of carcases. It was a horrid spectacle. When we arrived at the next filling station a number of locusts were still adhering. These were carefully scraped off by the Arab petrol attendant. He was collecting them for his afternoon tea. Ugh! Locusts and honey.

Pem's next dispatch recorded our arrival in Fez, by way of the hilltop city of Mulay Idriss, which the Moors regard as sacred. "It is an exclusive city," he wrote, "no unbeliever is allowed to remain in it after dark. Its superb gates are securely padlocked and there are all sorts of stories as to what happens to any Christian who fails to leave the place in time. The offence is certainly greater than getting caught in Richmond Park when the gates are closed."

We made our way through glorious country and in blazing
sunshine to Fez, which we reached after dark. The sunsets
especially appealed to Haj—"As soon as the sun dips behind
the horizon the sky assumes all the colours of the rainbow.
First gold changes to deep orange, then from orange to
lemon and then to deep purple. A few minutes later you can
switch on your lights, for there is only a pause between dusk
and complete darkness."

Within a few days we had crossed over the border into
Algeria at a frontier post called Oudjda, where all the business with documents was done in a small room which had
rifles fixed around the walls, and the officials were armed to
the teeth. "In fact," Pem reported, "so frightened was our
Map Reader that he declared two bottles of beer which he
had concealed under the back seat and we knew nothing
about until the customs officer asked if we had any dutiable
goods."

But even in sunny Algeria the rain sometimes takes over,
and on the remaining 150 miles to Tenès the relentless down-
pour continued. Eventually we reached the place, where on
the outskirts was what must have been one of the first, if not
the first, motel.

We put up thankfully here, with the storm raging and
flashes of vivid lightning, after a 150-mile drive along
precipitous roads with the Mediterranean far below—not
blue but a muddy grey. The Tenès motel was just what a
motel ought to be, its central headquarters with restaurant
and reception office, and a multitude of cottages spread
about a semi-tropical garden. Pem reported that the car had
remained watertight under "maritime" conditions.

All night the storm went on, easing off towards morning
but leaving a pale and watery sunrise in its wake. We had
to get to Algiers to catch the next day's boat back to Europe
and the motel manager's gloomy prognostication that the
coastal road would be washed away was not well received.

There was no other road, and as the boat sailed only twice a week we simply had to get through.

So off we set, up and down mountain passes where avalanches of mud-coloured water rushed down the gulleys. We had to stop frequently to remove rocks which had crashed down into the road, but the complete blockage we feared did not occur until we neared a little town called Dupleix.

On a narrow strip of corniche, with a sheer drop to the sea on one side and an equally sheer wall of mountain on the other, half a dozen great blocks of rock completely barred our passage. We would have to wait until a repair gang arrived with dynamite to break them up; meanwhile the Map Reader was sent to forage for food. He returned with a yard or so of bread and ditto of sausage, also a pièce de résistance which he said was brawn. The Owner said it was composed of goat and camel meat welded together by the goat's hair. The bread was good.

The repair gang arrived and surveyed the scene. They continued to survey the scene until we conveyed with gestures and the hands of our watches that time pressed us, if not them. Some franc notes were also produced, and work then started. The procedure was to chisel out a groove at the top of each rock, place a stick of dynamite in it and cover over with a shovel-full of mud. The fuse was lit, the charge exploded downwards and the rock split; this went on until the chunks of rock had been reduced to manageable size, when each section was heaved over the side and rolled down into the sea.

It took four hours and a good deal of financial encouragement before a passage was blasted through which Cosmop and the Vortic could squeeze. Then at the next village a French officer told us the road ahead was impassable. Onward we had to go, however, and soon came on the local omnibus stalled in flood water.

We estimated its depth by bribing some Arab boys to walk through it, and, as their heads did not disappear, decided to take the plunge. This we did, and, when water rose through the floorboards, thought we might have been a bit over-confident: both cars "made" it in bottom gear with engines revving hard, however. Thus we reached Algiers that night and relaxed our jaded tissues in the night club below the entrance floor of the Hotel Aletti.

Next morning saw us aboard the s.s. *Timgad*, crossing the well-mannered Mediterranean to Marseilles, whence we made hot-foot to our old friendly hotel at Brignôles where, as Haj always had it, "we lay the night". Then along the coast road by way of Cannes, Nice and Monte Carlo to the Italian frontier and on to Genoa. Here the first of Mussolini's autostrade had recently been opened, giving a clear passage by tunnels to the heavy vehicles making for Milan and points north by avoiding the twisty mountain roads on which they had previously been such an obstruction to faster traffic. It was called, in fact, an "Autocamionale", but we were only too glad to pay the toll to miss the narrow streets of villages wherein, at the time, murals featuring "Il Duce" were everywhere plastered.

During the winter months unemployment was rife and, there being no dole in Italy, whole armies of labourers were turned on to road-making. From the energetic way in which they were working, we guessed that Mussolini had issued a deadline for finishing the job, on the basis of "or else". As most of us remember, he made the railways run to time and even the civil servants to perform slightly more efficiently by the same formula.

North of Milan we passed by Lake Como, looking very different from the travel agents' posters in this wretched weather, when a white mist rose from a snow-powdered road. The Swiss frontier loomed up out of it and soon we were at the start of the Maloja Pass. Here the chains came out of the boot of each car, were fitted at a wayside garage specialising in this job and having the right type of jack for it.

A blizzard set in and both our cars were soon complete snowballs: as we neared St. Moritz, however, it stopped and the sun came out. Merry ski-ing parties were returning from their day's sport, but metaphorically crying Excelsior we pushed on through snow which became really deep whenever the road ran alongside the light railway. This, we learnt later, was because the mails went on the train and it was unnecessary to keep the road ploughed for just the few odd mad motorists who wanted to pass that-a way.

Out our spades had to come, and it was touch and go whether we would get through; at long last, however, the Austrian frontier post appeared and we thankfully crossed it and pressed on to Landeck, where the Hotel Post received and unfroze us—British cars did not boast heaters then. On again early next morning, for time now pressed, through Innsbruck and (with a slight deviation) Garmisch Parten-kirchen to Munich.

After here it was plain sailing to home—but, alas, when we arrived to our set time it was to find that production difficulties at Coventry had forced a delay in the Wizard's announcement, and so Pem's Cosmop story faded out into nothingness and its identity was never revealed. He had no "pay-off" line at the end and his finale to thirteen brilliant articles in three weeks' issues of the *Daily Express* had to be this:

We have come to the end of our narrative. We set out to prove that the modern British car is built for world conditions and to kill the absurd propaganda that has been spread abroad during the past few years that British cars are useless outside Britain.

Cosmop's conduct sheet remains unblemished after a vast variety of tests . . . Hot sunshine and desert tracks in

Morocco; fierce storms and rock-bound tracks in the mountains of Algeria; fast roads and spring-breaking roads, straight roads and roads strewn with hairpin bends; snow, ice, fog, frosts, floods, avalanches—what more could a manufacturer ask for testing his product?

I have known for many years from personal experience that the British car is equal to any rival, but manufacturers have been slow to counter the "no good in rough conditions" propaganda. They are beginning to take steps to remedy this, as will be seen by the organising of the great British car exhibition at Buenos Aires next month.

Once the bogy is finally laid our export trade, now that we have got down to price levels, will go ahead in leaps and bounds. FINIS.

It was to be almost three months later that the Wizard made its public début. Billy Rootes went about the preparations for the event in his typically grand manner. Meanwhile brother Reggie went over to the Argentine for the British exhibition, which was opened by the Prince of Wales (later for a brief period King Edward VIII), who always used a Humber Pullman for his official journeyings. So optimistic was Reggie about sales prospects that he took premises in Buenos Aires for a showroom and service station, and formed a company called Rootes Argentina S.A. He was, therefore, absent from the Wizard function, which took place at the Royal Albert Hall on April 27th, 1931.

The venue was fitting, because the Albert Hall had itself been opened in 1851 with an exhibition of British industries. No one had, however, given a large-sized luncheon there, although the Ford Company had held its own motor show in it, probably to assert its independence of the martinet who then ran the Society of Motor Manufacturers' annual motor show at Olympia (one J. C. J. Phillips). To hold a luncheon in the hallowed precincts involved removing every alternate

row of seats and substituting specially-made tables with long
legs. Also, catering was a problem because there were no
kitchens of the kind needed to prepare the "right" sort of
meal for a thousand V.I.P.s.

Billy overcame every difficulty in his characteristic style,
even to engaging stage hands from Drury Lane theatre to
unveil the batch of Wizards in the arena at the exact moment.
But one thing that kept him specially busy was the arranging
of the table plan, since protocol entered very largely into
this. Until an absolutely final list of acceptances could be
prepared there was a great deal of tentative placing done,
and much midnight oil burned in his office at Devonshire
House. A great board carried the host of cards that were
pinned on or taken off, or readjusted, as slowly the now
unalterable date approached.

Billy Rootes had his own staff working on all the arrangements for the great event: this was not a mere publicity
matter and I was only involved with seeing that the film
which had been taken on the Cosmop trip was edited, titled
and all ready, likewise the still photographs, Press releases
and so forth. But I was at Devonshire House on the evening
of Sunday April 26th to do whatever I might to help, when
the bundles of programmes were delivered from the printers
in readiness for the morrow.

I glanced through one of these handsome brochures,
which had a thick red cover with gold embossing, and as I
browsed over it some of the guests' names seemed oddly spelt
—for instance "Austin" Chamberlain instead of "Austen".
It so happened that Lord Waleran was handy, Billy Rootes's
personal assistant who had acted in the same capacity to the
Governor-General of New Zealand and therefore knew titles
and decorations like the back of his hand. I showed him the
programme and he confirmed my opinion—also discovered
more and more mistakes. We sought out Billy as soon as he
returned from dinner and showed him. Naturally, he went

up in the air in no uncertain way—"Well, what the blank blank hell are we going to do?" he asked, in an even more forceful manner than the expurgated words suggest.

I had been thinking the problem over during the preceding hour, and said, "Nothing for it but to get the job reprinted." "Don't be a blank fool!" Billy retorted, and certainly it did seem a faint hope. However, Billy agreed to let me have a try, and I phoned up a friend in London, one Sargent Pharaoh, an executive of the firm which had just got the contract to print *Modern Motoring*.

By this time it was about ten o'clock on Sunday night and the reception was at noon next day, with lunch at one o'clock—and the table plan was printed in the programme. My friend got through to his chief, who gave approval if the Garden City Press at Letchworth, Herts., could be got going. A telephone call to the works manager brought the reply yes, he thought he could get at the staff, who lived in the neighbourhood.

And so an S.O.S. went out; the monotype machines were started up, the tappers tapped as Bill Waleran telephoned the list to be set—it took him a solid couple of hours—and Dick Watney set out for Letchworth in his car (an Alvis, be it mentioned) taking a load of the programmes and a typed list to corroborate Bill Waleran's phoning. The latter also made a night journey to the printing works, taking the remainder of the programmes, and checked the proofs of the type-setting.

At 8 a.m., when the bindery staff arrived, they stripped the covers from the old programmes; the re-set interior sheets were running on the machines and soon were trimmed and inserted into the covers, which were stitched, parcelled up and by 11 a.m. the first van was on its way to the Albert Hall, arriving in company with the first guests.

The whole lot were delivered by 12.30 p.m., and the luncheon proceeded to schedule without any but the few of us knowing by what a hair's breadth the guests had a table plan and programme. The cost was astronomical, but Billy paid up and looked pleasantly at the people who had got him out of the jam—but fancy attempting to get something similar done today! Who the bunglers were I never found out.

Colonel J. A. Cole was Chairman at the luncheon; he was a dear old boy who had a wonderful knack of making a sonorous speech in a voice which was both impressive and carried extremely well. He had, incidentally, gained his seat on the Humber Board by being an obstreperous shareholder at an annual meeting, when the firm was playing around with an aeroplane department which, in more ways than one, never got off the ground. This was about 1910, when powered flight was being recognised as practicable by a few pioneers—among them the Hon. Charles Rolls, first of the twin Rs in Rolls-Royce, who crashed to his death at a flying display in 1911.

A cable from the Prince of Wales was received at the Albert Hall regretting that he could not be present personally and saying "British cars which I have used on my recent tours abroad have proved that this country can produce cars suited for overseas. But British manufacturers must not only produce such cars: good salesmanship and good service after sales must also be their keynote if they are to capture world markets. I wish the Industry every possible success."

In H.R.H.'s absence the guest of honour was the Right Hon. J. H. Thomas, then Secretary of State for the Dominions. Ambassadors and High Commissioners galore were among the thousand guests, together with dignitaries and V.I.P.s of every description. The government of the day was Labour, headed by Ramsay Macdonald, which was soon to become a National Coalition under Stanley Baldwin.

In the arena below the seats and tables the cars themselves were concealed in "property" packing cases. When the speechifying was over, the lights were extinguished in the hall and the film taken during our desert–arctic expedition was shown on a huge screen fixed up over the organ loft. During the time this occupied the scene shifters were busy de-crating the cars and, as "The End" flashed on the screen, floodlights sprang up and the array of Hillman Wizards was revealed for all to see and inspect.

It has, sadly, to be recorded that the Wizard did not live up to its name. Perhaps it had more than its share of teething troubles, and the pressed steel body's styling did not please everyone. The huge (for those days) advertising campaign, based on "The Car of the Moderns" theme, certainly brought in a large number of orders, and—at least to begin with—distributors overseas were enthusiastic.

One such was Thomas H. Moore of Cairo who, at the Albert Hall party, told me he wanted to make a real splash in connection with the Egyptian motor show due to take place in February. I asked him whether he thought it would create an impression if a Wizard arrived there from Coventry on its own four wheels. Moore was all for this, and I promised him I would go into the possibility of getting through to Cairo by road.

This proved a bigger problem than anyone would have imagined. Maps showed that the French had built roads down through Tunisia to the frontier with Tripolitania, and that there was a road on to Tripoli and as far eastwards as Misurata, about a hundred miles to the east of the capital. But, after that—what? (This was, of course, long before Mussolini had built his autostrada along the Libyan coast.) No one had a clue, even the touring authorities in Rome, to whom their London office referred our enquiry when their own sources of information proved unavailing.

Today the names Bengasi, Tobruk and Solloum are familiar; it was a very different matter in 1931. The thousand or so miles from Tunisia across Tripolitania and Cyrenaica to the Egyptian border seemed an unknown quantity—the existence of any civilisation, let alone a through road, seemed uncertain. At any rate, if we took the plunge and made the attempt it would be necessary to take our living quarters with us.

I sounded out a caravan-making firm and they were eager to have a go, and send along an expert into the bargain. Also, I tackled Harold Pemberton to see whether the *Daily Express* would like an exclusive story—by him. They would, he reported back, and he would too. So I put the idea up to the Rootes and they thought it was well worth while trying, so long as we did not disclose our intentions until we were within sight of being home and dry.

A 75 Wizard was prepared and the towing attachment fitted to it. "Make it a good strong one", I asked Hillman's chief engineer, who assured me that nothing would ever dislodge it. The caravan—a "Car Cruiser"—duly arrived and, amid the cheers of the workers, we departed from the Coventry factory on January 24th, 1932, full of hope that we would be at Cairo in time for the show's opening on February 16th. Down, then, to Dover and once again across the Channel on the Southern Railway's freighter, all five of our crew plus the car and caravan. The weather was filthy, and Pem said he hoped they'd soon get that tunnel built.

All was plain sailing through France to Marseilles and across to Tunis, then over a good road by way of Sousse, Sfax, Gabes and Medenine to Ben Gardane. Here, at the French frontier post leaving Tunisia they stamped our documents and refunded the tyre tax we had had to pay on entering the country (less the usual fees for stamps and formalities so dear to Gallic officialdom). But this was child's play compared with getting into Tripolitania. The officer demanded the full names of our fathers, mothers and grand-parents, their nationalities and also the exact status of the Foreign Office Minister whose signature appeared on our passports.

Next, the full details of each of our employments. What was a "Service Receptionist", as our man from the works had described himself? Conducted in broken English and badly fractured Italian it took fully an hour before the official was satisfied that we might enter the country, and so it was lateish when we arrived at the Grand Hotel, Tripoli. I suppose we looked a bit unkempt after our day-long run in dust and flies, and when I pushed open a door in the hotel which I thought might be the bar, there was a degree of consternation from an assemblage of smartly dressed Italians playing roulette.

So far we had taken the Italian touring office's assurance that, when we reached Tripoli, officials of the local auto-mobile club would supply us with maps of the route. There-fore when next morning the hall porter telephoned up to say that two gentlemen had come from the Tripoli Automobile Club to see me, I naturally thought good—now we're all right. But no. The two dignified gents had come to ask us if, when we got through, we would let them know whether or not there *was* a road. All the same, they performed one useful service in acquainting the military of our presence in Tripolitania, our route and expected dates of arrival along it. We were to bless them for this when we discovered at last what the country's conditions really were like.

Now, Tripoli is the centre of a region with a long history full of trouble and strife. Roman dominion lasted from the first to the fourth century A.D. After that it fell successively to the Byzantines, the Berbers, the Arabs and the Turks. In 1911 the Italians ousted the Turks and the following year the country was proclaimed under the complete sovereignty of the Kingdom of Italy.

Evidence of its greatness under the Romans is to be seen quite close to Tripoli, which we left about noon next day (February 2nd): on the road to Misurata there were the ruins of Leptis Magna, which must have been one of the finest cities in the Roman colonial empire. Many of the buildings were evidently faced with marble, and the vast extent of the city was apparent from the distant columns still sprouting from the deserted countryside.

At Misurata, about a hundred miles on our way, the road ended abruptly, and thence onwards we rocked and rolled our way along a bumpy piste which called for some expert stowage inside the caravan if any crockery was to remain intact. Even this was only a foretaste of what was to come, but we duly arrived at night at the fortified township of Sirte; we found we were expected and were comfortably housed and fed in the officers' mess. That night the padre brought along to the quarters in which they had installed us a bottle of Johnny Walker, which was very definitely manna from very nearly heaven.

We found the Italians most friendly—to us, but apparently not so to the local native population, who were presumably the Arabs they had pushed out. Each fort we came to was surrounded with barbed wire entanglements and it seemed that the country was being held down with a ruthless hand against insurrection. A story we heard—I cannot remember from whom—was that if any trouble broke out they would capture the local chief, fly him over his village and drop him into it from the 'plane, sans parachute. However, our departure was signalled by radio to the next fort along the route, and if we failed to turn up at the expected hour an armoured car would be sent out to look for us.

Since the caravan, and particularly its towbar, was taking such a terrific pounding, we were frequently having to patch up the latter with any improvised means we could think up. It was slow going, too, because we had continually to find out whether the rifts in the piste would bear the vehicle's weight or crumble into deep fissures; if so, we had to prospect on foot a way round.

To cover fifteen miles in an hour was splendid going— sometimes it would be one mile, even less. Here and there stretches of a kind of sandy "beach" would occur, when we could whack the speed up to possibly 30 m.p.h. for a while. We hoped to get as far as El Agheila the second night, but the fracture of a caravan leaf spring delayed us so much that we had to stop short at the little fort of En Nofilia, a hundred miles short of our target.

Here the commandant welcomed us, provided quarters and gave us dinner—an excellent one prepared in the Arab fashion. And outside the mess, as we broke up about midnight, a squadron of camels was encamped, the animals squatting in precise rows, completely motionless, in the brilliant moonlight. It was a sight never to be forgotten, with its background of flat, reddish desert against which the camels, bleached white by the hard glitter, looked like cardboard cut-outs in some theatrical scene. Next morning we were awakened by reveille and after a cup of coffee with our hospitable Italian officers we got under way before the sun gained strength.

It proved another day of struggle against the wretchedly weak towbar of the caravan, which was made of ash with metal fixings only at the front and rear ends of it. We had had to cut a portion of it out where the bucking and heaving of the component parts of the outfit strained the wood beyond endurance, and now we had yet another surgical operation to perform on it. The afternoon wore on, and it seemed that we would have to abandon hope of reaching our next planned destination.

When darkness descended it was impossible to carry on any further, because the headlamps' beam skimmed over the top of breakaways in the desert's surface. We decided, therefore, that we would have to camp out that night, so halted at the first likely-looking spot—pulling, through force of habit, off the piste to avoid obstructing the "road" for other traffic, unlikely though it might be.

Continued on p. 117

MILESTONES IN A MOTORING LIFE

From minimal wheeled transport at the author's Eton collar stage, to the self-propelled two-wheeler, then to three wheels. Middle left, *Giving instruction to a postman when the G.P.O. decided to*

adopt a motorised means of saving their employees' overworked feet. Bottom left, *A 3-speed hub-geared Rover sidecar outfit in King's Lynn when "nobbled" by Alexandra Day rose sellers while en route from Coventry to Cromer.* Below, *"Bush" Newsome in the saddle (Coventry 1913).*

Top, *The Paris shop of Lucien Psalty, with the proprietor, wearing his usual broad grin, just behind the handlebars of the machine on which the lady is sitting.*

Centre, *Author is active passenger to Rex Mundy in an 8 h.p. Williamson sidecar, having a*

little trouble getting up Rising Sun hill, Cheltenham. Alongside while author helps the engine is Geoffrey Smith, at the time Editor of "The Motor Cycle".

Left, *Testing a 1914 Rover Twelve (hood, sidelamps and bulb horn thrown in for £350).*

Genning up on a Daimler lorry chassis when about to join the A.S.C., M.T., in August 1914.

Back to the two-wheeler, the T.T. Rudge salvaged from the Le Mans café (page 48) with rifle slung should Huns cross my path (wouldn't have hit them, anyhow). Chorus in background are "Tiffies" from the workshops: big fellow on right was the blacksmith. Taken in the grounds of the Château de Chocques (1914).

"Bush" Newsome and self, now one-pippers, with Sunbeam car, about to depart on one of my film-collecting runs to Boulogne, outside the Château de Vilmarest at Arques (p. 54).

Vol. 2. — N° 19   June 4th 1916

Our 4th G.H.Q. Ammunition Park "in the field"—a mixture of "Ally Sloper's Cavalry" and pukka soldiers of the Royal Artillery. Left, The cover of the company's "Bulletin" showing the kinematograph machine and (on the screen) our orderly room with anti-aircraft shells bursting above (p. 53).

Below, *Unsolicited testimonial.*

Lt. D. H. NOBLE

As previously mentionned, the members of the Park recei a shock on Sunday when the new rapidly spread that Lt. Noble leaving, after having been with us for over seventeen months ; we almost got to feel that the Park belonged to him, rather than h the Park.

When Lt. Roach left us, Lt. Noble, or as he is famili known in England "Rover Noble" threw himself wholeheart into the work of carrying on the Sports club which included also Bulletin, Canteen and Concerts etc, with results every one is aw of, for never has the Park been better catered for in its leisure ments than during the last six months.

He brought over a cinema machine, arranged for the reg supply of films, organized Whist Drives, Revues, Concerts etc fact he has made life worth living during our period of waiting.

In everything in which he had a hand he left the stamp of personality and by his sympathetic nature, he endeared himse the men, who feel that they have lost a true friend and an excel Officer.

In leaving us he has the very best of wishes of the W Park for his future good health, happiness and prosperity.

C. W. Cross.

Dr. A. M. Low (extreme left) acted as my best man when I married in 1920 at the then Chapel Royal, Savoy (p. 66). My bride Pat Dunham's little sister on extreme right and various members of respective families grouped around My father is between Pat and myself.

Our olde-worlde cottage in Bridge End, Warwick, with Pat at door and 8 h.p. Rover coupé (with two-cylinder air-cooled engine) ready to take us to town— often we would drive the 95 miles each way just to have lunch at the old Trocadero.

Son John Dudley an early addict of the motor car and here behind the wheel at age of two.

A party for the Press to see and try P.A. Poppe's wonder car (!)—the 14/45 Rover (p. 78) at Burford Bridge, near Dorking. Managing Director J. K. Starley is leaning over the bonnet of the car on extreme right: I am sitting (apparently) on the starting handle!

Punters at a Brooklands race meeting putting their little bit on their fancy with one of the most popular of the bookies.

A 9/20 h.p. four-cylinder water-cooled Rover on the stand at Olympia, finished in the most attractive "strawberry and cream" colours which became quite a rage.

The Budapest trip (*p. 74*) to cope with worm driven axle troubles. Top photograph was taken in the "no man's land" between the frontiers of Germany, where one kept to the right, and Austria-Hungary where the drive on the left rule prevailed at the time. "Links Fahren" (drive on the left) caused vehicles and bicycles to wobble rather uncertainly as they met close by the German customs post.

The Rover in Buda, overlooking the modern city of Pest, across the Danube.

The 16/50 h.p. Rover Sportsman's saloon which Jackie Masters, secretary of the Motor Cycling Club, owned and drove for some 30 years. Looking out of it is Mrs. "Bee" Masters.

The 9/20 h.p. Rover on its R.A.C.-observed trial from London to Monte Carlo (p. 72). In its securely sealed "bag", with Observer R. W. Sprague and "Bush" Newsome on right, and Jack Starley (son of J. K.) on left.

Running into Monte Carlo, a more or less deserted town at this August period when the Riviera was considered too hot to be healthy!

Whole page advertisement which appeared in the "Daily Express",
"Daily Mail" and "Daily Dispatch" (Manchester)
to make sure that a good proportion of the public knew about
the prowess of the new 1930 Light Six Rover
(p. 81).

"*Cosmop*" (*p. 98*) *in North Africa to demonstrate that it could withstand torrid heat (actually, it was pretty nippy and we took our coats off specially for the photograph). Sharing a bottle of the local brew with me is George Bedford, who was well known for his efforts at Brooklands with pre-Rootes Hillmans.*

Below, *At least there was semi-tropical foliage to give the illusion of tropicality.*

When it rains in Algeria it sure does rain! Above, *The Vortic about to dash off back to last village for provisions (p. 105) while Harold Pemberton tries his hand with a shovel.*

Below, *The Vortic crosses the Cresta Run (note feet and head of fast-moving sleigh-er). In foreground Harold Pemberton; with pipe at back of car George Bedford.*

Top, The Essex Coach (p. 170) which offered such phenomenal value on the British market that the Chancellor imposed what were to become known as the McKenna Duties (p. 122).

Right, Although I have never found anyone who has heard of my first very own car, an Argo, this advertisement was reproduced in one of Floyd Clymer's "Scrapbooks" (p. 57).

"The Motor Car for the Millions"

ARGO
1918

5-Passenger Touring Car
$465
Electric Starting and Lighting, $60 Extra

An Increased Price— But an Increased Quality

2-Passenger Roadster
$405
Electric Starting and Lighting, $60 Extra

Yes! It is a Fast-Selling Car

No wonder the latest Argo Model, with every refinement, is in country-wide demand

We want dealers in every bit of unoccupied territory to help us bring Argo quality and Argo values to the public eye. That's all that's necessary for big business—the car itself will do the rest.

Think quick! How many people in your territory will welcome a car like the Argo at the Argo price? Dozens! Hundreds! Write us regarding your territory. If you're the right man, we'll be glad to reserve it for you until you've had a chance to investigate Argo plans and Argo possibilities.

Send in the Coupon for Territory

It's opportunity with a capital O. It's good now and backed by plenty of capital, ample facilities and extended manufacturing experience. It's going to get better all the time.

DO IT NOW!

Argo Motor Company, Inc.
127 Park Avenue
Jackson, Michigan

Send in the Coupon, It Means Dollars

Argo Motor Co., Inc., 127 Park Ave., Jackson, Michigan
Send me particulars of the Argo proposition.

My territory is ....
I am selling ....
Name ....
Address ....
State ....

When we started on our Monte Carlo Rally run from Glasgow in 1932 it happened to be just when the local medical students were holding their annual "rag", and we not unnaturally

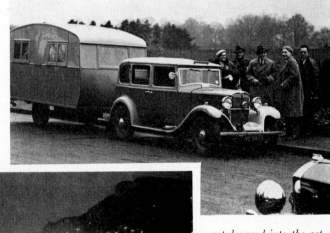

got dragged into the act. Centre, *On our way to Dover Reginald Rootes (centre of group) ran into us, metaphorically speaking.* Left, *All lit up: Monte Carlo from the Grande Corniche.*

On the way to Cairo (p. 113): in Northern France thick snow, but on the other side of the Mediterranean the weather was kinder but the "road" was not. The Libyan Desert is not a bit like the Sahara: dried clay rather than sand, but all the same it breaks up into fissures concealed by the scrub. Often the tracks which Italian army vehicles had made were

interspersed with deep holes and we had to prospect on foot to find a way round (centre).

Bottom, *We found the Italian military personnel very friendly and helpful; in this group at El Agheila (an isolated fortlet) I am between the N.C.O. and the officer, with Clive Scarff behind the officer's*

dog, Harold Pemberton in front of doorway and Hellyer, of the caravan suppliers, the giant on extreme right.

Top, *The Arab guide watches while our Service Receptionist (p. 119) puts planks and things under the back wheels to try and get the Wizard mobile again.*

Above, *We arrive at the Cairo motor show only a day behind schedule, and the President of the local motor club gives me the glad hand.*

Below, *Just to prove that this was Cairo, we went out to the Pyramids and flew our rather battered flag in the shadow of one of them.*

FROM ALFRED PEMBERTON'S PERSONAL SCRAPBOOK

Alfred Harmsworth (Lord Northcliffe to be) on tour in France with his Mercedes, 1905/6. His style in coatings was well suited to a driving seat with exterior gear- and brake-lever and no side protection. Above, Sir Max Pemberton on his early Quadrant motorcycle.

A spot of tyre bother. When both spare wheels were used up, the only thing to do was to stuff one of the covers with straw and hope for the best.

When Capt. Townsend started his car ferry at the Eastern Dock, Dover, the terminal consisted of no more than two sheds. The Sunbeam-Talbot Owners' Club returned from a rally (p. 147) when

a mobile Bowser was the sole means of refuelling. Centre, The "Halladale", successor to Capt. Townsend's first real car ferry, the "Forde", sailed from a wharf where now the Dover Harbour Board has built the extensive drive-on Terminal, through which pass far more than half a million cars every year. Below, A soirée of the Sunbeam-Talbot Owners' Club, with, in foreground, Georges Roesch, on right the

Marquess Camden, at left Graham Lyon with Mike Couper, Harold Pemberton, Geoffrey Smith and myself.

Maybe it was a bit of a "swiz", but in the "Ten Capitals in Ten Days" (p. 156) I counted Vaduz, capital of Liechtenstein as one. The chateau at the top of the hill is a famous landmark, while the Bank of Liechtenstein (below) has been a welcome haven for international financiers. This tiny Principality is, of course, sandwiched between Switzerland and Austria and a most interesting little country to visit.

Below, *Our Humber Snipe on its "Ten Capitals" trip passes through the impressive arches dedicated to the Austrian Emperor who reigned over this European monarchy in MDCCCXXIV (work it out for yourself).*

On the way to Lithuania we passed through Germany when Hitler was holding his plebiscite ("Vote for Me, or Else!"). Goebbels had instilled into the people how thankful they should be (p. 176). Even the railways played their part: the engine tender is inscribed "Dein Dank dem Führer" (Jolly well thank the Führer).

Centre, *As we crossed out of the Free State of Danzig on the ferry, Nazi cinema wagons were ready to tell the Danzigers about Hitler's peaceful intentions. Graham Lyon is standing by the car.* Right, *At the frontier between Lithuania and Poland (p. 178).*

Trailing across the U.S.A., Graham
Lyon at the site of the Battle of
Manassas, where Stonewall Jackson
held his position just over a century
ago. Centre, C. B. Thomas, chief
of Chrysler's export department, takes
a peek at our Sunbeam-Talbot
(p. 165). He was at one time head of
Chrysler's foothold in Britain at Kew.
Bottom, Leighton Noble, leader of
the band at Detroit's Statler Hotel,
says farewell to his English cousin

and two of his team take
advantage of the sunshine
roof (unknown then in
the U.S.) to strike up a
bon voyage chord.

When Switzerland in winter was believed in Britain to be one large heap of snow, our Humber Snipe penetrated to several resorts in the ski-ing regions of the Bernese Oberland and Engadine. Top, *Leaving Kandersteg on this January trip* (p. 149).

Below, *A wayside halt to admire Lake Thun. Back view on right is of George Throssell of the "Daily Telegraph" while James Skinner stands up through the sunshine roof to take in the beauty of the scene.*

Top, *The Turkish locomotive of the Orient Express* (*p. 157*) stands in Istanbul station, headlamps glaring, waiting to haul its load of diplomats, spies and so forth to the frontier. Below, *Bill Mackenzie (extreme right) shakes a farewell hand with the President of the Turkish Automobile Club, while Saunders and I perform similarly with other local notabilities. (Note.—The lady on left is not one of the beautiful blonde spies!)*

Sweden in the immediate postwar days (p. 202)—what a relief to visit a country not shrouded in gloom. Top right, The white gloved traffic policeman who controlled traffic in Stockholm with the finesse of the conductor of an orchestra from his pedestal in one of the main squares. Right, "Hugo", the 8 h.p. Standard coupé of immediate postwar days, with which Sir John Black kindly presented me, in a byway in Sweden's lush countryside.

In the course of developing heaters for British cars just after the second war (*p. 215*), Smiths sent first an expedition to Norway, where the fleet of different makes is here lined up near Tynset.

Centre, *The apparatus being readied for another night test.*

Below, *Mission achieved: Cliff Steadman drives in shirtsleeves in bitter North Canadian weather.*

The aftermath of the second war at (top left) *Boulogne*—the German U-boat pens made of reinforced concrete metres thick—(centre), all that remained of *Calais* when cross-Channel services resumed:

Below, On the way through liberated France to the Geneva motor show, *1947*, on a Lea-Francis (p. 212), a Mi-Carême village crowd.

the "Flèche d'Or" leaving.

When the Standard "Mayflower" was introduced in Sept. 1949 Sir John Black threw an impressive party at Coventry.
He is here greeting Mrs. Kay Petre, then motoring correspondent of the "Daily Graphic". Centre, I bought one of the

very first Standard Vanguards. Below, Henry Ford I and Harry Ferguson were at one time buddies (p. 196). When the split occurred Harry F. brought his "System" to England, prior to the lawsuit which made him a millionaire.

Sunset and sunrise in the Sahara (p. 140). Centre, Our desert cabaret, when the Ouled Naïl girls entertained us with music, song and dance, their golden ornaments jangling. Below, Ernest Appleby stands and contemplates the recesses where, in Ghardaia, candles have burned continuously for a thousand years or so.

Glimpses of Len Lord's three excursions for motoring writers. Top, At Banff Springs in 1951 (p. 223), when the party gathered on the terrace with a wonderful view into the Rockies.

A graphic road sign outside Johannesburg (1953).

The party at the Snowy Mountains Scheme in New South Wales in 1955 by the tunnel mouth which diverts the river from its original course to irrigate a potentially fruitful part of Australia (p. 230).

The Motoring Correspondents Circle (June 1945) visited Cowley at Lord Nuffield's invitation to hear about his last trip to Australia. Sir Miles Thomas on extreme left: he was then Vice-Chairman of Nuffield Organization.

The Guild's own private bar at the first race meeting held at Silverstone in 1950. The large figure on right is John Cobb, later killed on his water speed record attempt.

Below, Lord Rootes joking about the author at his Press party in Paris 1962. Harold Nockolds (extreme left) is amused, likewise Sidney Henschel (right).

His Grace the Duke of Richmond and Gordon presents the Harold Pemberton Memorial Trophy to the author at the Guild of Motoring Writers' dinner at the R.A.C. in 1951.

Right, *Len Lord (Lord Lambury of Northfield) as we all like to remember him—a happy snap at Heathrow in 1960, when he was leaving for one of his many selling trips to North America.*

Below, *The 50,000th member of the Institute of Advanced Motorists, Mr. Stanley Crame, is presented with a clock in December 1964 for having taken his Test at the right time by Lord Essendon. Mr. Denis O'Neill, C.B., of the Ministry of Transport (believed to have been the one who suggested a test diploma for motorists akin to the Master Mariner's certificate), is on left and Bob Peters, Sec. of I.A.M., centre.*

Lord Sempill, A.F.C., was a daredevil pioneer of light aircraft. As The Master of Sempill he made lone flights to demonstrate their capabilities. At his Craigievar castle he kept the 3-wheeled steamer made by the local postman in the '80s (p. 237).

Right, *Chairman of the Institute of Advanced Motorists, Mr. R. K. Munday* (right), *presents to General Lonsdale the I.A.M. trophy which is to be awarded for safe driving in the Army Championships and is to be known as The Lonsdale Cup.*

As a matter of fact, we had hardly got our meal under way, out in the open air (for it was stuffy inside the 'van) when a searchlight pierced the blackness and a siren wailed. It was an Italian military vehicle with four well-armed personnel aboard, which had been sent out by the commandant of the next fort—our intended destination—to seek us out and see if we had been set upon by unfriendly natives. We did our best to explain that we had been immobilised to our towbar, and could not move on, so after a while the military accepted the fact that we had got to stay put and would report (we hoped) next morning.

As a matter of fact, we never at any time experienced any hostility from the local population, which may have been due to our Union Jack bravely fluttering from our radiator cap. Strange as it may seem today, the British flag *did* mean something in those far-off times: even if the natives did not recognise it as the country for which it stood, at least it was not Italian!

Bengasi we reached on February 9th, after taking one whole week to cover the 800 miles from Tripoli. Even then it was only the car which arrived; the caravan was resting by the wayside twenty-five miles back because now the towing attachment on the car's chassis—which the chief engineer at Coventry had boasted would stand up to "anything"—had well and truly been pulled clean out of the chassis of the car.

We found Bengasi quite a well-developed little town, with a British Consul who proved to be a very helpful Maltese gentleman. He guided us to the best garage in the place, impressed on them the urgency of the work to be done, and within half an hour the proprietor had designed a new attachment.

By carrying on all through the night, the car was ready for us at 8 o'clock next morning. Wonderful mechanics, the Italians—they certainly made a better job of the repaired towing attachment than the factory had in the first place.

Incidentally, it was here, in Bengasi, that at the one and only good hotel (where we had a much-needed bath) I ran into Sir Harry Brittain, who was participating in the first trial trip of an Imperial Airways' service from England to South Africa—they had then been two days on the journey and hoped, after the machine had had some repairs, to complete the journey in another couple of days or so.

Back we went to the caravan, found its two occupants still alive and well, hitched up again and soon the castaways were revelling in *their* baths. Our trip from where the road proper ended at Misurata had shown us why it was that there was no knowledge about the possibility of driving from Tripoli to Bengasi—all traffic used the short sea route, which cut out miles of desertic going by steamer across the Bay of Sirte. Mussolini's autostrada certainly altered this quite considerably, but it was to be some while yet before it came into being.

Rainy weather set in after we left Bengasi, but we duly reached Derna, a very small town which we thought was the prettiest place we encountered on the whole trip. Here the military governor was very hospitable and we had the opportunity of sampling some choice local bananas, small but succulent. Then on and up something like a mountain pass, where at the summit the road ended abruptly and we were back in desertic country—but this time wet instead of dry. And here, we found, was where the Libyan Desert differs from the Sahara; when wet it becomes a slimy morass, being in the nature of clay rather than sand. Controlling the steering was just impossible; one turned the wheel and the vehicle slithered straight on.

Hereabouts Pem proved himself the hero of the enterprise —he stayed at the wheel for four hours, during which time we covered twelve miles—all in second gear. We had hoped to reach Tobruk, but again there was nothing for it but to camp by the "road"-side and dip into our tinned provisions.

Biggest problem was to deal with the mosquitoes—they were nearly as large as humming birds (and certainly did hum); our poor young Service Receptionist had bumps all over his exposed parts next morning which looked about as big as humming birds' eggs. We tried to console him by saying he was virginal food to the mosquitoes, whereas we were tough old meat by comparison.

The way ahead looked like a complete morass and our hopes of getting through were not raised by an Italian military vehicle driver, who indicated by signs that the flood water further along our route was at least a metre deep. I suggested to Pem that we might turn back and find the alternative piste, which ran a bit further inland. His reply was typical of the man—"I never turn back", he said. And he was right: we pushed on forward and in a few miles conditions did improve (although at one point we were forced to uncouple the caravan from the car and drag it out of a quagmire with block and tackle).

So we did get to Tobruk that night, to encounter the one and only offensive Italian officer of our whole trip. He—the commandant—more or less locked us in a compound for the rest of the night and let us fend for ourselves. This was no particular hardship, with still so much of Messrs. Fortnum and Mason's excellent tinned provisions in stock. Our Quartermaster had ordered a large and expensive case-full before we left England, and we certainly appreciated his forethought. There weren't so many mosquitoes that night, either, and our Service Receptionist's face had begun to look less like a pineapple when we set off again next morning.

We crossed out of Cyrenaica at Solloum, descending what was later to become known as "Hellfire Pass", to the Egyptian customs and immigration post. Here a Gippo medical officer wanted to vaccinate us; as he looked rather like an M.D. (Failed), and we felt we might pick up some disease from his attentions rather than he guard us against smallpox, we resisted. So the matter was amicably solved by our paying him for vaccinations we did not have. Then on to Mersa Matruh, with its de luxe hotel said once to have been a sultan's palace, where for the second time in a fortnight we had a bath.

No lingering in voluptuous luxury for us, however; we could just make it to Cairo for the opening day of the motor show if we pressed on, so dawn found us on the road again and, with no more than a brief stop in Alexandria, we arrived in Cairo during the afternoon. We had a great welcome, all the more so as the International Society of Tourisme was holding a conference, and had taken the day off to inspect the show.

Representatives from a host of countries were attending it, including some frightfully important wallahs who all seemed pretty impressed with this outfit of ours coming through from England on its own wheels. Moore Bros. Motors were highly delighted: they bought the whole caboodle from us, with Rootes' telegraphed consent, and we were free to return home by more comfortable means of travel.

During the past few days Haj had not been feeling too good, and now he was really seedy with what the British doctor at Shepheard's Hotel diagnosed as jaundice. When he checked in, however, there was a cable awaiting him; it read "Go on to Kenya investigate story of gold find urgentmost". The doctor gave him orders to stay in bed for a few days, but Pem, faced with this command from a News Editor who probably thought Kenya was a bus ride from Cairo ("It's in Africa, too, isn't it?") placed duty before his health and enquired when he could catch a plane for Kenya.

One was due to leave next morning, so he and I drove out to Heliopolis (Cairo's airport then) at seven o'clock and I saw him off an hour or so later. Haj was a man to whom nothing mattered except his work, and if any paper was ever lucky in its motoring correspondent that paper was the *Daily*

Express, for which he was eventually to die. It was an honour to have had a friend in him, and to me his memory is ever green.

Naturally, the motoring world outside my own particular segment of it had not been standing still during these post-first-war years. One of the most significant developments to popularise motoring occurred in 1924, when the Goodyear Co. gave the world a really practicable balloon tyre. Only the older among us can today recall the beaded-edge tyres inflated to about 50 pounds the square inch, which were until then universal. The puncture bogy was far more prevalent with them, and it was a back-breaking job to get those old covers off a rim, even with the help of great hefty levers.

The balloon tyre looked unwieldly to start with, and introduced some problems for designers of steering gear through the tendency to front wheel wobble at certain speeds. But its wider, flatter tread gave greater contact with the road surface, relieved stress on the suspension and lasted three or four times as long as the old high pressure ones.

At about this time, too, Ford of Britain, finding the growing demand for cars outstripping the capacity of its Trafford Park works at Manchester, decided it would have to move to a very much bigger site. Even though Henry I's dictum was that any plant of his must have waterborne facilities for carrying supplies and finished products, the choice of Dagenham came as a surprise, for the place was mostly low-lying marsh.

Its geographical advantages were inescapable, however, and so six years' constructional work was begun in 1925. Meanwhile the Model T "Tin Lizzie" continued coming out of Trafford Park until 1927, by which time Ford plants worldwide had produced more than 15 million of them. It was selling here as an open five-seater at £125 (no purchase tax then, of course), or £190 as a two-door saloon. The four-door ("Fordor") saloon cost an extra £25.

Meanwhile, more American interest was being shown in British and European markets. The General Motors Corporation, after failing in their bid for Austin, lighted on the ailing Vauxhall Motors at Luton, and acquired it in 1925. The old firm, dating as the Vauxhall Ironworks from 1857, had done good business with its 25 h.p. staff car in World War I, but demand was shifting down the price scale and the Vauxhall had not really made its number as an expensive car; also the Great Depression was casting its shadow before.

So a new sphere was entered under the ægis of G.M. when, in 1927, the Cadet, a six-cylinder model retailing at £298, supplanted the previous Vauxhall luxury types. But the original company will always be remembered for its magnificent 30/98, first produced in 1913, when it would lap Brooklands at 100 m.p.h. and won innumerable trophies in speed events. Revived after the war, it remained in production until 1923, and is now almost beyond price.

The move on the part of General Motors was prompted by the McKenna import duty of 33⅓ per cent to which I have referred, and while it helped greatly in bolstering the British motor makers against the threat from abroad, none the less price wars made news around 1930. Herbert Austin had increased the Longbridge factory capacity, and reached a record output of a thousand cars a week with a range of no fewer than twenty-four different models, starting with the Seven tourer at £130.

William Morris was breathing down his neck, however, and brought out the original Morris Minor which, as an open two-seater, he got down to the round hundred pounds. Austin counterblasted with a 7 h.p. "Ruby", and a little later Ford entered the fray with a £100 saloon—the lowest-priced car of this type ever to be marketed by any manufacturer in this country.

Sales of cars had to be fought for tooth and nail in this era of dismal depression. The Rootes had early realised that they needed a light car to augment the Wizard, and the outcome was a 10 h.p. water-cooled four-cylinder job with a saloon body that really would seat four people. It looked a winner right from the first glimpse, and Billy went off to the Continent with the prototype to see how it performed. He came back enthusiastic—but what was it to be called?

Well do I remember a meeting in the Humber boardroom at Coventry with Reggie in the chair, when various suggestions were debated. "Witch" seemed an obvious complement to Wizard, but was thought to lend itself too readily to synonyms, and eventually "Minx" won the day. As everyone knows, the name stuck for three decades and more from when, in October 1931, it was unveiled at the Paris Salon de l'Automobile at the Grand Palais on the Champs Élysées.

A family saloon with four doors and an engine of 1,180 c.c. capacity, in Britain it "attracted", as they say, an annual h.p. tax of £10 and sold for £159. There was a de luxe model, too, with sunshine roof and best leather upholstery, at £175, likewise a tourer at £170 and a sporting type saloon at £192 10s. Eleven feet in length, it appealed to the man who wanted something better and bigger than the quite tiny sevens and eights of other makes.

Also, it boasted one feature which was soon to become a standard fitment on practically every four-cylinder car, big or small—"cushioned power", as it was dubbed by the Rootes. This consisted of mounting the engine on rubber cushions instead of, as previously, bolting it rigidly to the chassis frame. A three-bearing crankshaft was further evidence of the Minx's modernity, for until then two main bearings had been considered adequate for at any rate a one-litre engine.

Although cushioned power was mentioned in Minx advertisements as having a patent applied for it, there seems a probability that it had made an appearance in the U.S. some time before. Chrysler had certainly featured "floating" power, mounting the engine in such a way as to allow it to rock, and controlling the amount of its movement by a leaf spring. Whatever the patent position was, however, the efficacy of the rubber mounting did smooth out the roughness of the average four-cylinder.

It probably accounted for the diminution in popularity of the small six-cylinder engine. Nevertheless, Morris—who had bought the Wolseley concern from the Official Receiver (and Vickers) in 1927—put on the market at about the same time the original Wolseley Hornet, with a six-cylinder engine of only 1,271 c.c., giving a tax rating of 12 h.p.

This Hornet set a fashion to the world by demonstrating that the way to get more body room on a given wheelbase chassis was to move the engine forward and bring the radiator well forward of the front axle. Up to then it had seemed like a law of the Medes and Persians that the radiator must be dead upright and in line with the centre of the front axle. By gaining those extra few inches, the little Hornet was able to sport a four-door saloon body on a quite short chassis.

While at the time we thought the forward radiator looked ungainly, today the old position for the radiator looks positively antiquated. The Hornet, as "scooped" by Harold Pemberton in the *Daily Express*, by arrangement with W. M. W. Thomas, then managing director of Wolseley, had another novelty—a sort of lighthouse on the roof which was the fore-runner of the winking trafficator. But it did not go on to production cars, being (I think) banned by the authorities.

The projecting nose of the Hornet, like the Minx's rubber mounted engine, was quickly copied by every other motor manufacturer without exception, and so, too, was the idea of having a dummy radiator shell concealing the utilitarian radiator proper, which was far cheaper than a genuine honey-comb one, specially shaped and well finished, which so often suffered in a collision.

Bumpers were only starting in the early 'thirties to make an appearance on British cars, and generally were flimsy things more for show than protection. The screenwiper was also a novelty; first hand-operated and then worked by vacuum from the induction pipe, slowing down and probably stopping if the throttle were opened, and flapping like mad when idling or running slowly. The screen washer was still to be a long time before it arrived in the U.K. from the U.S.

Two further new features were to make their appearance in the 'thirties—synchromesh to the gearbox, which the Vauxhall Cadet had in 1931, and the "knee action" or independent front wheel suspension introduced by the same firm on their 1933 Light Six. This was the first time independent front wheel suspension had been used on a quantity-produced car—Vauxhalls reached an output of 10,000 a year even in the days of the depression—but Lancia's Aprilia antedated the feature in a completely different manner.

It is interesting to realise that, even in those days, the problem of disposing of "old bangers" was in the public mind. Early in 1932, Massac Buist, motoring correspondent of the *Morning Post*, came out with the suggestion that a fund should be raised by levying the sum of £1 on every new car sold, from both manufacturers and agents, with which to buy old cars at, say, a tenner apiece and break them up for scrap. There was a stony silence from the motor trade!

Massac Buist, who had been the Editor of the *Autocar* for a short period, was ahead of the time when abandoned crocks would be left lying about in the streets and special machinery have to be designed to cope with the problem. The car population then, according to British Road Federation statistics, was 1,083,457, plus 626,649 motorcycles and 49,134 buses, coaches, hackneys and taxis, also 360,614 commercial vehicles. Yes, it was generally admitted that the car had come to stay.

Engine design was definitely making great strides in the direction of higher efficiency and improved reliability. One of the hardest international tests was the Alpine Trial, which

had been revived after the war but did not attract many
British entries. And for good reason—our engines were just
not made to cope with mountains, probably because we had
none.

In 1928, however, the Hon. Victor Bruce, with his wife,
drove an A.C. through the Alpine, and the following year
Mr. and Mrs. E. F. Leverett followed suit on an Arrol-Aster,
also Roy Franey and Humfrey Symons on a Riley Nine.
Humfrey was a well-known motoring journalist, who wrote
afterwards that "The first Alpine Trial was in 218 B.C., when
Hannibal entered several teams of elephants in the unlimited
c.c. class. Despite considerable opposition the Carthaginian
competitors that year swept the board, particularly in the
timed hill climb of the Col du Mont Genèvre. The trial lasted
fifteen days. Another famous Alpine Trial was in 1800,
Napoleon I being Clerk of the Course. This well-known
organiser of international events obliged the competitors to
cross the Alps in mid-winter and retirements were numerous,
although chains and other non-skid devices were allowed.
As the average speed imposed was high, the participants
were unable to find time for meals and arrived at the final
control starving and in rags."

Inter alia, it ought in fairness to be mentioned that Rolls-
Royce never had any qualms about the ability of *their* cars
to stand up to hard driving on mountains. Away back before
the first war, when the Austrians organised a series of
"Alpine Tours", with very strict regulations, a team of 40/50
Silver Ghosts had won the Coupe des Alpes. This was in
1913; the cars were most thoroughly prepared (as one would
expect, Claude Johnson being at the helm) and, with their
ultra-light bodies and narrow wings, the French called them
"très sport".

Reverting to 1931, the entry list included a team of Rileys
which came through without loss of marks, their drivers
being Victor Leverett, Jack Ridley and Capt. Riley. They

did very well again the following year, while in 1933
Triumphs went in for the Alpine in a big way. The firm was
then quite independent, and headed by Lt.-Col. C. V. Hol-
brook, C.B.E., who was all out for a new policy of high
efficiency and wanted to prove he was getting somewhere
with it.

The Alpine was to be the test ground for a model destined
to become famous and successful—the Triumph Gloria.
On one of them Donald Healey won the light car class of the
Monte Carlo Rally, starting from Athens, in 1934. Donald
had also, three years earlier, become one of the very few
British drivers to win the "Monte" outright—this on one of
Noël Macklin's Invictas.

It has to be borne in mind that all roads in the 'thirties
were very different from the smooth tarred highways of
today, and this particularly applied to the alpine passes.
They were rough, stony, dusty and exceedingly narrow in
their most dangerous sections. The Stelvio, with its forty-two
hairpins, was probably the best of a bad lot, mainly for the
reason that postal coaches had to surmount its 9,042 feet. Up it,
in the Trial, the cars were timed for twelve miles—which not
many British engines could then survive all out with equan-
imity. However, Donald Healey—later to design the Triumph
Dolomite—made fastest time of any unsupercharged car in
the 1,100 c.c. class on a Gloria.

Six Triumphs were put in, and all of them finished at
Munich without a single penalty mark, while a private
entrant—Capt. Maurice Newnham (then of the firm bearing
his name which was London distributor for Triumph) and
Donald Healey each won a coveted Coupe des Glaciers.
Incidentally, during the first war Maurice Newnham served
as a fighter pilot in the Royal Flying Corps and, as a Group
Captain, contributed greatly to the training of paratroopers
in the second war. Besides forming and commanding the
Parachute Training School at Ringway, near Manchester,

he was, also, responsible for training policy at all parachute schools abroad.

His book *Prelude to Glory* gives a vivid account of the vital part paratroops played in the war, once the inherent disdain of our War Office for anything savouring of modernity had been overcome. It was the old story over again, which I have related earlier concerning mechanical transport in World War I, and makes one wonder how on earth Britain has ever managed to come out on the right side in the face of the anti-everything-new attitude of most permanent civil servants and brass hats.

The 'thirties were, I suppose, the golden days of motoring, when governments had not yet got round to mulcting the well-off of the major proportion of their income and heritage. In Britain, Labour had gained power for a brief period in 1924, and when it was ousted after less than ten depressing months under Ramsay Macdonald, the trade unions staged the General Strike of 1926, with Stanley Baldwin's Conservative government in office.

Surviving this historic event, when those who rated our country higher than the shibboleths of socialism turned their hands to whatever job needed doing to keep the wheels turning, in the 1929 General Election Baldwin was swept out with the Tory party largely because they adopted the unappealing slogan of "Safety First". Labour got back, but in 1931 a crisis of loss of confidence in sterling (how familiar it all sounds!) caused Macdonald's resignation and the formation of a National Government which lasted to 1935. Despite these upsets in the political field, the motoring scene was on the whole sunny.

Abroad, both Mussolini and Hitler, with a similar load of unemployment trouble on their shoulders, had offset a lot of it by embarking on the construction of special motor roads but we, of course, could not do anything like that because any road in this country was bound to be open to all and every form of traffic, pedestrians included. (It should be recorded here that it was a certain Labour Minister of Transport, Alfred Barnes, who piloted the Special Roads Act through Parliament after World War II which enabled the first motorway to be conceived in this country, and I don't think he has received a sufficient amount of praise for his work in this connection.)

But to return to the 'thirties, these were years when beautiful cars with really lovely coachcraft-built bodies could flourish throughout Europe—Rolls-Royces, for instance, with bodies by Barker, Figoni and Falaschi of France, Kellner of Berlin, Freestone and Webb, Mulliner, Hooper and Park Ward. Then there were the beautiful productions of Hispano-Suiza, Isotta Fraschini—the latter with sedanca de ville coachwork by Castagna of Milan—the Mercedes 36/220 and 38/250 with supercharger that whined like a jet aircraft, and Bugattis made by an Italian who lived his life as a Frenchman in a German-speaking province of France which twice was overrun and occupied by the invader from next door.

There was W. O. Bentley, too, with his magnificent models ranging up to the eight-litre before he had to give up producing them in 1931 (Rolls-Royce after taking over put out their first successor bearing the Bentley nameplate in 1934). Across the Atlantic, a certain Lobban Cord decided to market a front-wheel-driven car—not that this was an invention on his part. Alvis, for instance, had brought out a f.w.d. racing job (nicknamed the Tadpole) in 1925, which scored successes in hill climbs and on Brooklands.

But the general public fought shy of a car that was pulled by its front wheels. André Citroën, who adopted it, said with some logic that the most rudimentary of all mechanical principles is that it is far easier to pull a cart than to push it. The Cord was nevertheless highly thought of during the years it was made—1929 to 1938—and is today a collector's piece. It may, indeed, have inspired Citroën to go and do likewise; not that he got away with it save by relinquishing control of his business to the Michelin financial giants.

As the Great Depression passed over, competition—and outputs—increased. The public had become motor-minded in a big way; probably as the result of so many learning the ins and outs of mechanical transport during World War I. The workings of the internal combustion engine were no longer a mystery to the average man in the street: *his* main problem now was to raise the money to buy a car. Even though motor manufacturers reduced prices, and there was no purchase tax to pay, the great mass of working class simply could not produce the "ready", and hire purchase was in an elementary state so far as cars were concerned.

Automatic transmission had not made its presence felt on this side of the Atlantic in the 'thirties, but the epicyclic gearbox, the Wilson pre-selector, was in use on the Armstrong Siddeley, the Daimler and the Talbot. In the Humber-Hillman-Commer combine, predecessor of the Rootes Group, attention was being paid to another type of epicyclic gearbox devised by Capt. Edgar de Normanville.

Former motoring writer and publisher as well as being a clever and creative engineer, de Normanville greatly impressed the Rootes brothers with his design for a somewhat similar type of box to the Wilson, but which was not pre-selector. It gave, however, instant changing "without tears"; there was a steering column lever working in a simple quadrant, i.e., without a gate, and all the driver had to do was to place it in whichever notch he wanted.

Edgar de Normanville worked in the Humber drawing office for a time and eventually produced his gearbox, which certainly operated very well under routine tests. The Rootes decided to go ahead with it on a new Humber model, and the slogan "Motoring's Sixth Sense" was coined for advertising purposes. I was allocated the task of reassuring the public as to its reliability and general merits, and it seemed that a test was called for which would place an unusual strain on the transmission.

After my experiences in the Libyan desert it sounded a good idea to have a crack at the Sahara, towing a caravan through soft sand and thereby multiplying the load that had to be pulled. I discussed the suggestion with E. J. Appleby, who was then Editor of *The Autocar* and originator of its very popular feature called "Occasional Jottings" under name "The Scribe". His son Barry did—and still does at the time of writing—the thumbnail sketches for it. At all events, Ernest Appleby liked the Sahara plan, and Geoffrey Smith, his editorial director, gave it his approval. The Rootes likewise.

First, however, I had a personal matter to attend to. Having been a widower for three years, and not liking it, I was fortunate enough to meet someone in a similar position and with the same ideas. Ashley Courtenay, my old friend from Grove Park days, who was now the proprietor of a flourishing guide to hotels called *Let's Halt Awhile*, played Cupid by introducing me to a very charming lady who hailed from Ireland but had lived for long periods on the Continent with her first husband, in the Diplomatic service.

On August 28th, 1933, therefore, Margot Saxton and I went to the Registry Office at the Guildhall in the City of London and took the step which neither of us has since regretted. Soon afterwards we set up house in Coventry, on the Kenilworth Road, the move from London being due to the fact that headquarters of the H-H-C combine was now at the Humber factory. Reggie Rootes was firmly installed there as managing director, and it seemed appropriate that the publicity department should be on the spot.

Almost every day, as I drove home for lunch (catering arrangements at factories not being the accepted thing a that time), I was overtaken by a newcomer to Coventry who lived at Warwick and was even more anxious to get home for lunch than I was, for he drove at a speed that had little regard for the 20 m.p.h. legal limit. When I say a newcomer, I mean that he had only comparatively recently started up in the motoring world in the Midlands, having previously operated from Blackpool.

This was, of course, William Lyons, who was producing a very smart saloon called the S.S., combining his coachwork with a Standard chassis. Originally called Standard Swallow, using the name of the sidecar he had been making up north, it was listed for the first time as a separate make—the S.S.— in *The Autocar* Buyers' Guide of 1933. Jaguar was adopted several years later, after Hitler had given the original initials a sinister sound. And, as everyone knows, the success of Bill Lyons, ably abetted by his chief engineer Bill Heynes, has been phenomenal.

Humber's new gearbox having passed out of its experimental stages, was being readied for production when our expedition to the Sahara got under way towards the end of 1933. I had made very special arrangements with the caravan makers that our mishaps with the previous 'van should not be repeated—likewise with the car's towing attachment. So off we set with an extensive stock of tinned provisions, crockery, water cans and bedding.

As technical expert we had a man from the factory who had been working on the de Normanville gearbox assembly and therefore was reputed to know what went on inside it. A typical Midlander, who I don't believe had ever been even a dozen miles away from Coventry (and it's interesting to mention here that, in spite of there being a five-shilling excursion train every Saturday afternoon from Coventry to London, a large proportion of the locals had never paid a visit to "Smoke", as they called the metropolis).

Hence mechanic Idlans, as I will call him, ought to have been suitably impressed at the opportunity of seeing a bit more of the world. He didn't seem to be, however, and maintained a kind of bored distaste for the Channel ferry and the parts of France (wot, no fish and chips?) through which we passed en route for Marseilles.

All went well, however, and in due course we were aboard the Mediterranean steamer bound for Algiers. "Gleaming white against the hills", wrote Appleby in his Disconnected Jottings as a foretaste of the stories that were to follow under the title of Land of Pastel Shades, "the queen of the Barbary coast seemed to smile a welcome. Our good ship glided in between two low breakwaters a bare stone's throw from the market place where Christian captives were sold as slaves not much more than a hundred years ago."

Ernest Appleby was a man with a poetic soul, despite a hard childhood in Canada selling newspapers on the streets before he migrated to England; a dear and charming companion who made the best of his opportunities. Never out of temper, always ready to do his stint of whatever had to be done, he revelled in this release from everyday chores and really did let himself go in his writings about what was to prove a pleasant, if somewhat strenuous, trip.

Typical of his impressions following a sight-seeing tour of the Algiers neighbourhood was this gem ". . . The little cemetery hidden in the midst of this rabble town (a junk market on top of a nearby hill), is a survival of Mussulman poetry and love of tranquillity. It is called the Cemetery of the Three Princesses where, beneath aged and fantastically formed fig trees, lie the remains of three obscure little princesses of love, of whom nothing is known and who have found immortality by chance in a harem of death amid the peace and verdure of the secret gardens of Islam."

What a vast continent Africa is! We have to revise our ideas of distance when we plan itineraries in a land where England, Scotland and Wales could be dropped into a corner and hardly noticed. With the invaluable aid of Michelin's admirable map of Algeria, plus a large one of the Sahara at sixty-three miles to the inch, we had plotted out a route. The local Shell office had given us a useful guide to their petrol pumps in the desert, which naturally were few and far between.

One fine morning we departed from Algiers with our store cupboard full to bursting, also some rolls of stiff wire netting. This last was the result of a tip from the R.A.C.'s representative there, one Captain de Malglaive, who had told us that it might come in mighty useful if we encountered deep drifts of soft sand, as were prevalent after a sirocco. First came a long ascent from the coast for some fifty miles to a township called Aumale, and on to the summit of the Col du Dirah (3,396 feet). This was quite a different countryside from the Foreign Legion sort of thing we had been expecting, with mountains—some snow covered—towering in the distance; in fact, winter sports were a regular thing in due season, they told us.

But, as we dropped some hundred miles down to Bou-Saada a big change came over the scenery and when we eventually arrived at the place, where we were to stay the night, it almost looked as if we had reached the edge of the Sahara. This was an illusion, however. It proved that there was not only an excellent hotel at Bou-Saada, run by the Compagnie Transatlantique mainly for American tourists and one of a chain originally laid down for tours by Citroen-Kegresse semi-tracked vehicles some years previously, but a verdant oasis into the bargain.

And it happened to be washing day; a weekly outing for the local women, who carried the family linen to the edge of the tiny stream, placed it in the water and proceeded to dance on it. We were rather fascinated, and set up our ciné apparatus to film the process. Our local guide looked a bit uncomfortable about this, but said nothing until I asked him to request the nearest lady to continue her dance. He shook his head with the remark "I cannot speak to another man's wife". Fortunately for our film the right husband came on the scene; some francs changed hands and all went off happily.

A funny thing did, however, happen to us in Bou-Saada oasis. A cheerful voice behind me wished us good evening and I turned round to find it came from a young Arab who, it appeared, had every intention of attaching himself to our party. He told us he had been in Hollywood, had filmed with Rex Ingram, spoke French and German in addition to American English and was familiar with Russian—at least, so he said, a Russian princess had made love to him ("but she was too old").

Aged about twenty-two, he strongly denied being married but owned to possessing certain attachments in the female line. He offered to show us around the desert if we would let him come with us, and after we had discussed terms and so forth we felt he would be a very useful addition to our crew. And so he proved, assuming the role of chief steward, navigator, kitchen staff and general factotum.

In the course of showing us around the Sahara, Rex, as we christened him, led us over camel tracks where deep soft sand alternated with rocky outcrop and rutted, hard baked clay. Mile after mile and day after day we careered over pistes which justified the legend "Impracticable for Motors", and gave us (well, me at any rate) qualms as to whether the car and its transmission would stand the strain.

Idlans took it calmly and so, fortunately, did de Norman-ville's gearbox, as well as the rest of the outfit. At night, when the desert turned cold, we would park in the great open spaces and keep snug in the caravan while Rex juggled with tins and served us with meals that were not to be despised. Sometimes he was able to buy fresh provisions, including bread, at insignificant little "villages" which we ourselves could not possibly have discovered.

At one oasis Rex was evidently *persona grata* with the local chief: we were greeted by a deputation of solemn elders and in our honour (and at our expense) the ceremony of the "Mechoui" was laid on. A sheep was killed and spitted lengthwise with a thin tree trunk, then roasted over the embers of a fragrant wood fire. When done to a turn we sat round in a circle with the sheep, still whole, in the centre. Knives and forks being strictly taboo, each of us had to tear strips off the carcase and consume them with relish and appropriate burping. The eyeballs, a special delicacy, were offered to me as the presumed leader, but I managed to get Appleby elected to the status of co-leader and made to eat one of the things—ugh!

Then followed a desert cabaret: while we digested the somewhat stringy meat (how the sheep exist, on the parched herbage, seems a mystery), a troupe of Ouled Naïl girls appeared, accompanied by flute and tam-tam players. They proceeded to entertain us with native music and the danse du ventre. With their robes, which glittered with threads of gold and silver woven into them, sparkling in the sun and their necklaces of coins jingling, they made a wonderful sight. But the thing which intrigued us most about the dancing girls was how come, these young women who went openly about among men, unveiled and unashamed? Rex, of course, could supply the answer.

The Ouled Naïls, he told us, were not ordinary Arabs but a race who inhabited the mountains of that name which ran from east to west in the Laghouat region. They had quite distinct views on the subject of their women and it was the custom for a young girl to be sent by her family to one of the towns, where she earned her living in special cafés in the "reserved" quarter.

Not at all unattractive to western eyes, they radiate sex appeal in a curiously marked way, and their ambition is to tempt the matrimonial advances of the desired young man of their tribe. They did not bank their "takings" but (in those days) translated all the currency they won into gold coins and jewellery, which they wore on their persons. Round the neck of each of "our" girls we saw strings of gold coins— pre-war sovereigns and five pound pieces, five-Napoleon French ones and what have you. Most of them seemed about ready for retirement and wedding bells.

But wait, said Rex; I will show you *the* most beautiful of all the dancing girls. Her name was Djemila and she was, he went on, the toast of all the beaux in the Territoires du Sud (the northern part of the Sahara). So on we journeyed, crashing and bumping our way along vile pistes and in due course arrived at the township which housed Rex's special sweetie. His preparations for the coming encounter were thorough; he vanished into a Turkish bath (we were surprised to learn that nearly every place, however small, had one of these, patronised by the better types of inhabitant once a week).

When he had had his bath he scoured the local market to buy fitting robes, and a little later reappeared clad most gorgeously in a silk burnous and fine new turban. But then— tragedy. Djemila had gone. She had achieved her dowry and claimed her man. Poor Rex: he was heartbroken—and the effects of the hurried bath and thin new raiment gave him a cold. Gloom descended on the entire company, for we had taken Rex to our hearts and mourned with him.

From here he took us into a little known part of the desert, the home of the M'zabs, a mysterious tribe quite different in appearance from Arabs. They look Jewish, rather, with (in the case of the men) a black beard forming a complete fringe to their faces and a sallow brown skin. There is a school of thought which holds that they may be a lost tribe of Israel; another that they are the descendants of the inhabitants of the ancient city of Carthage, who were forced to flee when the place was sacked by Scipio in those far-off days of history.

A third authority on the subject of the M'zabs, about whom none of us was erudite enough to have any theory at all, says that they are Berbers pure and simple—and purer, perhaps, than they are simple. For they are keen businessmen and act as moneylenders and merchants in not only their own region but elsewhere in North Africa. Yet whatever they may be in origin, they are a people of very pronounced characteristics.

Their towns, seven in all and spread over a fairly large area, have one feature in common; they are built on a mound-shaped hill surmounted by a mosque of obelisk design. To my mind there was one outstanding mystery about the M'zabs, and that was how they could have existed while they built their "cities"—really they are townships with populations of perhaps a thousand or so.

Being a peace-loving race, opposed to fighting or the use of arms, they had, apparently, been chivvied about the desert by more aggressive tribes. Wherever they settled, enemies would soon appear and drive them out of the communities in which they had created the amenities of existence.

When the M'zab elders made their decision to find sites for their towns right away from civilisation they had to discover the one thing that makes life possible in the Sahara —water. In a desert which, vast though it may be, the oases are limited in number and have been known from the beginning of time, they had to find untapped sources. Maybe a thousand years ago there were water diviners with extra sensory powers who could trace the course of the underground rivers from oasis to oasis.

At any rate, as we stood on the mound which is Ghardaia and gazed on to the sun-baked, arid, vegetation-less desert stretching in every direction, we had to admire the courage of those ancients who determined to create their own oases. For that is what they did, but the mystery is how they lived while they laboriously dug their wells, spadeful by spadeful, in the burning heat until they reached the precious water.

We watched as it was brought to the surface in the same way as it had been through the ages. A goatskin with three of the leg apertures sewn up is lowered down the well at the end of a rope, with a second rope keeping the fourth leg's open aperture pointing upwards. The other ends of the ropes are harnessed to a donkey, which walks down a well-worn path and, when it reaches the equivalent of a stop sign, the goatskin appears at the well's mouth, the open-ended leg is drawn over the edge and disgorges the skin's contents into a stone cistern. From here it runs along channels to the various "subscribers" and irrigates their allotments, one at a time. We bought about ten gallons to refill our cans and it cost a pound's worth of French currency.

The indefatigable Rex, now better of his cold and heartbreak, unearthed a M'zab guide, and he introduced us to some of the local customs. I thought the quaintest was the way in which the goats—and every inhabitant kept one or more of them—knew what to do when their master's frontdoor was opened at the crack of dawn. No doubt relieved to get a breath of fresh air after being cooped up all night (the same probably went for their masters), the goats made their way, alone and unguided, in ones and twos and very sedately, along each narrow lane in the town, eventually congregating peacefully in an open space on the outskirts.

Here they would wait patiently until the goatherd arrived, when they "fell in", so to speak, formed fours and marched behind him to the local grazing ground. Presumably they managed to get a modicum of sustenance from the dried-up-looking sage scrub (rain only fell at the rarest intervals), and as the sun dipped in the heavens the goatherd rallied his charges, returned them to the parade ground, "dismissed" them and they strolled back to their respective owners' residences.

Then there was the locksmith, who made front door keys

for his clients of a type that Mr. Yale could never have thought up. A chunk of wood, suitably shaped with a primitive plane and chisel, had a quantity of headless nails embedded in it, their positions coinciding with the holes bored in the counterpart, which was attached to the door's lintel. Each key was fully nine inches long and about four wide, and possibly was a method of restricting one citizen to one home, for he certainly could not have carried any number without some discomfort.

But apparently the M'zabs are a strictly moral race, and anyone who goes a-travelling has to return once a year and must not marry outside of his tribe. Report has it that they are a wealthy lot of people, and that millions of gold pieces are buried under their cities. We had no opportunity of confirming this.

In the Sahara the sunrise and sunset are miracles of Nature's hand at her most artistic. The gold in the western sky at night turns to orange and becomes suffused with pink, then red, until finally the sun vanishes completely and indigo blue spreads over the horizon. One day I found our mechanic, Idlans, who had seemed immune from any matter approaching the ethereal, gazing intently at a sunrise, which is, of course, exactly the opposite of what I have just tried to describe. "Isn't it wonderful, Idlans?" I said to him, "What does it make you think about?" "Well," he replied in his ponderous, matter-of-fact way, "this is Sunday again, and I'm wondering if I'm being paid overtime for weekends." Exit for breakfast.

Dear old Appleby had been swotting up the history of the M'zabs, and proceeded to give of his learning during a highly satisfactory dinner Rex prepared from our collection of tinned goods. "According to Georges Rozet," he declaimed, "there was trouble in the Islam camp in the first century of the Mohammedan era (A.D. 622). A puritan sect refused to accept Ali, the prophet's son-in-law, as their Caliph.

"Beaten in their argument, they murdered Ali and fled from the east into Barbary. The remnants of the tribe fled to Ouargla, where they aroused the jealousy of the locals, who drove them out. They had put eighty-five miles between them and their pursuers when they found themselves on a ghastly limestone plateau amid arid hills, upon which nothing grew and where water could only be found by digging deep for it. Here they built their cities.

"The people now live in peace, but quite apart from Arab, Berber, Nomad or Sudanese, upon whom they look with contempt. They are the Quakers of the Islam faith and have retained their rigid laws and customs, which among other things demand that every good Mozabite must reappear in the Heptapolis every other year, no matter where he may have wandered in the meanwhile. To the mosque he must go to be strengthened in his religion, thence to his home to keep contact with his family and to acknowledge as miraculous the children born unto him during his absence.

"And to his home he must return to die, to be buried in an orderless cemetery, unprotected by shade or verdure, where crematory sun beats down upon the sacred ground." Added Appleby: "Let me say that Rozet knew more about the Sahara than the average Londoner knows about his own suburb."

There was a little lane near the mosque, and in it an open-air shrine where a candle has burned every night for a thousand years (and probably still does); there was the Kaid's house with a view from the roof of the camel square with a ring of stones wherein the elders sat and made their decision to build the city (but, again, what *did* they do for water meanwhile?).

Then we were jerked back to modernity by the arrival of a decidedly dilapidated Ford containing four bearded young British officers and a mountain of baggage. They had started off from the Gold Coast with a brace of old cars picked up secondhand in Accra; had been forced to abandon one in the desert and so far had been sixteen days on the trip. They were going home on leave, and apparently this counted from the time they actually arrived in Britain, so they were not hurrying unduly.

Rex gave them lunch in the caravan and they then waved a cheery goodbye and went dustily off northwards, while we hitched up and went the opposite way, leaving the M'zabs and their old Mozabite customs behind us. We had filled up with gasoline at the local Shell pump—the Algerian (then French) Shell Company had done much exploration of the Sahara and laid down pumps at strategic points along the three "lines" which were practicable for motor vehicles during the months when the French authorities allowed any traffic to pass—November to May.

These lines are the "Tanezrouft", the most westerly, the "Hoggar", the middle one, and the "Ajjers and Tibesti" to the east, running almost parallel with the (then) Italian–Libyan frontier. They are not roads, or even pistes, for the frequent sandstorms merely blot out wheel tracks in an incredibly short time.

Perhaps the most "glamorous" of the filling stations was "Bidon Cinq", a pump dumped down in the completely un-inhabited southern section of the Tanezrouft line, hundreds of miles from human habitation in any direction. It formed the indispensable refuelling point which permitted motor vehicles (and aircraft too, in those days) to travel between Algeria and the French Soudan, on a stretch of desert where otherwise there would have been a gap of 500 miles.

The Compagnie Générale Transsaharienne had researched the Tanezrouft line in 1923 and had installed huge bidons, or steel petroleum drums of some 500 gallons capacity, along it at fifty kilometre intervals. Bidon Cinq was the fifth one after leaving the Soudan frontier going northwards, and here C.G.T. and Shell between them maintained a filling station, with two Arabs in charge, during the desert's open season. A tanker of Shell's fleet—ordinary four-wheeled five-tonners—kept the pump and its attendants provided with petrol, food and water; this last the "gardiens" were not to dispose of to anyone except in case of dire emergency.

Shell of Algeria issued a Guide to the Sahara, and this is how it describes Bidon Cinq: "You should first know that the 'Free Town' of Bidon-5 has as its flag a wind sock, that its wide boulevards are those of the Infinite; that its Place du Silence is ornamented by a petrol pump for motorists, that its Grand Hôtel of today—overnight staging post of *grand confort*—was once a coach body, and that its most artistic Monument is an aviation fuel pump.

"You should also know that Bidon-5 is lost in the middle of the Tanezrouft, that frightful desert of thirst devoid of animal or vegetable life. But do you know why it was created, and why it has been given such a name, this replenishment depot which is unique throughout the world? In 1923 an expedition organised by the Compagnie Générale Trans-saharienne found it possible to traverse the Sahara by the route of Tanezrouft.

"A few years later, in order to facilitate travel along this route, a refuelling point halfway between Reggan and the first post in the Soudan was laid down. The government also made it a wireless telegraphy point, and thus it became famous, and year by year has assumed still greater importance." It did, in fact, make possible the establishment of a regular, if infrequent, service of public transport across the Sahara.

Well, the Humber Snipe and its caravan, as well as the de Normanville gear, stood up to this sandy adventure, and Idlans had no delving to do inside the box of tricks, as we irreverently called "Motoring's Sixth Sense". I taught Rex to drive it, and he cottoned on in no time to the gear-change. And so we eventually returned to Algiers, regretfully—very—

bade farewell to Rex and sailed off across the Mediterranean back to Marseilles and home. I felt we had done our stuff as far as establishing the de Normanville gear's reliability was concerned, and Appleby's story week after week in the *Autocar* certainly confirmed this.

As for me, I persuaded John Gordon, then Editor of the *Sunday Express*, that the M'zabs would interest his readers, and he gave me a whole page in two consecutive issues to do so. It was rather sad, however, that Humbers had to abandon the gear because of difficulty in manufacture. De Normanville went on to design his overdrive, which at the time of writing is still going strong, and deservedly so.

Midway through 1935 the Anglo–French combine Sunbeam-Talbot-Darracq was in difficulties: the Rootes acquired the first two companies in October, leaving Darracq to go out of existence. Talbot was doing fairly well, with a range of five models, all six-cylinders, from 13·8 to 23·8 h.p., priced from £395 to £850. At the works in Barlby Road, off Ladbroke Grove in West London, the famous designer Georges Roesch was in charge of engineering, and some very fine jobs he turned out. Appointed just before the end of World War I, this (then) young Swiss from Geneva had served with Delaunay-Belleville and Renault in France, and with Daimler in England.

The firm of Clément-Talbot had been founded in 1902 by the Earl of Shrewsbury, whose family name was Talbot, in association with a talented French designer, M. Clément. A link-up with Darracq came in 1919 and the following year a further merger was concluded with Sunbeam of Wolverhampton, making the first big motor combine—"S.T.D." Roesch's 14/45 Talbot was produced in 1926 on a meagre capital outlay; it was an immediate success, largely due to the skill with which he employed top quality materials to make component parts light in weight but with a high reserve of strength.

Unfortunately, the S.T.D. combine fell upon evil days financially and Roesch's talent in designing the Type 105 Talbot, with its automatic traffic clutch and his own particular revision to the Wilson pre-selector gearbox whereby the next higher gear was selected automatically ready to engage when the pedal was pressed down—to say nothing of one-shot lubrication and built-in jacking system—was his last effort in the purely Talbot line.

Under the Rootes' regime he was given one very major designing task, going by the name of Sunbeam. King George V having died on January 20th, 1936, Edward VIII succeeded to the throne and, as Prince of Wales, he had long been a friend of Billy; he owned a Humber himself and bestowed a Warrant of Appointment as suppliers of motor cars to his Household on Rootes Limited.

He also paid a visit to the factory at Coventry where, to the great delight of everybody, he rode the very Humber tricycle which had been owned by his grandfather, Edward VII. Now that he was king, however, he would need a really majestic vehicle, larger than anything Humbers had ever produced, and Billy made up his mind he was going to get it.

The outcome was an eight-cylinder-in-line engined Sunbeam, of $4\frac{1}{2}$ litres capacity developing 150 b.h.p. The engine was shown to the Press at a reception held at Claridges on October 8th, 1936, and a complete car at the Olympia motor show a week or so later. The 11-ft. 4-in. wheelbase chassis had independent front wheel suspension by transverse leaf spring, and, with Thrupp and Maberly limousine body, the listed price was £800 (£750 for a "Continental" model). Another car with the same chassis was shown by H. J. Mulliner with their bodywork.

Stanley Baldwin's first National Government was now in power, having succeeded Ramsay Macdonald's second Labour government in June 1935. And, as we all know,

Edward VIII was never crowned king; he abdicated on December 11th, 1936, and his brother succeeded as George VI. The result of all this was that never another word was heard about the eight-cylinder Sunbeam; it was sunk without trace.

Nor did Georges Roesch himself survive much longer with the Rootes: rationalisation of products decreed that there was now no scope for an individualistic designer, no matter how skilful, and he departed from Barlby Road. To succeed his creative art some rather nondescript cars with the name Sunbeam-Talbot on the radiator appeared, composed almost entirely of the same components that went into Humber and Hillman models.

During 1936 I was beginning to feel that Coventry was rather a boring place to live in; that I wanted to get back to London; also that merely being an employee was not quite my cup of tea. Maybe the Rootes thought the same, for Reggie very pleasantly agreed that my services as a freelance publicity man could be of more use to the firm. So I formed a private limited company with Bill Owen, at that time the motoring correspondent of the *Daily Mirror* and equally anxious to strike out on his own.

Press and Allied Services Ltd. thereupon came into existence, with offices in New Square, Lincoln's Inn, and we were among the first British "public relations" firms (only we hadn't then heard this magniloquent term—it came from across the Atlantic during the second war). We picked up a few more accounts, the one which interested me the most being Autocheques Ltd., the motoring travel firm started by Graham Lyon and then occupying offices in Piccadilly Circus House.

Graham Lyon's system was to enter into an arrangement with numerous hotels all over the Continent whereby they would accept his Autocheques in payment of dinner, room and breakfast, and he was most punctilious in seeing that the cheques, when sent in, were paid immediately to the hotels. There was, of course, no currency rationing in those days, and many a British motorist touring abroad found it more convenient to pay his hotels by way of Autocheques than to juggle with foreign money.

Also, if one were robbed, or lost one's cash—or overspent and had nothing left for the last night or two on the homeward journey—it was comforting to know that one could at least have dinner and a bed. The prices of the various hotels naturally differed, and the method of overcoming this was to put a basic value on the cheque and to stick on "crowns", to the number specified, in the case of the more expensive places. Any unused Autocheques and crowns could be exchanged back into sterling on return home, less a small commission.

A very enterprising man was Graham, with a keen eye on publicity, and he and I got on famously. He had worked in the United States for some time after the first war—before that he was a salesman for Wolseleys in their showroom in York Street, Westminster, and was an ardent motorist—and while in the U.S. he had devised a similar sort of cheque scheme in connection with long distance buses and coaches.

Returning to Europe after a period spent in North Africa organising tours for Americans on those Citroen-Kegresse half-trackers which I have mentioned earlier, he went in hot and strong for encouraging British motorists to take their cars abroad. He found a kindred spirit in Capt. S. M. Townsend, the originator of the cross-Channel car ferry.

Capt. Townsend's family business had been concerned with shipping, added to which he too had been addicted to motoring abroad since he was "so high". In 1906 his father took him to Spain, having sent his car on ahead securely packed in a wooden crate: it was delayed en route for three weeks. As he grew up he went to the Continent with his car regularly in spite of all the formalities.

But he steadily got more and more irked with the evident

desire of the Southern Railway to make it as difficult as
possible to take a car across the Channel. Rates were high
and cars had to be taken aboard by crane (which meant tips
all round for the gang who performed the operation), while
petrol tanks had to be drained and no provision was made on
the other side by the railways for fuelling on the quayside.

In 1927 Capt. Townsend made a study of the possibility of
running a car-ferrying service and discovered that, if he
charged only half the railways' tariff, he ought to break
even and perhaps make a profit. He tried the plan out with
a chartered coaster—the *Artificer* of 386 tons—and, although
both the A.A. and R.A.C. were apathetic, he embarked on a
month's experiment that July.

The little coaster could carry fifteen cars but only a dozen
passengers, so he shipped the human surplus across on the
mailboat and they picked their cars up on arrival of the
Artificer. She took two and a half hours on the passage, but
cars could keep their full quota of petrol. Dover Harbour
Board welcomed the Townsend Ferry and provided berthing
facilities at the Eastern Arm, which was little used then
except for loading Kent coal on to cargo ships.

On the first working period Townsend made an £80 profit,
and decided to branch out the following year. He bought an
ex-naval vessel, the *Forde*, which the Admiralty sold him as
scrap for £5,000. She was renovated and converted for car-
carrying; a company was floated to run her with a capital of
£15,000. The gallant captain was disappointed with the
public's response to the offer of shares and he had to take up
most of them himself: they eventually fetched £15 apiece for
a cost of £1. The railways pulled their thumb out somewhat
when they saw that they were missing business by their
antiquated attitude to car-ferrying and started in with a
freighter and a tariff to compete.

Enter now Graham Lyon and his Autocheques. He "sold"
the idea of joining forces to Capt. Townsend, who gave him

a tiny office in his Leadenhall Street premises to begin with. G. L. told me that it was so small that, when his secretary came in to take letters, *he* had to go outside to dictate. In return for the accommodation, G. L. routed all his Autocheque customers across the Channel by Townsend Ferries.

Graham Lyon built up business by persuading the French authorities to issue a Laissez-Passer and avoid having to deposit a sum of money with the A.A. or R.A.C. sufficient to cover any possible Customs' claims from abroad if the car's owner did not remove it from the country concerned inside the permitted touring period. In due course this led to the abolition of cash deposit or banker's guarantee for Autocheques' users, and the two motoring organisations were forced to fall into line. It opened the way to the much bigger migration of British motorists to the Continent which is now so very evident.

Talking one day with the director of the Swiss National touring office in London, I realised that the roads to the ski-ing centres were not by any means all impassable in the winter months. Wherever possible, they were being ploughed and kept open, and he pointed out on the map such places as Gstaad, Adelboden, Kandersteg and Grindenwald in the Bernese Oberland, and St. Moritz and Davos in the Engadine, all of which were normally accessible by road. This was not generally known at home, where the popular idea of Switzerland in wintertime was that it was just one large heap of snow.

There seemed scope for a bit of trail-blazing here and a newspaper story to go with it. When I next met George Throssell, motoring correspondent of the *Daily Telegraph* (which had a readership attuned to winter sporting as well as motoring) I sounded him out and he soon 'phoned me up to say his Editor thought it a good idea. The Rootes felt the same way about it and had a Humber Snipe allotted for the jaunt.

13—MIAML

We set forth on January 18th, 1937, in good weather, drove down to Folkestone and next morning crossed on the S.R.'s cargo boat (Townsend did not run in winter). As "supercargo" I took, with Throssell's agreement, a certain James T. Skinner, who was motoring correspondent of the Westminster Press and wrote for literally dozens of provincial newspapers. My wife came with us, too. Once across in France we made for Reims, stayed the night there and next morning fell for the hotel manager's suggestion that we should see over the champagne "works" of Pommery and Gréno. This is something everyone ought to do while in the district—not necessarily P. and G.'s cellars, for most of the big firms welcome visitors.

If I may digress for a moment, I would explain how one first of all sees the vast casks from which the grape juice, once fermented, is drawn off, blended and put into temporarily-corked bottles where in due time the second fermentation will take place (hence the greater strength of champagne bottles compared with those for still wines). One follows the bottles underground, into a labyrinth of passages, all lined with racks which hold their bottles in a slightly neck-down position. Each day every bottle is turned just a fraction until eventually the sediment produced by the second fermentation—which transforms the wine into "bubbly"—is resting on the inside end of the cork.

Then comes the fascinating process whereby this sediment is whisked away and the final corking done, without the loss of the precious bubbles. A trolley with a refrigerated base is wheeled along a selected line of bins and filled with bottles of the wine adjudged mature by the experts, their necks (the bottles'!) in the freezing tank. This creates a little blob of ice around the cork, with the sediment securely imprisoned in it, and the trolley is pushed on into the "operating room".

When its turn comes, the cork is smartly extracted, complete with ice blob, a little ladle-full of special champagne poured in to make good what has been taken out, and the bottle placed in a corking machine which forces the proper cork into place under strong compression. The bit left exposed assumes the familiar domed shape, which is capped and wire sealed.

One perhaps wonders why, when the temporary cork is whipped away, the bubbly does not froth out. I asked our guide this and for reply he told me to look up to the roof of the cavern, a hundred feet or more above us, where a small round patch of daylight could be seen. He explained that the air pressure down below, coupled with the low ambient temperature, took the fizz out of the wine, which now lay dormant until it graced some festive table. Back above ground a courteous sales promotion man invited us to sample various vintages and specialities. Luckily, Skinner was T.T., and drove us to Vitry-le-François, where we recovered during a typically French lunch stop. Then on to Basle for the night.

There was not a headache among us when we set off again next morning and, via Berne and the shores of Lake Thun, started climbing into the Oberland. We arrived without incident at Adelboden (4,450 ft.), then on to Kandersteg (3,853 ft.), Grindenwald (3,470 ft.) and Gstaad (3,480 ft.). Eastwards then alongside the Lake of Brienz, sheer perfection in its beauty, with a brilliant sun glinting on the water, from which a faint haze rose in the morning light.

The gamut of colouring—mauves, purples, pinks and blues—left us all exhausted of words with which to call each other's attention to some new vista at each bend in the road. That afternoon, beside the Wallensee, our marvellous visions were repeated, in mellower tones; the colour harmony was pitched in a lower key; gold had turned to orange and mauve to rich deep purple. The white caps of the mountains were tinged with rosy alpen-glow which, as dusk fell, became really brilliant and made us stop by the roadside to gaze entranced.

It was dark by the time we reached Coire (or Chur as the German-Swiss call it), and as we entered the town Skinner woke up and enquired "Where's this?" "Coire", we told him, and thereafter every time he awoke from a doze when we were passing through a town he would ask "Is this Coire?" Poor Skinner; he died shortly afterwards and on this trip, he told me, he was having the time of his life. We never got to know him better; never called him Jim, Jimmy or even James—always Skinner.

In his office he was bossed by an insatiable and un-pleasant London Editor, and it was complete heaven for him to get away from his everyday grovelling. And, although he seemed always to be dozing, he turned in some really splendid stories about the trip, which appeared in the dozens of provincial papers his group controlled.

Coire is the gateway to the Engadine, and although today nobody worries much about climbing the Julier Pass, in 1937 it was quite something to climb to its 7,500-ft. summit in January. The road winds easily up to Tiefencastel for the first twenty miles and then there is a gradually steepening climb for thirty miles to the watershed, followed by a few miles' descent to Silvaplana, where one joins the road coming up from Italy via the Maloja Pass and turns north-east into St. Moritz with its altitude of 5,977 ft.

The old Grand Hotel, kept by an English couple, had not then been burnt down and we celebrated with the Famille Martin that night. On next day to Zernez and via the Flüela Pass (7,817 ft.), which was subject to occasional closing in time of blizzards but not this particular day, to Davos (6,105 ft.). Had the Flüela been closed we would have returned to Tiefencastel and taken the alternative road via Glaris.

We found it quite fascinating, this visiting of one winter

sports centre after another while the places were full of holidaymakers acquiring a deep tan in this the depth of winter. A few of them, mostly Italians, had come by car, but never one with a G.B. plate on it did we see: I doubt very much if you could have bought a ski-rack in Britain at that time.

But time pressed and so it was with greatest reluctance (as James Fitzpatrick used to say in his Travelogues) that we said farewell to the Swiss Alps and headed towards home. Zürich was our first stop and on the second day we passed out of Switzerland with infinite regret, only alleviated by the recovery of the petrol rebate (which foreigners received at the frontier when leaving).

Soon we were once more on the cargo boat from Boulogne, with the faithful Humber Snipe showing close on two thousand miles on the clock as a result of our fact-finding winter expedition—out of which the Rootes got full value for money publicity-wise.

Hitler's Shadow Solidifies

ANOTHER WAR CASTS ITS SHADOW BEFORE—AND
INVOLVES THE MOTOR INDUSTRY IN A "SHADOW
SCHEME". BUT UNTIL WAR ACTUALLY BREAKS OUT
THERE IS STILL SELLING OF FACTORIES' OUTPUTS
TO BE DONE AND PUBLICITY GOES ON UNABATED

Luckily there were some in Britain who were not completely gulled by Führer Hitler's protestations of having no territorial ambitions and—as usual in time of national stress—the Government looked to the motor industry to lend a hand to make up for its own indecisions. Stanley Baldwin's National Government had been superseded by a Conservative one under Neville Chamberlain in May 1937, but there was at no time an effective counter to Hitler's sabre-rattling since he seized power in Germany soon after World War I. Now at last, thanks largely to Winston Churchill, it was being realised that Britain was in no shape to cope with the Nazi menace, and that in particular our Royal Air Force had insufficient backing in respect of aero engines.

In 1936, however, the Air Minister (Lord Swinton) put up to our principal motor manufacturers a plan which became known for short as the Shadow Scheme. Its intention was to provide productive capacity and know-how to be kept in reserve for emergencies. Briefly, what the motor firms were asked to do was to establish new factories in juxtaposition to their existing plants, tool them up and train a nucleus of staff who, if and when the crunch came, would quickly get production going and train further staff. The

Shadow factories would be built with Government funds, but their design, erection, management and staffing would be the concern of each "parent" motor firm. Once in physical being, and proved capable of their intended function, they would remain "shadows" until their active co-operation in aero engine manufacture was demanded.

Austin, Daimler, Morris, Rover and Standard backed the plan, and Billy Rootes went into it whole-heartedly. Aided by Colonel Cole, who was still Chairman of Humber Ltd., he got cracking with typical alacrity. The site chosen was alongside the main Coventry–London road at Ryton-on-Dunsmore, then a completely rural area some few miles south-east of their main plant at Stoke, a Coventry suburb.

On it buildings rapidly took shape and, in May 1937, were nearing completion. Meanwhile, a smaller Shadow factory had been built alongside the goods entrance of the Humber works, and here test production was in hand during that year. One of the Air Ministry officials who, with the Minister himself, paid a visit of inspection to the Rootes' nuclei shadows at this time was the same Owen Clegg who had designed that successful 12 h.p. Rover car in 1910.

At this period the R.A.F. was being expanded to implement the Government's decision to raise its strength very considerably, and so the motor industry's shadow factories went to work immediately they were completed instead of just waiting for the emergency to happen. Between them they manufactured all the parts for the Mercury and Hercules engines used in the then current bombers, and their contribution to our country's meagre supply of aero engines at a time of desperate need may well have been the deciding factor in turning the scales of air power in Britain's favour.

Not content with engines, Billy Rootes also laid down plants for making complete aircraft; one at Speke, near Liverpool, and the other at Stoke-on-Trent. Herbert Austin did likewise so far as air frames were concerned, while

William Morris also started a works at Castle Bromwich for aero engine repair.

[I should here mention that, in addition, the Rootes turned the Talbot works at Barlby Road, North Kensington, into a repair plant for the Rolls-Royce Merlin engine when war did break out. Sales manager Jack Scott acted as liaison officer with Derby, and so well did he get on with the Rolls-Royce executives that, soon after war ended, he was asked to join the firm in the capacity of sales manager, and succeeded so ably in introducing modern methods to that position that he later was put on the R-R Board.]

While all this extra activity was going on, cars were still being made and had to be sold; publicity, therefore, perforce carried on in its accustomed way. I suggested to Reggie Rootes that a quick run round some of the capitals of Europe on a Humber Snipe might be useful if we could get the *Sunday Pictorial*—which then had a huge circulation—to send a photographer along and condense the effort into a picture feature. He agreed, and I put it to the management of the paper, who also thought it was a good idea and sent one of their best photographers to go along with me.

Starting off on a sunny day in the spring of 1937, we went over to Calais, drove to Paris (capital 1), and eastwards to Berne (capital 2), then still further east to Vaduz (capital of Lichtenstein—3), Vienna (4) and Budapest (5). This last was always a favourite city of mine, with its wonderful mixture of ancient buildings in Buda and modern streets in Pest on the other bank of the Danube.

In the middle of the river was the delightful St. Margaret's Island, where hot springs bubbled out of the ground and the Café de Paris had a fine large band of young gipsy girls who discoursed tzigane music in all its many moods, from soothing to exciting. Next, northwards to Prague (6), then renowned as the Bohemia of so many musical comedies, and on to Berlin (7), where black-shirted Nazis and their

swastikas were too plentiful and cocky for my liking. West-
wards then to The Hague (8), Brussels (9) and home to
London, the 10th and final capital. "Ten Capitals in Ten
Days" the feature was titled, and it was given two whole
pages of travel-glamour in consecutive issues of the *Sunday
Pictorial*, of which the rate for advertisements was £1,000 a
page—quite good publicity for the Humber Snipe at
negligible cost.

The Motor Show of 1937 was to be the first held in the new
Earls Court building, and a month or so before it opened a
request came from the Humber sales manager that I think up
something calculated to arouse interest in a revised Humber
model due to make its debut there. Remembering the
success of "Beating the Blue Train" seven years earlier, I
looked up the timetable of the Orient Express, on which
beautiful blonde spies were reputed to hold continual vamping
sessions with stolid British diplomats carrying highly secret
dispatches to our Embassies in the eastern yonderland.

I found that the express started the European section of its
run at Istanbul, went through Bulgaria, Yugoslavia,
Hungary, Austria and Germany to arrive in due course at
Ostend, and that it did not hurry itself unduly on the early
stages of its journey, but quickened its pace after Budapest.
Anyhow, there seemed a chance of making a close race of it,
and once again the Rootes agreed it was worth attempting,
so long as we did not say a word about our intentions until
we were back successfully.

Poor Pem, as his brother Alfred has said in the first chapter
of this book, had met his death the preceding February; his
successor was something of a "new boy" and I had to think
hard about whom to ask to come along and make a convincing story out of the effort.

I had had some more or less minor interludes with other
of the national daily papers' motoring correspondents: with
the Hon. Brian Lewis (later to become Lord Essendon), who

was motoring correspondent of the *News Chronicle*, when we paid a running visit to Europe's three major motor racing circuits—Montlhéry, Monza and the Nurburg Ring—on a Talbot Ten, likewise Tommy Wisdom, then of the *Daily Herald*, who accompanied me on a modernised Grand Tour of Europe in a Hillman Minx.

Each of these trips was productive of good publicity and the company of both these friends delightful. For the Orient Express effort, however, it seemed as if Bill Mackenzie, the *Daily Mail* motoring correspondent, would be most suitable. Accordingly I tackled Leonard Raftery, advertisement manager of the *Mail*, and he backed the suggestion after promise of due recognition in the advertising columns of their Motor Show supplement.

As it was to be carried out just before the show, when autumnal weather and the possibility of fog and frost had to be reckoned with, it might not prove an easy trip. Mackenzie, however, was an enthusiastic and hardened motorist abroad; we also took with us a young man from the factory nominated by chief engineer Bernard Winter, by name Saunders. I invited a friend, one George Bell, to come along: he too was a keen motorist abroad, and I felt we should need all the help we could get on the driving side. We looked like having two long nights on the road, and in the more easterly countries the roads were probably going to be what is now euphemistically called under-developed.

Off we set one misty September morn—it was Saturday the 4th, I remember—and crossed from Dover to Dunkirk on the night train ferry. Disembarking at some ungodly hour, we reached Frankfurt in the evening and were at Passau the next night. In the morning George Bell was complaining about bad toothache, which grew worse during the day, and when we arrived at Budapest he had to call in a dental surgeon right away. This resulted in strict orders that he would have to have his jaw operated on immediately, so we had to leave him in medical hands and go on one short.

Yugoslavian roads proved to be pretty grim, and Bulgarian ones the same only somewhat deeper in dust. Dense clouds of it rose from our wheels, and Saunders got worried about it finding its way up the engine's breather pipe, which for some inscrutable reason the designers at Coventry had so arranged that its lower end terminated a few inches behind the off-side front wheel.

We entered Turkey at Adrianople, and from then on to Istanbul, except for the final stretch into the city, the roads were the worst yet. We had now been about a week on the outward journey, which on the return trip we would have to cover in about sixty hours if we were to reach Ostend before, or even coincidentally with, the train.

While Saunders attended to the car in the best local garage we could find, I went to the Turkish Touring Club office and told them about the object of our visit. They were most interested, promised every help, and their President very courteously agreed to come and give us the "départ" at the railway station, alongside the express, on the next Tuesday night at ten o'clock. He advised me to go to the Bulgarian Consul and ask him for a letter written in Cyrillic characters in case we could not make ourselves understood at the frontier, which we were due to reach in the wee sma' hours. Very excellent advice it proved, too.

Meanwhile, Saunders had found his worst fears realised. He had had the sump off and discovered a mass of dust among the sludge. It was all cleared out, of course, but he was afraid some of it might be lodged in the crankshaft oilways, and ungetatable without completely dissembling the engine, which was beyond the bounds of possibility. Otherwise the car had stood up splendidly to the hard going, and Saunders telephoned Coventry to assure the chief engineer that nothing had gone amiss save the inhalation of so much unexpected foreign matter.

Now we could relax for a day or two, and we found Istanbul a good place for this. The open-air beer gardens, with their bands and music-hall shows, were reminiscent of the same sort of entertainments that London used to have in Vauxhall, and Copenhagen has today on a more lavish scale. Mosques were everywhere, also hordes of small boys demanding baksheesh; Asia was just across the Golden Horn and altogether the time passed very quickly, what with buying provisions for the (we hoped) non-stop 1,800-mile run through to the Channel coast. We sent a telegram to George Bell at Budapest warning him to be ready for picking up the next morning, and Tuesday night found us all set to get under way the moment the train made its first move.

So on the platform a small party gathered beside the wagons-lits bearing a plaque "Istanbul–Budapest–Wien–Frankfurt/Main–Oostende", while alongside, but in the station yard, stood the Humber all raring to go. As the preparatory whistles shrilled we hurriedly shook hands, doubled round the barrier to the car and, when the massive Turkish engine gave its first throaty puff, Saunders let in the clutch and we were away. Hands waved from some of the carriage windows, but I must mention that none of them seemed to come from delicately manicured fingers attached to beautiful blonde spies.

Soon we were clear of the city; the minarets and mosques faded into the background and we were speeding along beside the Sea of Marmora with a vividly golden moon floodlighting the scene with liquid fire. Alas, the good macadamised road petered out in a very short time and we were back on those unmade tracks across what seemed like open fields. The moon vanished and a night mist came down; we were reduced to a painfully low speed over literally a river of potholes—some so large that a bathtub could have been buried in them.

Thick dust eddied round the car, made us cough as it

poured in through the open windows, the heat being so sweltering that we just had to get some air. Behind us a dust cloud stayed suspended in the still atmosphere to mark our passage through the desolate countryside. This persisted for best part of a hundred miles, until eventually we thankfully reached Adrianople.

It was long past midnight as we entered the city, when suddenly an official with upraised hand leapt into our path and we stopped abruptly. By gestures he explained that he wanted to come aboard, and that he was the local chief of the Customs who was to see us across the frontier. Excitedly he seemed to be yelling "On, fellows, on!" and we bumped over the potholed country track which had now replaced the town streets, crashed our way over crazy wooden bridges that looked unsafe at any speed, through water splashes and gullies that sent everything in the car jangling and hurtling about the floor.

After half an hour of this we came to the frontier post, where our passenger leapt out, taking our documents and passports with him; they were stamped at express speed and we were waved off as if it really was a race we were engaged upon. Evidently our good friends of the Turkish Touring Club had notified the Chief of Police that we were out for a record run.

At the Bulgarian frontier a little farther on it was an altogether different story. The country was locked up for the night, with a hefty gate across the road very securely fastened. Nothing moved on the far side until, after much headlamp flashing and horn blowing a sentry appeared in the distance and strolled towards us, cigarette dangling from upper lip and rifle slung over his shoulder.

I poked through the bars the letter the Consul had given me; the sentry took it, pored over it for about five minutes and then turned it the other way up to see if that made it any more comprehensible. He probably couldn't read anyway, but he walked off towards the guardhouse taking the letter, and presently there appeared an officer bringing the key to Bulgaria, into which we were permitted to enter.

All now went off happily; our documents were stamped yet again, we shook hands all round and in no more than about half an hour were once more on our way. Through the sleeping town of Plovdiv (formerly Phillipopolis) we passed and came into Sofia just as the new day was starting. A wash and some quick coffee, plus a fill-up of the tank and we left Bulgaria's capital behind us.

We wanted to get to Dragoman, the frontier station on the railway, before the train and just managed it. The Bulgarian locomotive was unhitched and a Yugoslavian one substituted: some of the passengers who had seen us at Istanbul looked out and waved again (but still no beautifully manicured fingers, etc.). We completed the climb of the Pass, checked into Yugoslavia and prepared for another night on the road.

Still that dust cloud rose from our wheels, and, as daylight gave way to dusk, the red-gold sunset contained a very definite hint of fog. For hours we thumped our way over a murky track and then, at last, spots of rain spattered our screen. Soon it was pouring, and at the same time the road developed a steep camber, laid with infernally greasy pavé.

If one did not keep the car on the middle hump, its tail slithered sideways down towards the gutter. Oh, a nasty night when one felt as tired as we did, and with nothing but sticky frankfurters, now-stale bread and bottled beer to sup on. The three of us took turns at the wheel and luckily there wasn't much fear of getting off the right road, because as far as we could see it was the one and only.

Came, yet again, the dawn and with it the Hungarian frontier; once through it a fine autobahn type of road stretched ahead. There was joy in our hearts at the thought of breakfast at Szeged, the first town along the route, and the speedometer needle crept up. But the oil pressure did not do likewise: "That b—— dust in the sump", muttered Saunders, and even as he said it there was a nasty rattle from beneath the bonnet. No need to ask whence it came; all too obviously a big-end had given up the ghost for lack of oil.

So once again we slowed down to a crawl, hoping we could make it to Szeged. We did, and as the proprietor of the first garage we saw raised his shutters he found customers on his doorstep. He cottoned on in a flash; made it clear that he knew exactly what to do and would see it was done pronto. We left him and his staff getting down to it with a little general guidance from Saunders, and went off to the local hotel for breakfast.

It meant, however, the end of the race with the Orient Express; we could never make up the hours we now had to sit idly waiting. All we could hope to do would be to get the car home, because even a new big-end would not eradicate the rest of the dust still lying around in vital oilways inside the engine. We told Saunders what we thought about breather pipes sited just where they would catch all the dust, and dared him to tell the designer chaps at Coventry what we thought of *them*.

By late afternoon the garage pronounced the car ready— and a jolly fine job they made of the repair—so off we set again, with hawklike gaze fixed on the oil pressure gauge, for Budapest and George Bell. Also, I might add, the Hôtel de Paris there, for we certainly were not now going to spend another night on the road.

We did, in fact, have one more big-end go, at Aachen on the German–Belgian frontier, and so were again delayed. No one, however, luckily knew about our train-beating plan, and Mackenzie still made a useful story for the *Daily Mail* about motoring in eastern Europe, so all was not lost. His "Balkan Adventure" was reprinted as a pamphlet for the Motor Show; the new model was launched at Earls Court and in due time that breather pipe was curtailed and fitted with a filter. No one, as far as I know, got the sack over the original gaffe.

The year 1938 was a jumpy one for everybody in Britain, with all of us hoping they could believe Hitler when he so definitely stated he had no further territorial ambitions once he had swallowed Poland, Czechoslovakia and Austria. We hadn't had so much experience of dictators in those days! But the object of this book is not to recap. history which is common knowledge: so far as the world of motoring was concerned in this, the last complete year of peace for seven years, the motor industry carried on fairly normally.

Even while the firms in the Shadow Aero Engine scheme were very much occupied with their new plants and ironing out the bugs, production of cars was not suffering all that much. Whereas in 1935 output of motor vehicles had just topped 400,000 and in 1936 was 461,000, 1937 was a complete record with 507,749. In 1938 it was 447,561, of which 342,390 were private cars and taxis (these are figures issued by the Society of Motor Manufacturers and Traders, for the years dating from October 1st to September 30th).

The Motor Show took place as usual in October 1938, and almost immediately after it Graham Lyon and I set off on a trip to which we had both been looking forward somewhat eagerly. A "Cavalcade of British Cars" to the U.S.A. had been organised by the Junior Car Club (later to become the present British Automobile Racing Club, or B.A.R.C.) and, headed by Sir Malcolm Campbell, was to go across the Atlantic on the maiden voyage of the (then) new *Mauretania* in June following.

Meanwhile, hotels had to be booked for the large party on its arrival in New York and throughout its tour thereafter. This was to be via Washington, West Virginia, Ohio and Indiana to Chicago, thence back through Michigan, a brief detour into Canada by way of Niagara, and ending up at

New York after passing through part of New England and Boston. Graham Lyon had been charged by "Bunny" Dyer, the J.C.C. secretary, with fixing up hotel accommodation at all overnight stopping places, and I smelt the chance of some good ancillary publicity out of this tour.

The Rootes very sportingly let me have a two-litre Sunbeam-Talbot for this prospecting jaunt, and Cunard's equally obligingly gave it a return passage at single fare. So, on a foggy morning in November, G. L. and I drove to Liverpool and were alongside the 20,000-ton *Samaria* that afternoon, sailing at midnight on an oily sea to Belfast, and thence to Greenock. Thereafter the Atlantic seemed just to have been waiting for us to get into its clutches before boiling up into waves "mountains high".

There was only a handful of passengers aboard, including a party of theatricals who certainly livened up an otherwise dull voyage—Leslie Henson was one of them. At the end of ten days we were decanted into a New York whose streets were piled six feet high on either side with snow swept from the roadway. G. L. already had his "operator's licence": I had to attend at City Hall and go through some eyesight tests before getting mine—my driving ability was apparently taken for granted by the fact of holding a British licence.

A day or two's acclimatisation in New York prepared me for American road conditions, and a comfortable Sunday's run brought us to Washington, where the A.A.A.—tipped off by their London office—gave us a taste of what American hospitality can mean. They were wonderful, and it took us most of the next day to recover from it. But we nevertheless won through to White Sulphur Springs, via the Blue Ridge Mountains of Virginia, and stayed the night at the magnificent Greenbrier. No ordinary hotel this, but a gracious collection of Colonial-American lodges spread out in most splendid grounds.

A central mansion contained restaurant and conference

rooms, and it so happened that a medical organisation was holding a conference there at the time. When we went in to breakfast next morning a most grisly array of every conceivable surgical instrument was laid out on display at the entrance to the dining room, presumably by their enterprising manufacturers—no doubt of great interest to the surgeons but somewhat off-putting to the layman about to break his fast.

While G. L. did his bookings for the Cavalcade I looked over the Sunbeam-Talbot, now displaying its New York state 1938 licence plates ("NY 30-05"). We got under way about 11 a.m., and on a good concrete road winding through beautiful country covered best part of a hundred miles before deciding that lunch would be quite an idea.

There seemed no prospect of finding a hotel, so we risked a wayside shack which said it was a diner—"Joe's Place", it was called. But what unexpectedness once we got inside: instead of the miserable sort of "caff" one would find on our side of the Atlantic, this was a modernly-equipped lunch bar. In no time at all we were served with soup and a hot sandwich (hot grilled bacon between layers of crisp toast), all produced on a spotlessly clean stainless steel electric grill plate.

The proprietor, surprised to find he had a couple of limey visitors, entered into a long diatribe about the way we were letting Hitler get away with what he was doing in Europe. We apologised for the vacillations of our government, told him about the purpose of our visit to the U.S., advised him to have plenty of food on hand when the Cavalcade passed his door the following June, and hit the trail once again.

At this place—Gauley Bridge—we met up with the Kanawha River and our road ran alongside it, gradually rising until we were a thousand feet above it. Fine vistas of the rocky gorge that confined the stream far below could be glimpsed here and there, and especially at Hawk's Nest,

where a parking place for rubbernecks made us halt awhile.
Then on through Charleston as dusk was falling to our
overnight stopping town—Huntington, pronounced Hun-
nington—Indiana.

Away early next day, and now following the banks of the
Ohio River, we passed through townships with familiar
names—Portsmouth, Manchester, Aberdeen and Ripley.
London showed up on the next signboard; it was merely a
few houses, and "Unincorporated" at that. Oxford's name
plate had the grace to mention that it was named after
Oxford, England.

The Ohio River teemed with floating traffic, mostly steam
tugs which pushed their barges ahead of them: there was the
railway, too, running alongside the road and without any
dividing fence. A large locomotive with, in American fashion,
all its "works" on the exterior, was standing on the track
conveniently for a photograph with our car, so we pulled up
beside it. Down stepped the engineer to inspect our "purty
little auto", and nothing would satisfy him but he must have
a ride in it.

I had taken him perhaps half a mile when a train appeared
coming towards us. "Gee!" cried our friend, "that's what
I've got to hitch on to," so we quickly did a U-turn, over-
hauled the lumbering freighter and he clambered back on to
his footplate. This was some little way outside Cincinnati, a
huge place mainly populated, apparently, by ex-Germans,
and from there to Indianapolis it was only a little over a
hundred miles. This was our night's goal, and I had a
special personal reason for wanting to stay there so that I
could meet up with one George Marott, a leading citizen.

Had it not been for an unfortunate incident, my father and
his elder brother might likewise have been citizens of
Indianapolis or some other U.S. city. Over half a century
before my present visit—several years before I was born in
England—they were to have accompanied George Marott

across the Atlantic (in the days when America was crying out for immigrants, particularly British). The evening before they were to sail, however, they had all gone out for a row on Southampton Water and a steamer cut their small boat down. Marott and my father were saved, but the elder brother was drowned; he is buried in Freshwater cemetery, Isle of Wight.

Not unnaturally, my grandfather stopped my father from going, but young Marott, a penniless boy, had had his fare paid by my grandfather and given a hundred pounds into the bargain. He duly sailed next day, eventually settled in Indianapolis and started to work in the boot and shoe trade; he wrote to my grandfather and assured him that his loan would be repaid "with interest" when he had made good.

This he did, and to the extent that he now—an old man—owned property in the town, including the largest hotel. We were to stay there that night, and Marott's strange quirk was (I hoped) going to be fulfilled: it was that he would repay only in person to a member of my family.

My father had died the year before, and had never found an opportunity of making the trip to Indianapolis, so Marott had cordially invited me to be his guest that evening, which happened to be his eightieth birthday; he made it a big night and threw a wonderful party in my honour. At it he handed me an impressively sealed package, assuring his guests that it contained scant repayment for the "English gentleman" who had made it possible for him to get a start in these "Glorious United States".

When I broke the seals in the privacy of my room, there were 5,000 dollars in crisp new 50-dollar bills inside the package. Good old George Marott! But I was sad to learn that, before he could welcome the Malcolm Campbell Cavalcade, he passed away. He had promised to give "those English boys" a right royal time when they came to Indianapolis—and I bet he would have done, too.

Next morning it was sleeting, but we accepted the invitation thrown out by Mr. Myer, the general manager of Indianapolis race track, at the previous night's party, and have a run round it. The all-brick surface was quite roughish in places and I would certainly not have liked the idea of driving even the Sunbeam-Talbot all out on it, at any rate under the prevailing weather conditions. However, as we had about a couple of hundred miles to cover to reach that night's destination—Chicago, the farthest point west on the route—we decided not to have a go but to press on in case the threatened snow materialised.

We made it by five o'clock, went straight to the Blackstone Hotel and the moment the baggage was off the car was whisked away, American fashion, although (as usual) it was necessary to show the driver where reverse gear was "hidden". Four-speed gearboxes were then unknown in the States, and the puzzlement of these American drivers when they did not find reverse in its accustomed place, where our first gear is, always amused us.

That night I paid my first visit to an American burlesque show, the "barker" outside proclaiming the attractions of "Twenty gorgeous gals wearing a great big smile". Strip-tease was the latest thing in Chicago—it was banned in New York—and hadn't of course penetrated to Europe (as far as I know—definitely not to London, or even Paris). I thought it was just as boring as I do today, in spite of being thirty-odd years younger.

Prohibition had not hit the U.S. as a whole then, although there were several "dry" states. Illinois was not one of them and so there did not seem to be any gangsters around in Chicago—I thought it was rather a dull sort of place, in fact. One thing did impress me, though, and that was Lakeside Drive, an express highway built along the shore of Lake Michigan on land reclaimed from this great inland sea. Its outstanding novelty was that hydraulically-operated ramps were raised and lowered to suit inward and outward traffic flow morning and evening. The idea is no longer novel, of course, and has been superseded by the use of traffic lights—the cost of the hydraulic mechanism must have been colossal. But it worked very effectively.

On the following day, Sunday December 11th, we started to head eastwards and, when we left the capital of the Middle West, found ourselves running just ahead of a snowstorm. We wanted to keep it behind us, as we had been warned that, on this open section of highway, blizzards could be pretty fierce and we didn't carry snow chains or even a spade.

So we kept going, abandoned lunch and crossed into Michigan state to reach Detroit and the shelter of the Statler Hotel in good time, despite losing the hour between Central and Eastern time. It so happened that the hotel's orchestra was headed by one Leighton Noble, who, when he heard that a namesake was in the restaurant insisted that his "English cousin" should be his guest to the extent of a bottle of (Californian) champagne.

Next morning his boys turned up to give us a musical send-off, and our sun roof so intrigued them that two of the trumpet players stood up on the front seats and did their stuff through the open roof to show it off for the cameraman. We had a date at the Chrysler works, the first American motor plant I had ever seen over. It may not have been the largest, but its immensity compared with ours at that date greatly impressed me—and not only the factory itself but the enormous offices where serried ranks of clerks were working, in one particular section on exports only.

Head of this department was C. B. Thomas, who had for several years been chief of the Hudson set-up in Britain at their Kew (Surrey) works where the Terraplane was handled. Previously the Essex coach, a great seller in the

U.K. before the McKenna duties, started a trend towards closed cars at a popular price.

The original Chrysler car had made its appearance in 1924, when it created a sensation on both sides of the Atlantic with its peppy, highish compression-ratio engine which gave a performance far ahead of any other make at anything like the price. Walter P. Chrysler himself had gained plenty of experience in motor manufacturing through his connection with various other firms—notably Maxwell and Chalmers—all of which had hit difficult times during the post-first-war depression of America in the early 'twenties.

Chrysler's adroit financial juggling conjured fifty million dollars out of the Chase Securities Corporation and, as he himself said at the time, "What was already in my heart, but still called Maxwell, was out of the wood." His Chrysler Corporation came into existence in 1925, took over Maxwell in its entirety and, needing still more production capacity, bought up Dodge, whose two brothers John and Horace had both died a few years earlier.

This put Chrysler firmly on the big-time manufacturers' map, and he battled through the Great Depression of the 'thirties, which extinguished most of the remainder of those outside Ford, G.M. and Chrysler, even though production did on occasion go down to 40 per cent of capacity. The Plymouth, introduced in 1928, was intended by Chrysler to catch the lower-priced market and was, incidentally, the first car to incorporate a free-wheel and rubber mountings for the engine (in 1931, just about when Rootes were busy on the original Hillman Minx).

At the time of our visit to Detroit, Walter P. was in poor health and he did, in fact, die during the following year. He was a man I would dearly have liked to meet: his start in life had been as a farm boy in Kansas, but machinery fascinated him and he changed to repairing locomotives. When the motor car came on the scene he transferred his mechanical passion to them and worked his way up to being head of the Buick Company (which had been started by David Dunbar Buick, a Scot from Arbroath, in the early years of the century). A controlling share in this firm was acquired by William C. Durant, who was the founding father of the General Motors Corporation, and who thereafter played a considerable part in the future of Chrysler.

However, we had not come to Detroit to see Thomas just to discuss the history of the American automobile industry, although one interesting thing he showed us was a complete list of the more than two thousand different makes of car that had been manufactured in the U.S.A. since the Duryea brothers ran their first "buggyaut" at Springfield, Mass., in 1892–3.

We got round to talking about the forthcoming autocade of British cars, and C. B. promised every help when it arrived in Detroit, with co-operation from the Michigan Auto Club. It had been a morning of great interest to all three of us, and it was with great regret that we simply could not stay longer.

Snow was falling heavily as we nipped through the tunnel which brings one out in Windsor, Ontario, the only town in Canada which faces northwards into the United States, and where the Customs' men looked just like our own officials but with a rather more fanciful cap. There was very little formality and soon we were on "The King's Highway No. 3" bound for Welland and the Niagara Falls.

In summer one could miss this not very interesting trip by taking ship across Lake Erie from Detroit to Buffalo, but it did not run in winter, and then the distance by way of Canada was less than keeping on the U.S. side and having to negotiate Toledo and Cleveland into the bargain. We used the Whirlpool Rapids bridge and raced a snowstorm all the way to Syracuse, where we stayed overnight.

Next day was finer but freezingly cold: we were only a

little way south of the Adirondacks at Utica where, having stopped for a warm-up, an interested passer-by asked "Don't you British have heaters in your autos?" We didn't, of course, but we wondered why. The Americans seemed to be driving in their shirtsleeves while we shivered in our overcoats. At Albany we were back in New York state, but we still had to visit Boston so kept on through Massachusetts, admiring the New England scenery under its coat of hoar frost.

Graham Lyon made his last hotel booking in the city where the tipping of English tea into the harbour precipitated the War of Independence—Boston—and we set off anxious to reach New York city and avail ourselves of the hospitality offered by cable while we were in Chicago from the Waldorf Astoria. American hotels never lose any chance of business and, once news of our mission spread around, rooms were "complimented" to us at all the hotels along the cavalcade's route—which our speedometer showed to total 2,500 miles.

It was December 21st when we bade farewell to the U.S., mission accomplished, and sailed aboard the Cunarder *Ausonia*. She made one call, at Halifax, Nova Scotia, on Christmas Eve and we went ashore and bought Christmas presents. Off the Banks of Newfoundland on the Day itself the foghorn wailed continuously and the ship rolled in heavy seas, but a good time was had aboard by (nearly) all. My good luck was to win the prize for the nearest guess to the distance actually run—317 miles—and on Boxing Day the distance proved exactly the same, but I hadn't the courage to repeat my guess. At least, however, I won seven bob at Keno, after dinner.

On the last day of 1938 we arrived at Plymouth, where G. L. disembarked with the case of Blue Point oysters he had bought in Halifax, and went on to a West Country hotel to join his wife. I arrived at Tilbury on New Year's Day, and by noon the car had been disembarked and I was en route for home.

Within a week or so I was off again—this time on a new Humber Snipe to cover the Monte Carlo Rally and incidentally to show off its paces to Geoffrey Smith, then editorial director of the *Autocar*, and his chief photographer Donald Osmond. The Rally was now over a stiffer course than when, in 1932, I had dragged a caravan through it from Glasgow; then it was just a case of going by direct main roads all the way. A certain amount of mountainous stuff had since been incorporated in the route—nothing nearly as stiff as has been included of recent years, though.

In late 1937 Gordon Wilkins (just then a "new boy" on the *Motor*) and I had made a survey of this fresh section on a Humber Snipe. It was practically the ordinary winter Route des Alpes, with the Col de la Croix Haute and the Col de Leques the only two sticky bits, plus four timed stretches. Gordon and I went out and did a report, with photographs, on this innovation a month or so before the 1938 Rally started. Oliver Stewart, who was then editing the *Motor*, gave it a big show.

The 1939 Rally was plotted over the same route, and our little party cruised comfortably down to Digne, where we were to stay the night prior to going over the course next day, and had arranged to meet up at the Ermitage Hotel with Mrs. Kay Petre and Major Reggie Empson, who were covering the Rally for the *Daily Sketch*, and all have dinner together.

We duly arrived in good time, and waited for the others to join us: we waited and waited, however, until eventually we decided they must have broken down or gone somewhere else, so we dined and went to bed. Next morning, as the competitors came through Digne, we had hot coffee ready outside the hotel for any who cared to stop: Tom Wisdom was one, and he asked us if we knew who the English Press people were who had had the bad crash, for he had heard on his radio a report of it.

In a little while the facts became known; there had been a collision at crossroads between the *Daily Sketch* car and a lorry, and Reggie Empson had been killed on the spot, Kay Petre badly hurt and in hospital. So there was nothing for it, in the absence of specific information, but that we should carry on to Monte Carlo, which we did with deep sorrow in our hearts, for Reggie had been a close friend of both Geoffrey Smith and myself. This was to be the last "Monte" for ten years and it was won by two French entrants, tying in a Hotchkiss and a Delahaye, starting from Athens.

In April 1939 news was published that the frontier between Lithuania and Poland was to be reopened after having been sealed off for eighteen years following a Polish "putsch" just after the end of World War I. The Poles had annexed a slice of Lithuanian territory which included the ancient city of Vilna, claiming that it rightfully belonged to them. The Lithuanians begged to differ and a row blew up. As a result the frontier between the two countries had been closed to all forms of communication: railways and roads were torn up, telegraph wires pulled down and the only way to travel from Poland to Lithuania was to go via East Prussia, of which Königsburg was the chief town.

Now, it appeared, the squabble was patched up and the main road between the two countries to be reopened to traffic. I thought there might be a good "story" in being the first to cross it—at any rate, the first British car. So, too, thought the *Daily Mail*, likewise the Rootes, hence Mackenzie and I made up a party, which included Graham Lyon, also my son John (now fifteen) for make-weight, so to speak.

We chose a 14 h.p. Hillman for the attempt, because it needed a bit of a "putsch" itself and, as the Orient Express effort had proved, Mac could be relied on to write a highly

readable piece even if things went haywire. First we had to
find Kaunas, the capital of Lithuania, on the map, and
getting there was a fair journey across Europe in itself.
Germany was then boiling up with Nazi fervour and the day
we chose to traverse it was the very Sunday on which Hitler
was holding a national plebiscite to make sure the people
elected him their leader.

Everywhere the Nazi flag flew in profusion, and all the
towns were thickly plastered with Dr. Goebbels' slogan—
"Ein Volk, Ein Reich, Ein Führer". Mass meetings of black
shirts dominated the landscape and we were rather
suspiciously received in hotels, restaurants and filling stations.
We countered as best we could by raising our right hands and
shouting "Heil Hitler" to all and sundry, which at any rate
gained us an unhindered passage from the Dutch frontier
through Hanover, Berlin and Stettin.

At that time there was a Polish Corridor separating
Prussia from East Prussia, and adjoining it the Free State of
Danzig, which had more or less nominally a British Governor.
Gdynia was being made into a new Polish port to side-track
Danzig and, as we went through this place, I was intrigued
by the many large buildings going up, so stopped the car here
and there to take photographs. James Bond not then having
been heard of, I suppose it never entered my head that I
might look to the Poles like a spy.

When we arrived at their frontier with Danzig, however,
police were waiting for us and just would not believe that we
were not Germans spying on them. Our British passports
were of no avail; we had to go back to police headquarters
and wait there while my films were developed. After close
scrutiny of them we were allowed to go on, but the films
were impounded (I only got them back several months
later).

Danzig was quite a gay little place, with a resort atmosphere and a casino at the adjacent seaside town of Zoppot.

We paused here for a late lunch—very late on account of the photographic interlude—and, as we waited for the ferry to carry us across to the East Prussian side of the Weichsel (also called the Wista and Bug along its winding course) river, a couple of huge Nazi lorries forming a mobile cinema were coming over it into the Free State. No doubt to show pretty films and try to convince the Danzigers of the benevolent intentions of Hitler towards them. By this time, from what we had seen in Germany, we were pretty well convinced that war was not far away. Our job, however, was to press on and reach Kaunas via East Prussia's Königsburg.

It was spring officially, but the countryside was cold and wet; Nature hadn't yet awakened to any show of life. The road was not too bad, and Königsburg (now Kaliningrad) offered civilised comforts. Once we left it to go southwards into Lithuania there was a big change, and quagmires abounded on roads which might once have done justice to Mr. Macadam but which for apparently the last quarter-century at least had not had a visit from a steam roller. The way to Kaunas led over a vast, flat and desolate countryside, for the most part barren. Sparse trees leant in the direction of the prevailing wind and looked as bare and gaunt as the blasted poplars lining the Flanders' roads during World War I.

Twilight brought sleet, which turned to snow while our road became a glutinous, slippery bed of mud, and whenever we crashed into a particularly deep pothole it smothered the windscreen—and screen washers hadn't yet been invented. Kaunas, formerly a mere provincial town but for the past eighteen years the Lithuanian capital in place of Vilna, was pretty grim.

We went to the hotel they had told us was the best, where we found a couple of American cabaret artistes bemoaning their bad luck in having had an engagement here foisted on them. Food and a bed were, however, available and afterwards we strolled around the place; one thing that made Kaunas seem such a one-horse town was that no building had more than two storeys—a relic, we were told, of the days of the Czar and his aversion to high roof tops which could conceal snipers with anarchistic tendencies.

We started off on our assault on the Polish frontier next morning, over a road which made that of the preceding day seem almost like an autobahn. It was as if all the tractors in Europe had ploughed it, and the countryside grew bleaker and lonelier as on we pounded. Waterlogged stretches we did our best to dodge, or alternatively to rush them in bottom gear with engine racing; the floorboards were just that—no monocoque construction of sheet metal then—and so we tried to keep our feet dry by raising them off the floor. At one point we had to climb a ditch and take to the heath to get past an ancient lorry which must have been abandoned at about the time the frontier was closed. Then down came a heavy fall of snow and it was next to impossible to tell hard ground from quagmires. To make matters worse it was getting dark; we hadn't the foggiest notion how far we had to go to that frontier, or even if we *could* go on.

The sight of a tumbledown shed close beside the "road" prompted the suggestion that we had better put up for the night in it, in case the worst happened and we were stranded away out in the open country. We prospected and found it was reasonably weatherproof but bitterly cold; we brought all the rugs, coats and seat cushions from the car and made ourselves as comfortable as possible, which was not very.

Neither were our tums, after a foodless day with not much in the way of breakfast at that half-baked hotel. But then Graham Lyon performed something of a miracle, like feeding the multitude with fishes—he produced a can of bully beef and a few bread rolls. Always a born caterer, he had had an intuition that something nasty might happen and had provided against it without saying a word to the rest of us.

Somehow we passed the night in that depressing, smelly shed until at long, *long* last dawn broke. The snowstorm had abated, the important parts of the car were cleared of its leavings and there was not too much in the way of drifts to make driving impossible. The engine did not sulk and quite soon we were under way again. A few miles further on we came to an improvised frontier and, as far as we could make out, the Hillman was the first car to make a civilian crossing of it.

Soon a fairly decent road appeared and we drove on towards Warsaw with just one stop at the first place we came to where there was a restaurant of sorts—a funny little town whose name I can't remember but where the menu was of vast size, and the food would have done credit to a good hotel. And so to Warsaw and back home without any specially memorable incident, except that in Berlin we were invited to a party in a private house, given by some Germans whom I did not personally know, but who apparently knew that Mackenzie was from the *Daily Mail*.

I should add that, soon after I was back in London, I was asked to call at the War Office, where I was quizzed about our trip and its object: the upshot was that I was discreetly warned to keep out of Germany unless it was absolutely necessary for me to go again, in which case I was told to notify this particular department of the W.O.

Britain's R.A.C. Rally used then to be held in the spring, and for the 1939 one a secret section in Derbyshire was to be introduced to stiffen it up a bit. Obviously, there could only be a certain number of "sticky" hills available in the area for such an event, and Gordon Wilkins and I felt it might be a good idea to go up to Buxton and have a peek at any we could discover from the one-inch Ordnance map.

This offered a chance of him trying out for the *Motor* the new four-litre Sunbeam-Talbot, it being then just getting on to the market. Off, therefore, we set and made for Buxton where, on the surrounding hills, the snow was pretty deep. We managed nevertheless to unearth a few possibles and Gordon did a nice piece about the car, coupled (I nearly said padded out) with a potted history of Buxton and its surroundings based on a map dated 1610 which we happened to find in our hotel.

When the Rally actually took place, Jack Barclay lent me his own personal Rolls-Royce Wraith (bearing his famous "JB 1" number plates) for the event, complete with a very charming young lady from the staff of the *Queen* magazine. We also had Jack Bergel with us; he was then motoring correspondent of the London *Evening News*. Nothing too terrifying in the shape of hills or tracks came our way and the Rolls gave us a nice comfortable ride, devoid, as was the Wraith's wont, of any fireworks in the shape of lurid performance on the test hills; really, of course, the car had been entered with an eye to the Concours d'Elégance.

This was held on the Madeira Drive at Brighton after the conclusion of the road section, and the Wraith certainly did bristle with gadgets. There was Jack Barclay's backgammon board elegantly enshrouded in walnut in the rear compartment, together with a cocktail cabinet, a smoker's companion suitably furnished with a stock of Havanas in the armrest and—great novelty—a glass roof underneath the normal one; the latter slid back at the touch of a switch to allow the occupants to have sunshine without draught.

Equally novel was the interior heater and demister for the inside of the windscreen, specially imported from America to amaze the poor untutored British. Naturally, JB 1 won the Concours hands down—and, at the same moment as the judges gave it the award, Jack's other mount—an equine by the name of Salmon Bar—was winning the 3.30 race at Hurst Park by three lengths, Gordon Richards up.

The Germans had, as the result of that poll I recorded when we passed through on the way to Lithuania, voted

Hitler full dictatorial powers over their country and their lives to the extent of practically 100 per cent of the population. It would indeed have been strange if there had been any back-sliders or non-voters, and doubtless unhealthy for them!

The shadow of war grew darker as the summer progressed, but the Cavalcade of British cars to the U.S. went off successfully in June with Sir Malcolm Campbell heading it. Some good may have been done in letting a proportion of Americans see that this little old country (which was going to more or less ruin itself holding the fort for them whilst they dithered about entering the fray) really did make automobiles. At any rate, Hitler's blow fell on us on September 3rd, 1939, and once again in most people's lifetime we were at war with Germany.

A Second "Post-war"

THE SHADOWS OF WAR TURN INTO SUBSTANCE.
THE MOTOR INDUSTRY ONCE AGAIN PROVES THAT
IT IS VITAL TO THE LIFE OF OUR NATION. BUT THE
SELLING OF NEW CARS CEASES AND ANCILLARY
ACTIVITIES SUCH AS PUBLICITY AND SERVICING
FACE A HARD TIME

It was a foregone conclusion that the making of civilian
motor cars would cease almost immediately war was
declared and that any need for publicising them would do
likewise. Equally obvious was it that motoring holidays on
the Continent were finished for an unknown period and—in
my case—that neither Press and Allied Services nor Autocheques was going to stay in business much longer. The
Rootes very sportingly gave Owen and myself three months'
notice instead of shutting us off overnight, as they might well
have done, so I had time to sit back and try to think up
what to do.

Meanwhile, my son John was over in America, where he
had been paying a visit to some friends I made in Boston on
that pre-Cavalcade trip with Graham Lyon. I hoped he
would stay there, as his hosts very kindly suggested, but he
wanted to come home, and sailed back on the last voyage the
Mauretania made in civilian guise. It did not add to our peace
of mind to hear "Lord Haw-Haw" say on the German radio
that they knew the *Mauretania* was about to sail and would
lie in wait for her. We heard no more until a telegram arrived

from Liverpool from John saying that he was safely back in his own country.

I personally was then nudging fifty and not at all anxious to join anything connected with the government, even if a chance happened along. Graham Lyon quickly went off to Devon to try to find a likely place where he could open an hotel, and came back with a very promising offer of an empty country house at Totnes, about halfway between Exeter and Plymouth. Some ten miles inland from Torquay, it was well situated, remote from the town and practically isolated, therefore likely to be immune from bombing (which everyone expected to start immediately war was declared). There followed, however, the period of the "phoney" war, when nothing much happened to prove that Europe's best armed country was gunning for us.

G. L. got his hotel, which he named "Château Bellevue", into working order just before Christmas 1939; he invited me down to see it and I was the first guest to sleep in it—alone, in fact, for his only staff was Nellie Pamplin, who had been a faithful member of Autocheques for several years, and she, together with the Lyons, lived in the lodge at the entrance to the drive. Hence I, the mice and whatever ghosts there were had the "Château" to ourselves. Christmas Eve saw some guests installed, and soon after I returned to London to follow up an invitation from the Motor Agents' Association to think up a campaign whereby retail motor traders and garages might be saved from what, in many cases, appeared imminent bankruptcy.

The first six months of the war was a very curious period: petrol was rationed but there was no ban on pleasure motoring. Many private owners nevertheless felt it was the patriotic thing not to use their cars, and the government ignored any potential warlike services which the retail motor trade might be able to offer. Prominent in M.A.A. affairs at the time was George Lucas, a Southampton motor trader (later Lord Lucas), and he presided over a committee specially set up to deal with the problem; members of this committee were the Editors of *Motor Trader*, *Motor Commerce* (now *Motor Industry*) and *Garage and Motor Agent*. The idea of a Motor Trade War Executive was conceived to put the case for the retail motor trader before the country at large, and the chairmanship of it was accepted by Herbert Austin (who was by now Lord Austin of Longbridge, K.B.E., LL.D., J.P.).

I was appointed to look after the formulation of the campaign, the publicising of it; this I did from the M.A.A.'s offices in Great Portland Street. Inaugurated in the opening months of 1940 it was greeted with strong support from the Press at large. *The Motor* put it thus: "Hail to a new Stenson Cooke. In this year of grace, 1940, he has arisen in the person of Dudley Noble.

"Not since the days when the young Automobile Association fought with great energy and determination for the freedom of motoring from the thraldom of the horse age have we seen such a fight put up as the campaign organised by the Public Relations Officer of the Motor Trade War Executive." (Incidentally, this must have been one of the very first times the term P.R.O. was used in Britain.)

I went round the country making impassioned speeches at meetings, luncheons and Press conferences, and the "Keep the Road Wheels Turning" campaign, as we christened it, certainly made its case heard. In the end it did bring about the desired results.

As 1940 drew on, the phoney side of the war gave way to Nazi aggression. They invaded Denmark and Norway on April 9th, and Belgium, Holland and Luxembourg the following day. The British Expeditionary Force evacuated France between May 31st and June 4th, and Paris fell on June 14th. France surrendered three days later, with General de Gaulle safely ensconced in London, where he sheltered for the next few years. Italy entered the war on the side of the Germans on June 11th.

The big blitz on England started on September 7th/8th, peaking in raids on London when thousands were killed and immense damage done. While the night raids continued, my wife and I regularly spent the dark hours in the well-appointed shelter deep down in the M.A.A. offices, where we could hear bombs dropping all around but never had a direct hit. Meanwhile, son John, too young still to join up, had taken on a camouflaging job with the Lonsdale Hands' organisation and was away in the West Country.

During the daytime, when I would be working in my office on the third floor of 201 Great Portland Street, it was possible from the balcony to look southwards towards Oxford Street and northwards to Regent's Park; often there was not one solitary vehicle to be seen on this whole stretch of at least a mile. Eventually the M.A.A. decided the War Executive's campaign had been successful, at about the end of 1940, with the enlistment of machine shops at suitable retailers' servicing facilities working on production or repair of war material.

My engagement was terminated. What next to do?

I went down to Totnes to give Graham Lyon a hand running his hotel, as he was feeling the strain and wanted a holiday. When he returned it seemed to me that a good line of country for my wife and self would be hotel management, and in no time at all we found ourselves in charge of the Possingworth Park Hotel at Heathfield in East Sussex. This was a large country-house type of place, the guests being mainly wealthy refugees from the bombing of London—one of them happened to be Jack Barclay's mother, and he visited her quite often.

It was pleasant for a time, and we paid frequent visits to Eastbourne on our car to do shopping, but soon the general atmosphere and some of the old grumblers got us down. We

therefore transferred ourselves to a much livelier setting—
the George and Dragon at Wargrave, Berkshire, right on the
banks of the Thames, between Henley and Reading. This
was a compact place with bars as well as a few residents in
a mere five letting rooms.

Coping with a bar trade was something new to us, but I
solved that problem by getting a very old friend and his wife
to help us out. They were Jackie and Bee Masters, who were
feeling the war just as much as we were, mourning the days
when one could motor as one wished. Jackie had been
Secretary of the Motor Cycling Club, which ran the historic
trials from London to Exeter at Christmas, to Land's End at
Easter and to Edinburgh at Whitsun. He had taken on a
job with the Hotels and Restaurants Association, but Bee was
at a loose end. She jumped at my invitation to take charge
of our bars—her dream of a perfect job.

So the Masters came and lived at the George and Dragon,
where Bee was a wonderful success and soon built up a
devoted clientèle among the locals and the hotel residents.
Rationing was a nuisance, of course, especially meat, but
I discovered that the local butcher badly needed sugar, of
which we had plenty, whereas we equally badly needed more
meat. I flatter myself that we gave jolly good value for the
five bob we were allowed to charge for a main meal!
Rationing of spirits was also a decided nuisance, but it so
happened that one of our residents who went up to town
every day was the director of a wine company, and the dear
old boy would stagger home every so often with a decidedly
heavy knapsack.

Our "bar flies" were many and various, starting each
morning with the local postman, who came in about
ten o'clock (opening time) for a pint of mild. On Bee's first
morning he looked at his mug and growled, "Wot's this,
mum, gone all 'oly?" She hadn't a clue what he meant
until he added, "Got a parson's collar on, ain't it?"—for as

the froth subsided the level was down about half an inch. He never had to mention it again, and before long he, like most of the customers, had succumbed to Bee's cheery chatter. I should add that, at this writing, Bee is very much as she always was, though nearing her century and everyone hoping she will make it.

Not far distant from the George and Dragon was White Waltham aerodrome, from which quite a lot of our old friends—and some new ones—would pay us visits. Notables were Tommy Wisdom, then in the R.A.F., and Tommy Rose the famous pilot, while Bud Flanagan lived only down the road and I was able one after-closing-time to alleviate his raging toothache with an appropriate spirituous potion from the bar.

And so the war years rolled along until, in 1943, there were signs of peace being within hailing distance. From the Rootes came an intimation that they were thinking about restarting their publicity and as, by this time, hotel-keeping had lost most of its glamour, we said farewell to Wargrave and returned to London.

I have already noted that the Rootes went in for the Shadow aero scheme in a big way, and had airframe factories at both Speke, Liverpool, and Stoke-on-Trent. Billy wanted to have a film made of this war effort—he was knighted for it, also for his services at the Ministry of Supply, in 1942. To cope with this, and also with the mounting degree of what I may term pre-post-war motor publicity, I persuaded the Rootes that I needed an assistant and could suggest nobody more suitable than Jackie Masters, who joined on January 1st, 1944, in that capacity.

This left me free to go from factory to factory with the filming crew and, as cost was increasing all the time, Billy decided that a new contract must be drawn up with the producing company. He gave me definite instructions that no more film was to be shot until this had been done.

It so happened that I had arranged with Harold Heath, in charge at Stoke, that filming would start there on the following day, and when no film gang appeared he naturally asked Billy why he had been let down. The next thing was a furious telephone call to me from Billy at his suite in Claridges. I reminded him of his instructions, but his only reply was "Don't be a bloody fool!"

Now, although Billy called most of us at some time or another a b— f—, it got me on the raw on this occasion: I slammed the receiver down, collected my hat and walked out of Devonshire House for ever (at least, so far as being on the staff of Rootes was concerned). Off to the Northumberland Avenue Turkish baths I went, for I knew from past experience that Billy's temper would subside as quickly as it had arisen. At least he couldn't get at me there.

I had made up my mind some time before this that there was not much more future for me with the Rootes, as at this particular time (May 1944) I was already well over fifty and Billy had outlined plans for publicity once the war ended. "I'm going to have all young men here," he told me one day when we visited the mezzanine floor offices which had been shut off since 1939, and, with no pension to look forward to, it sounded ominous. My ponderings on the subject had made me feel that I should work on a freelance basis from my own office, and I had already got one in mind, in Fleet Street. Now I was able to settle for it and the main problem was to pay the rent and so forth.

At this point in the war the R.A.F. and U.S.A.F. were mounting massive attacks on Germany in preparation for the Allied landings in Normandy on June 6th, but we too were at the receiving end of robot bombs. Every day over a hundred people were being killed in London by them— first the V.1 ram-jet pilotless missiles coming over from launching pads in Northern France, and later the V.2

rockets which kept up a succession of attacks on London and the southern areas of England.

The worst part about these V.2s was that they arrived without any warning, whereas the V.1s could at least be seen as they crossed the Channel coast and were often intercepted by fighter planes. One became almost unconcerned about the sirens, even at night, and the general exodus to London tube stations practically ceased in 1944, while during the day one went about one's business almost normally. But it was not until the end of March 1945 that the V.2s finally ceased to fall, some six weeks before the German surrender.

Plenty of commissions came my way once I was installed at 107 Fleet Street. One of the first (for reasons I can't now remember) came from the Polish Forces in Britain. The Motor Agents' Association and the Society of Motor Manufacturers and Traders were also early clients, while H. J. Cunningham, Editor of the *Export Trader* (an Iliffe publication), was overjoyed to find someone who could help him with his then single-handed job of getting it, and the *Motor Trader*, out every so often.

The same went for the man who was running the *Commercial Vehicle Users' Journal*, now known as *Commercial Vehicles*, while Hector Caird, owner of the *Queen*, wanted to resume a regular motoring article. Off my own bat I decided to publish a digest of all the news likely to interest firms in the motor and allied industries every week, and brought the *Automotive Press Digest* into existence. It still goes strong, and many are the tributes to its utility which continually reach me today.

What stands out in my mind most, though, was the conception, as the result of meeting up at the Press Club in 1944 with Laurie Cade, then Food Correspondent of the *Star*, of the Motoring Correspondents' Circle, now called the Guild of Motoring Writers. Laurie was telling me about the "Circle" to which all the F.C.s of the newspapers belonged—

rationing, of course, being one of the most topical subjects in those days—when, with motoring likely to be possible soon, we both simultaneously came out with the thought "Why not start one for Motoring Correspondents?"

Discussing the idea further at the Press Club, we decided to approach such of the pre-war motoring pressmen as were still on their papers, or whose whereabouts we knew, and get their reactions. These proved favourable, and so we called a meeting and drew up a statement which would go out to everyone likely to be interested, saying that a Motoring Correspondents' Circle had formally come into existence.

Meanwhile I had been writing some potted biographies of leading motor industry personalities for the *Export Trader*, and had done one about Billy Rootes. It brought a telegram threatening a libel action although I must say that *I* thought it had been couched in a most amicable way. So to Devonshire House I went, saw Billy and talked things over, and we parted on good terms; in fact, thereafter we were more friendly than ever before.

He asked me to take on the launching and editing of a magazine devoted to Guernsey cattle, in which he was very much wrapped up at this period, at his estate at Stype, near Hungerford in Berkshire. (Brother Reggie, I should add, was equally engrossed with a pedigree Jersey herd at *his* estate near Maidstone. Farming during wartime was a favourite and not unrewarding sideline of most business tycoons, even if not a financial success—which was usually the last thing desired!)

The autumn of 1944 drew on: Brussels was liberated on September 3rd, Lyons and Antwerp the following day and Ostend on the 8th; but then came the tragedy of Arnhem and a hiatus in the Allied advance through Europe which went on until mid-October, and even in December the Germans were counter-attacking in Belgium and Luxembourg. Christmas Day, my diary tells me, was frosty, with snow in the country, but it was a day of liberation for British motorists too, for they no longer had to use masks on their headlamps. For my wife and myself it was a day of special rejoicing because son John, then just turned twenty, was home from Canada, where he had been training for the R.A.F. and had brand new wings proudly displayed on his tunic.

Life in London was beginning to assume some semblance of pre-war in spite of the occasional V.2 the Germans were lobbing over; the motor industry was girding up its loins in preparation for a return to car production. The Society of Motor Manufacturers and Traders, where Reggie Rootes had succeeded brother Billy as President, felt it should prepare a volume of self-congratulation to be issued in 1946, when the industry would commemorate what it was agreed was its Golden Jubilee.

I was asked to write the portion dealing with private cars, while G. McKenzie Junner, then Editor of *Commercial Motor*, dealt with the heavies. The title of the book was chosen with much circumspection—*Vital to the Life of the Nation*. It related the history of the various firms which had played such a big part in winning two wars, with special emphasis on the Shadow Aero Engine scheme. I may, perhaps, be forgiven for quoting one or two passages from this book:

> Self-reliant and experienced in a hard school, the motor industry, by its own endeavours, raised itself from an experimental institution, dependent upon the patronage of the rich few, to a universal supplier of a commodity which contributes to the economic life of the nation to the extent that this cannot exist without it at all in war, and hardly less in times of peace. The motor car is inextricably bound up with the security of our country, and the industry that makes the car is an essential ingredient in the prosperity and economic future of Britain . . .

There are, however, certain major obstacles in the way of the realisation of bright prospects for the future. One of the greatest is taxation . . . In the last complete pre-war year this totalled, from all forms of mechanical transport, no less a sum than £87,674,000. So far as private cars were concerned, the yield of the horse-power tax (at the rate of 15s. per h.p.) was £16,819,373, an average of £8·78 per car. From the petrol tax of fourpence per gallon the contribution was £51,600,000 . . . Yet that tax has since been increased by 66⅔ per cent, while, under the cubic capacity basis due to be imposed on January 1st, 1947, it seems improbable that there will be any alleviation . . .

The purchase tax, too, which is now levied on all new cars, will undoubtedly prove a deterrent in the home market once the immediate abnormal demand is satisfied . . . The third major obstacle in the way of the motor industry realising its full potentiality in the nation's economy is that of roads . . . All signs point to the urgent need for the planning of better highways without the least delay, and it is to be hoped that the Motorways which road users and authorities alike have been demanding for many years will begin to take shape before long.

At the beginning of World War II the total number of motor vehicles in use on the roads of Britain was somewhat over two million (*vide* the S.M.M. & T.'s year book for 1938, issued in July 1939).

The war ended on August 13th, 1945, with the surrender of the Japanese, and the British motor industry commenced its rather painful return to civilian activities with—as in the case of post-first-war days—very much enlarged factory capacity, plus the problem of divesting itself of aero engine mentality and machinery where the firms concerned had participated in the Shadow Scheme.

Striding Forward—Whither?

POST-WORLD WAR II BRINGS HOME THE INESCAP-
ABLE FACT THAT BRITAIN MUST PAY FOR HER
IMPORTS BY SELLING GOODS ABROAD BECAUSE HER
FORMER INVESTMENTS OVERSEAS HAD HAD TO BE
SOLD OFF TO FINANCE THE WAR IN ITS EARLY
STAGES, WHEN THE U.S. INSISTED ON "CASH AND
CARRY" FOR THE ARMS AND STORES SHE SUPPLIED.
THE BRITISH MOTOR INDUSTRY PULLS ITS SOCKS
UP AND RISES TO THE EMERGENCY

Internally, most British motor factories had undergone a
ruthless change; nevertheless, in a remarkably short period
cars were coming off the assembly lines. They were to all
intents and purposes the same as the ones in production when
war had broken out—in other words, the 1940 models which
would have been at the 1939 Motor Show, had it been held.
In a transport-starved world the demand for them was overwhelming, and the Government required the industry to
send not less than half its production to overseas markets.
During 1945, in fact, a new car could only be bought by a
U.K. resident with a permit issued by the Ministry of War
Transport. A basic ration of petrol was restored, sufficient
for about 200 miles per month for pleasure motoring.

Rumours of brand new cars floated around, and in the
autumn of 1945 I was commissioned by the then popular
weekly journal *Picture Post* to go and report on a "People's
Car" due to be manufactured at Grantham. I went up there,
to a factory operated by William Kendall which had been

manufacturing anti-aircraft guns, and found that Mr. Kendall was not only the Member of Parliament for the borough in which his factory was located, but also a member of the Institutes of Mechanical, Automobile and Production Engineers.

He had been, before the war, works manager in Paris for Citroen, and so it was reasonable to suppose that he had a pretty comprehensive knowledge of the making of a motor car. Kendall showed me the prototype of his new job—which I believe was the only one ever to be built—and it certainly had some novel points. First was that its engine was a three-cylinder *radial* mounted at the tail, air-cooled and with the exhaust directed on to vanes projecting from the fly-wheel.

Suspension was by hydraulic buffers all round and the saloon body was in pressed steel with two doors, each with sliding windows, and hinged rear quarter lights. Air to cool the 700 c.c. engine was drawn in at the front and passed along the underside of the floor. Sixty miles an hour was claimed, and forty miles to the gallon. There was one head-lamp only, with a side lamp on each wing, and altogether it was not at all a bad-looking car for its time. Kendall hoped he would be able to sell it for around a hundred pounds, but the recently introduced purchase tax made this seem an impossibility, in spite of talk about large scale production.

But alas for Kendall's hope of keeping his wartime staff employed: never another word was heard about the car to which he gave his name. The same fate overtook an American attempt to build a "People's Car" at this time; called the "Playboy" it had a small four-cylinder water-cooled engine at the rear, independent suspension on all four wheels, and was about the same size as the original Austin Seven.

On the other hand, Dr. Ferdinand Porsche's Volkswagen, built to Hitler's command and well-proven in wartime use by the German Army, was restarted on what was to prove a wildly successful civilian career. British R.E.M.E. officers got the shattered plant at Wolfsburg going as a means of relieving the destitution which existed in 1945 in a defeated Germany, and, incidentally, one of the first production Volkswagens was sent to England with the suggestion that it might be a good idea if the design were taken over by our motor industry and the VW Anglicised.

Inspected by what was said to be a team of "experts", their verdict was that the car was too ugly, noisy, flimsy and unorthodox. Billy Rootes, then the President of the Society of Motor Manufacturers and Traders, together with other of our industry's chiefs, accepted this verdict. They predicted that, if the Germans went ahead with the VW design of Porsche "It would mean no undue economic competition in world markets vis-à-vis British products." It should, in extenuation of this apparently poor judgment, be mentioned that Henry Ford II, assisted by *his* technical advisers, had previously come to the same conclusion.

Meanwhile, with so much devastation in France, Germany and Italy, we were the only nation able to supply any tangible quantity of cars and unfortunately they were definitely sub-standard in quality. Strikes were prevalent and there was a general air of discontent among the workers: a Labour government under Clement Attlee had taken over from Winston Churchill in July 1945 and Sir Stafford Cripps was inflicting pet Socialist theories on the country, crippling it in similar fashion to a more recent experience.

One amongst the motor manufacturers who was influenced by Cripps was John Black of Standards—now a knight for his services to the Shadow aero scheme. He was urged to get out of the British rut of building only small cars at popular prices, with the result that the Standard Vanguard was planned and put on the market in 1947. With 1,850 c.c. four-cylinder overhead valve engine developing 65 b.h.p., and having a claimed top speed of 80 m.p.h., petrol consumption of 27 m.p.g., six-seater body, independent front

suspension and Lockheed hydraulic brakes, it was expected
to sell for around £500, inclusive of p.t. However, a new
model took as long then to bring to the production stage as it
does today, and meanwhile Sir John wanted something to
fill the big new factory near Tile Hill where aero engines
had been in occupation.

Enter then one Harry Ferguson, just back from the U.S.
after breaking off relations with Henry Ford I in regard to
his tractor—or, rather, the Ferguson System as Harry used
to insist on calling it. He himself was a North of Ireland man
whose connection with motoring went back to motorcycling
days before World War I (when both he and I had ridden in
the then "classic" Irish End-to-End trial). He invented a
lightweight farm tractor of which the outstanding novelty
was an ingenious hydraulic lifting mechanism at the rear,
allowing various farming implements to be attached
and manipulated thereby without much human effort being
required. This Ferguson System was taken up by Henry
Ford I and Harry Ferguson struck up a personal friendship
with him—which, as so often happened in the Ford organisation, abruptly ended.

The two H. F.s had (to quote from a pamphlet issued in
1944, which contained a photograph of them smiling at one
another across a table on which was a model of the Ferguson
tractor) "reached an agreement to mechanise the world's
farms, with Ferguson's new and revolutionary, small, light,
low-cost, indestructible tractor and implements that would
eliminate animal power on the farm and produce at half the
cost.

"This, in turn, will proportionately reduce the cost of
living and raise the standard of life. It will cut the vicious
spiral of ever-increasing wages and prices. It will start the
greatest wealth-creating, employment-giving era in the
world's history and benefit the whole of mankind." (This is
an excerpt from a speech Harry Ferguson delivered to

delegates of the International Food Conference at Bethesda, Maryland, on June 5th, 1943.)

He further stated that Henry Ford agreed that his Fordson tractor did not meet "our objectives", and that General Motors' tractor was "an even greater failure". In fact, Ferguson went on, "All the companies making tractors today are scarcely touching the fringe of the possible world tractor business."

It is obvious from the foregoing that Harry was no mean spell-binder, but he could not swing his first contact in the U.K.—Lord Nuffield—into taking up his System for Britain. John Black, however, proved more amenable and entered into negotiations to manufacture the tractor, and here I was invoked to lend a hand. Black had, as a matter of fact, asked me to join him at Standard when I left the Rootes, but I had had enough of tycoons and replied that I would do anything in my power to help him without actually becoming a member of his staff. The first thing he wanted me to do was to act as a go-between with H. F., as the two men seemed to have taken a dislike to one another after the tractor negotiations had begun.

Sir John Black thought that he should be making overtures to the farming community if he were to become a member of it, and I think my editing of that Guernsey cattle magazine for Billy Rootes indicated that I knew an oxtail from an ox tongue. At any rate, I wrote speeches for Sir John to deliver to farmers' meetings, and the routine was for me to present these to him over breakfast at Mallory Court, his (or, rather, the Standard Co.'s) mansion near Leamington Spa.

Next, I would hear from him the things he wanted to convey to Harry Ferguson, apart from what he put in writing, and it was then my job to go to Claridges, where H. F. was living with his wife and daughter while negotiations were in progress. After telling him the various points which Sir John wanted cleared up, Harry would discuss these with Mrs. F.

and eventually daughter would be told to get her typewriter out and put down on paper what the *Famille* Ferguson had to say in reply. This I conveyed to Black's holy of holies at Banner Lane, Coventry, works, where his large, de luxe office was, I imagine, similar to Mussolini's in his heyday. In due time the match of wits ended with the tractor going into production at Standard's ex-Shadow Scheme works, and the productive capacity gap was filled to everyone's satisfaction for several years at least.

The "System" was introduced to the farming and general Press with a demonstration of typically flamboyant Ferguson publicity flair. Up the steps from Brook Street, in the heart of Mayfair, H. F. himself drove his tractor into the ballroom of dignified Claridge's Hotel, wherein a small square area had been roped off. Inside this he proved—to quote his own words again—"The Ferguson System can be operated by a child in small fields and awkward corners, and makes the horse look as foolish in a field as he would now look in a factory." Ferguson was at this time instigating Court proceedings against Henry Ford in the States for contravening his patents and, as we all know, the outcome was to make him a millionaire.

Meanwhile, the Motoring Correspondents' Circle was well under way, and I quote from the *Newspaper World* of June 16th, 1945: "With the return of the basic petrol ration recently and the announcement of plans for car production, the Motoring Correspondent is beginning to resume his former activities and can look forward to a position of still greater importance. He now has his own organisation, the Motoring Correspondents' Circle having been formed last year as a purely social link between those engaged in writing about motoring for the lay Press. It is not a 'Group', and does not seek to impose restrictions upon members as to individual initiative in news-getting."

We had a regular monthly luncheon, to which one (or more) leading personality in the motor industry was invited. These were very informal affairs and there were no speeches but, naturally, if a guest had some item of news to expound it did not fall upon deaf ears. Our first guests were Sir William and Mr. R. C. Rootes, and we held the party at the Cheshire Cheese in Fleet Street, which seemed an appropriate setting. Later came Sir John Black, bearing a scale model of the Triumph Ensign which he was planning to follow the not very successful Vanguard.

Then there was Sir Bernard Docker, at the time head of Daimler, with George Hally, his managing director. Mr. L. P. Lord and Mr. E. L. Payton from Austin were our next guests, while Emanuel Shinwell, who was at the time Minister of Fuel and Power, came on one occasion and talked to us like a Dutch uncle, sipping the while at a second bottle of whisky (which I had to beg from the restaurant's management, for spirits were then still very hard to come by and one only was our quota). Two esteemed guests were Capt. Phillips, general manager of the Royal Automobile Club, and his opposite number of the Automobile Association, W. V. Gibson, or "Gibbie" as everyone knew him. To quote again from the *Newspaper World*:

Chairman of the Circle is Laurence H. Cade, who has been a motoring reporter for more than thirty-five years, and is the doyen of motoring correspondents [this was in 1945, remember]. Other members are Mrs. Kay Petre of the *Daily Sketch*, Major Oliver Stewart of *The Tatler*, Ronald Strode (Kemsley Group), James Stuart (*Evening Standard*), F. J. C. Pignon (*Daily Mail*), J. N. Bennett (*Daily Herald*), J. Jellen (*Scotsman*), Basil Cardew (*Daily Express*), Sidney Henschel (*Financial News*), John Prince (*The Times*), Alan Tomkins (*Sunday Dispatch*), the Hon. Maynard Greville (*Country Life*), Frank Hardy (*Irish*

Times), Ralph Feilden (*The Recorder and Imperial Review*), W. A. Gibson Martin (*Liverpool Journal of Commerce*) and Dudley Noble (*The Queen*). Members who are temporarily in the Forces are Antony Johnson (*Daily Mirror*), John Prioleau (*Observer*), T. H. Wisdom (*Daily Herald*) and R. H. Walling (*Evening Standard*).

Poor Jack Bergel of the *Evening News* had been killed in a flying accident, and not yet replaced.

The photograph which accompanied this story was captioned "Motoring journalists recently visited Cowley, where Lord Nuffield told them about his tour of Australia. On the left are Sir Miles Thomas, vice-chairman of the Nuffield Organisation, Basil Cardew, H. J. Cunningham (*Motor Trader*), Walter Boyle (*Garage & Motor Agent*) and, on Lord Nuffield's left, Laurence Cade, Dudley Noble, Ralph Feilden, R. Strode, Kay Petre, Geoffrey Smith (Iliffe Press) and F. J. C. Pignon."

The actual photograph is one that I naturally treasured as a landmark in the Circle's history, since it was the first such record in the M.C.C.'s existence. I sent it to the Guild of Motoring Writers' archives, inaugurated and once carefully supervised by that veteran of the motoring world, St. John C. Nixon, who as a boy actually went through the famous Thousand Miles' Trial of the A.C.G.B.I. in 1900.

In passing, I must mention that this outing to Cowley was not the first get-together of such motoring correspondents as were active in their jobs towards the end of the war. Whilst I was still with the Rootes, and they were making war vehicles, Billy agreed it would be a good idea if we ran a little Press party to let the chaps see how the things could nip around on rough country. So we took about forty representatives of all sorts of publications, many of them specially for overseas, up to Stafford from Euston early in November 1943, and had half a dozen vehicles dash about the rougher parts of Cannock Chase and sample the kind of stuff these Humbers would tackle.

One of our party was from *Motor Cycling*, and he added some local colour by reporting in his issue of November 11th, "I have just got home from a day spent trying out four-wheeled military vehicles in the wilds of Staffs. The show had been arranged by the Rootes Group, and Dudley Noble invited me to go along. Older readers will remember him as a most successful rider of Rover motorcycles just before the first war . . . I did not feel so sure that a motorcycle could have got round the course that these Humber cars took, and in any case no rider could possibly have endured the physical strain for very long."

A little while after this Sir Bernard Docker invited the Circle to go to Coventry and then on to Stoneleigh Park to perform similar antics with Daimler Scout cars, of which his company had turned out a considerable quantity for the Army. Lunch was served in one of the shops at the Daimler factory, and after we were all seated Sir Bernard strode in accompanied by a huge dog. At that time he (Sir B., not the dog) wore an enormous moustache, and Laurie Cade christened him "Tally-ho", a nickname which stuck to him in Press circles for a long while, until he became clean-shaven.

This was just before the final relegation of war products to the limbo of forgotten things so far as the motor industry was concerned, and everyone's thoughts were turning back towards the joys of peace, including tourism. We had had a Travel Association in Britain before the war to stimulate visitors to come to the U.K., and this had been kept faintly alive with an office in Arlington House, where the Secretary —and his secretary—whiled away the time (possibly) playing noughts and crosses.

When peace loomed ahead, plus the necessity for this country of ours to earn foreign currency in a big way, a crash publicity programme had to be thought up to let the

world know that we were not completely in ruins, and anyhow such ruins as there were made interesting viewing for
visitors who had not been bombed day and night for a few
years. Hotel accommodation was difficult, because government departments infested most of those which still stood,
but it occurred to me—and I had now been appointed Press
Officer for the Travel Association—that liners might lie in the
London Docks and serve as floating hotels.

The first enterprising company to adopt this plan was
Swedish Lloyd, and among the various Press parties which I
organised to beat up publicity was one for visitors from the
first of its ships. The company's managing director came
over for it, and we struck up a friendship, the outcome of
which was that my wife and I were invited to go over to
Gothenburg with our new small car and have a bit of a tour
round Sweden.

What a change it was to go from dingy, damaged, still
darkened London to a city where everything was just as it
had been in 1939—except that certain items of food were
rationed (bread, butter and meat, if I remember rightly).
But petrol was to be had for the asking, and very cheaply, so
for the next few weeks we revelled in being able to motor
where we liked, staying in excellent hotels and living like
civilised beings once again. I think we covered fully a couple
of thousand miles on our gallant little Standard 8 coupé,
which we called "Hugo" because his registration number
was HGO 77.

Photographs today give it a somewhat antiquated look,
and I'm afraid poor Hugo has long been on the scrapheap,
but he served us faithfully and well, with his folding roof
which allowed us to bask in the Scandinavian sunshine. Our
holiday gave Margot, my talented wife, scope for her literary
ability, and soon after we returned home she laid the
charming little piece which I am going to print here on
my desk.

Lax, sill, snapps—three little words, and little words—
but what magic they conjure up; what a wealth of beauty,
what sweet memories of places and friends, in a world of
peace and plenty, lusciousness and bountiful nature—of
forests beyond compare, feasts on board the prettiest ship
I have ever sailed on, feasts in beautifully appointed restaurants, in gardens bright with flowers and trimly kept;
feasts in charming teashops and in lovely homes.

The joys of the table were, however, only some of the
delights of this, our first real holiday since 1939 when war
descended on us. They tasted so much sweeter because of
the grim interlude, but none the less I say with my hand on
my heart that nowhere else in all the world could a better
holiday have been spent than in Sweden . . . Perhaps it
was the knowledge that, 'tween decks, there reposed
Hugo, the sturdy little car we knew we could trust and rely
on to take us anywhere we might seek to go.

The people of Sweden I fell in love with straight away,
from the moment the *Saga* docked in Gothenburg and we
were welcomed with flags and friendship . . . They are an
attractive folk; very hospitable and enamoured of the
open-air life—and as regards this last well they may be, for
they have every outdoor amenity on their doorstep.
Lovely lakes and inland seas for sailing and bathing; end-
less woods of great variety in which to ramble; gardens
brilliant with flowers in which to bask.

To make the most of these delights the great mass of the
Swedish people go from the towns at weekends and holiday
times in the summer, never losing a moment of the short
time that their northern climate permits. Very much did
we notice the deserted air of cities and towns during the
great Midsommer Fest, when everything was at a stand-
still and the great god of Pleasure held sway. The sun shone
with Mediterranean intensity, and never a shaft of it was
lost. Out into the parks, of which every populous centre

had one or more, where restaurants brightly lit after dark provided for the various purses of the inhabitants; the ordinary dining rooms in the hotels closed down to enable staff to work in these "summer houses".

Hugo took us one evening—it was that of the longest day —to a beauty spot called Langedrags, a few miles out of Gothenburg where, of course, there was every facility to eat and watch the sun go down into the sea. Here, perched on the very edge of the water that flows in between the innumerable skerries [rocky islets] that pepper the Sound, hundreds of pretty little yachts sailed colourfully around the sea-girt verandah on which we ate a tasteful meal of freshly-caught fish.

If we hadn't had Hugo with us we would never have seen one half of the loveliness of Sweden. When one day we set off after lunch, his tank full almost to overflowing with unrationed petrol, the road led us up hill and down, round corners and bends, into shadowy woods, past gleaming blue lakes and through tidy little villages. We soon had to give up counting them—the lakes, I mean. They were in such profusion. We would ascend a hill and there would be a lake on our right; we would top the rise and there, below on the left, would be another. Sometimes we could see two or three at the same time, all quite separate and indepen- dent, of varying size and equal beauty. And Hugo was so obliging, with his open-and-shut roof which gave us all the air we wanted but kept out draughts when the sun sank on the horizon and the air turned chill.

Overnight, on our run of about 400 miles from Gothen- burg to Stockholm, we stopped at a delightful motel, called the Gyullene Uttern, or Golden Otter, a very well-known resort on the shores of Lake Vattern, a lake so large that it might almost be called an inland sea. It was growing late when we swung round a bend in the road and there, just ahead, was a castle-like building. Checking in at the reception office, we were given a young "chasseur" who conducted us along a private road descending towards the lake to one of the chalets which, we now saw, dotted the hillside. By the time we had washed and smartened ourselves up a bit it was close on ten o'clock and we were rather shaky about the reception we might get in the dining room. But we need not have worried ourselves—we were served with an excellent meal and with the politeness and complete disregard for time that we had already sampled in Sweden. The chef never seemed to "have gone to bed and locked up the fridge".

Next morning on to Stockholm, "Venice of the North", with its little white steamboats flitting here and there—they say you can go anywhere in and around the city by boat. Everywhere you look there is water and still more water ... But one of my favourite sights was a certain traffic policeman in a little cylindrical box at a busy junction. In it he was raised about three feet above the road and from this daïs he would control the various streams of vehicles with artistic sweeps of white-gloved hands.

He had a technique worthy of the conductor of a large orchestra, who brings on one bank of instruments, or another, with expressive waves of his baton. This young man was both handsome and polished, with dazzlingly white teeth and an engaging smile—but woe betide the driver, cyclist or pedestrian who disobeyed or took the wrong channel; instantly the smile would disappear and be replaced by a dark frown of angry disapproval. All traffic would be halted while the wrongdoer was made to repair his error and listen to a crushing public admonition.

But back to Gothenburg and homewards we had to go, with that couple of days at sea on the *Saga* to soften the blow of leaving the good life of food and petrol aplenty behind us. And so we landed at Tilbury, were reunited with Hugo and made our way into dark and gloomy

London . . . Thus ended our first revival of motoring holidays abroad, and on a £50 travel allowance.

During 1946 Britain's progress towards peacetime functioning was interrupted frequently by strikes and general unrest on the part of the working class population. They voted Winston Churchill out of office as a reward for his magnificent leadership during the war and put a Socialist government under Clement Atlee into power at the General Election on July 26th, 1945. The country's condition rapidly deteriorated: rationing of food grew worse, even bread—which had been free throughout the war—was put on ration. But a small allocation of paper was made available to those who wanted to start new publications (which had been rigorously banned), and after a lot of thought I decided to start a motoring magazine which would appeal to the frustrated British motorist who liked taking his car abroad.

What should its title be? There's so much in a name: I wanted mine to conjure up vistas of the open road and the joy of seeing the milestones flit by—yes, that was it—*Milestones* let's call it. So I went ahead and got out a "dummy" to send around to firms likely to be sufficiently interested to advertise in it, also to the journals dealing with publications generally. The *World's Press News* was kind enough to give it a notice—"something entirely new in the way of quarterly motoring magazines", it said: "Dudley Noble makes *Milestones* smack of the romantic, convey the thrill of driving towards the blue haze of distant mountains and pausing awhile on sunlit shores or in quaint villages and remote cities . . ."

Others were equally welcoming—and remember that this was at a time when all publications, old established or new, were severely rationed as to the quantity they could print. One could seldom buy on a news-stand either the *Autocar* or *Motor* unless one had had an order in years previously.

Except for the commercial vehicle, motor trade and motor-cycling journals, the two mentioned and also the *Light Car* were the only ones in existence (I believe *Practical Motorist* was incorporated in another title during the war years).

At any rate, *Milestones* seemed generally liked, and some faithful subscribers have remained since the first issue, while as for advertisers I would like to mention as staunch supporters Austin, Dunlop, Jaguar, Joseph Lucas, Morris, Rolls-Royce, Rootes—and one whose name has since faded out—Lea-Francis.

This last I must sorrowfully recall for its very human chief, George Leek, from whom I was always sure of a hearty welcome when I was in Coventry—to say nothing of an equally hearty lunch. George, who was formerly the Buyer for Rileys when Victor Riley ran the firm—one of the first in Coventry to produce a rather glamorous small car—had a tiny house adjoining the works in Much Park Street. Here he had a cosy little dining room and a cook whose products (I must say it) were rather more satisfying than those which emanated from the works. Not that the Lea-Francis was too bad a job for its day, and, of course, *any* car made at that particular time could be sold over and over again. In fact, when one was lucky enough to be allowed to buy a new car, an agreement had to be signed with the Motor Trade Association undertaking not to dispose of it within one year. Depending on the make and model, it would then fetch two or three hundred pounds more than one had paid for it new. It can be understood, therefore, that friendly relations with motor manufacturers were something to be fostered.

The book about the motor industry's war effort which McKenzie Junner and I had written, and which was most handsomely produced by my old friend Alfred Pemberton, was published to coincide with the Jubilee celebrations laid on by the Society of Motor Manufacturers and Traders. These included a cavalcade of ancient and modern cars in

Regent's Park on July 27th, 1946, in the presence of King
George VI and Queen Mary, with much pomp and circum-
stance. A week later the basic petrol ration was increased by
half and the roads started to get busy again over the August
Bank Holiday at the beginning of that month.

The first post-war Paris motor show was held in early
October 1946, at the Grand Palais on the Champs Elysées,
and was more or less dominated by British firms, who were
still the only ones with any real production yet under way.
Signs of things to come appeared in certain prototypes,
notably the 750 Renault with rear engine, which had been
designed secretly during the German Occupation.

According to Saint Loup's biography of Louis Renault, a
prototype had been in existence since 1941, when the
veteran motoring journalist Charles Faroux (later to become
a member of our Guild of Motoring Writers) was invited to
have a trial run in it. Renault's trusted designer, Serre, told
Faroux they had made it "in the Tricoche workshop. It's
verboten. You have no idea what tricks we played to keep the
Germans away."

In 1944 Louis Renault was denounced by the newspaper
Humanité after the Liberation; he was imprisoned, broke
down in health as a result of a conspiracy of ill-treatment in
Fresnes prison and died on October 24th, 1944. The accusa-
tion of collaboration is believed to have been unfounded, but
the outcome of Renault's death was that his factories were
nationalised in January 1945 under the title of Régie
Renault, and have so remained.

At any rate, France was recovering at a remarkably rapid
rate, and most of the main roads were motorable, although
déviations were numerous on account of blown bridges. But
tourism was being encouraged, and visitors from abroad
with cars could get petrol coupons entitling them to 100 litres
on landing and then apply for further supplies at the rate of

fifty litres weekly from the Banque de France in most large towns.

Graham Lyon had gone back into the travel business again, supplementing it with an hotel in Dover, from which port one car ferry a day was making a round trip across the Channel. The hotel, now the White Cliffs, had been before the war the Brown House, and I was able to introduce G. L. to Mr. Cecil Byford, general manager of the Dover Harbour Board, whose property it was. Though in a pretty horrible state when we first inspected it, despite the prolonged bombardment from across the Channel, the fabric was not seriously damaged, although the interior was a shambles.

To furnish an hotel at that particular time was not an easy matter, with soft goods on ration and coupons difficult to come by. Luckily, however, through my appointment with the Travel Association, I found it possible to get Graham a special allocation, but by roundabout means, for Attlee's government had no policy for encouraging visitors to come to Britain.

Indeed, the whole country seemed to be sinking lower and lower into the Socialist mud. At any rate, the White Cliffs Hotel opened its doors eventually; the only proper one Dover then boasted, for all the pre-war establishments had been blitzed. Mrs. Lyon, a Frenchwoman, played a big part in its décor; she was really quite a marvel in this sphere and made a little go a very long way in the furnishing line.

But, once the White Cliffs was in good working order, Graham itched to get into something else—a hotel in France, somewhere near the Channel ports. One day he made me an urgent telephone call: would I run over with him and look at a château he thought he might be able to acquire? Naturally, I was game and so off we went to Calais and on to Étaples by train, where we took the one daily diesel railcar (of which only rumours had yet been heard in Britain)—to Montreuil-sur-Mer. The mer retreated centuries ago, and the once fortified town stands at the top of a long and winding hill which is still Route Nationale no. 1, even though where it passes through a short tunnel in the fortifications there is only room for one vehicle at a time.

We climbed wearily up the hill in the breaking dawn, since the train landed us at Montreuil station early on a winter's day and, at the summit, found the Château de Montreuil. This was the old original one, which a brief inspection showed to have been so neglected during the Occupation that it would take a mint of money to put it back in habitable order.

In the grounds at the back, however, stood a modern "dower house", a moderately large villa which seemed in pretty good condition. It was inhabited by a caretaker with a swarm of children, whose nappies and other intimate garments hung from numerous clothes lines. Inside we found no extensive damage—it appeared that a German officers' mess had been housed there—and it had quite a number of rooms on the upper floors, probably enough to sleep thirty or so people. The entrance hall was sufficiently big to make an adequate dining room, and off it opened a smaller one suitable for a bar.

The problem now was to find the owner, but we did ascertain that his name (believe it or not) was Wooster, and that he was probably somewhere in Paris. Off we set the next morning, therefore, and Graham went straight to the Ritz Hôtel bar, which he said was the best place to find anyone's whereabouts in the capital. Sure enough, when he asked George, the barman, if he knew a Mr. Wooster, the reply was, "Certainly, sir, he should be in any moment."

And it was so; introductions were effected, negotiations proceeded. The Woosters never wanted to live in the château again because it had been "tainted" by the presence of Germans under its roof. They had several other residences scattered around the Continent (being wealthy members of

the family owning the European yeast monopoly or something similar) and G. L. could lease it if he wished and turn
it into an hotel. Which, of course, he hastened to do and
thereby achieved his ambition of having an hotel for
British motorists on each side of the Channel. Of course,
there was none of that clothing coupon nonsense in France:
one just paid the price asked for what one wanted, and got it.

The revival in motoring sparked off by the Jubilee
celebrations caused the Royal Automobile Club to feel that
they should commemorate *their* fiftieth anniversary, having
been founded (as the Automobile Club of Great Britain,
with Ireland tacked on a little later) in 1897. I was asked to
edit this and willingly accepted, for Harry Stanley, then
assistant secretary, was a great friend. The plan called for
the head of every department to compile a history of his
particular section, while I would open the book with a
comprehensive account of how it all started and generally
edit the whole story into a coherent narrative. This would
involve having a room set aside within the clubhouse in Pall
Mall, where all the old documents and archives could be
assembled and referred to, without ever leaving the building.

It may be remembered that the winter of 1946/47 was one
of the very worst Britain ever went through, starting off with
snow and frost in December and, after a brief let-up,
following on with unbroken hard weather until early March.
During this period I worked daily at the Club, where a bedroom (with bed removed) was laid out as an office and each
morning, arriving half frozen, there would be a blazing coal
fire roaring cheerfully up the chimney.

Work proceeded steadily and cosily and, by the end of
February, nearly everything was with the printers for setting.
This was nicely according to plan, for we—my wife, Kay
Petre and self—had decided we would drive across France to
the Geneva motor show, the first since 1939, and opening on
March 13th, 1947. We aimed to get there in time for the

girls to have their longed-for bout of shopping in neutral, prosperous Switzerland.

We had borrowed a Lea-Francis from George Leek, and at midday on the Friday preceding show week set forth over still frostbound roads to Dover. Crossing the next morning we found road conditions if anything worse, and only just managed to scramble up some of the hills on R.N.1 which, under normal circumstances, one hardly notices. We got through to Compiègne by evening, where an hotel called the Palais (now out of existence) took us in.

The place was freezingly cold, and they explained there wasn't yet any fuel or gas for heating, and very little for cooking, so we had to make the best of it. On next day towards Switzerland, with a lunch stop at Châtillon-sur-Seine, where the kindly propriétaire brought footwarmers for Margot and Kay. They had been perished in the car—no heaters yet!

The weather and roads had now cheered up a lot, and we arrived in Geneva by early evening to be gladdened, as in Sweden, by neon signs, well-stocked shops and nice food, even if ration tickets did still have to be given up for meat, butter and bread. The Lea-Francis had brought us through without a hitch, and I made some good publicity for George Leek in both the *Queen* and the *Sunday Observer* (for which I was writing now that John Prioleau had decided to retire).

Here at Geneva, as in Paris, the show contained little other than British cars available for reasonably early delivery. With its hard currency, Switzerland was a much sought-after market, and it was a great pity we sent so many dud cars to them in those early post-war days—they have taken a lot of living down.

I seem to have been pretty busy that summer, for I see a cutting in *World's Press News* of July 17th, 1947, said, "Dudley Noble, one of the most active writers in Fleet Street on motoring, was televised in B.B.C.'s picture page programme last week on motoring in post-war Europe—his points covering condition of roads, petrol supplies, food and accommodation. His quarterly magazine *Milestones* is now developing into a publication catering mainly for motorists who like touring the Continent—shortly after this B.B.C. engagement, Dudley dashed off to it again. Apart from that activity, he is just finishing up the R.A.C.'s Jubilee Book to commemorate the fiftieth anniversary of that body this autumn. He is doing a book on London for the Travel Association, has recently done one on road signs for the British Road Federation and is now engaged on another dealing with the intimate operating side of London's Underground for publication by Clarence Winchester with the co-operation of the L.P.T.B."

In 1947 the Guild of Motoring Writers continued its monthly luncheons to notable personalities both inside and outside the motor industry. To one of them the Editors of the leading motoring journals were invited, with a view to making it clear that the Guild would welcome their membership. This had been withheld because of some malignant rumours put about on the formation of the Circle by one of their staff in the Midlands. But even after this olive branch, it was obvious that the "big boys" of the two main publishing houses were still "agin" members of their staffs joining. Indeed, it was to be another dozen or so years before the old generation passed away and with it a more enlightened attitude came about.

Early in 1948, Tom Wisdom now being Chairman, he put forward the suggestion that the Guild should become international by inviting distinguished foreign personalities of the motoring Press to accept honorary membership. Charles Faroux, who had been the originator of the Le Mans 24-Hour Race and was justly regarded as the Grand Old Man of French automobile journalism, gladly accepted, and the Guild was all the richer. It was, alas, short-lived, for he was then eighty years old. Jacques Miral and Maurice Henry were two more who accepted from France, while Robert Braunschweig likewise honoured us, he being the Editor of Switzerland's principal motoring journal *Automobil Revue/ Revue Automobile.*

At about the same time "Bill" (W. F.) Bradley, retired from the Paris staff of the *Autocar*, but still living in France, became a member. As I have mentioned, he had reported the ill-fated Paris–Madrid among other epic races of the very early days, and stayed on in Paris under the German Occupation. Thrown into a concentration camp in spite of his advanced age, he had luckily survived to see peace break out once more. Another distinguished motoring writer in France—Jacques Loste—joined the Guild, and gave it invaluable service by organising, at the time of every Salon de l'Automobile, a dinner for members and their guests in the historic premises of the Automobile Club de France overlooking the Place de la Concorde. And yet a further influential addition to the Guild's overseas membership was Count "Johnnie" Lurani, of Italy.

His Grace the Duke of Richmond and Gordon, who had been prominent in the motoring world before the 1939 war, when among other activities he wrote for the *Sunday Referee* as the Earl of March, was invited to become the Guild's President. He accepted, and was of tremendous help to the Guild in these its formative years. When Tom Wisdom, who had proposed him as our President, likewise suggested that the foreign journalists who were to visit the first post-war Earls Court motor show might be invited to "have a go" on British cars at the Goodwood circuit, the Duke most readily agreed. Thus came into being, on Sunday, October 31st, 1948 (my fifty-sixth birthday, incidentally), the event which has acquired international stature and been widely copied abroad. I remember it well, as Maurice Chevalier used to say—the thick fog in the morning which rolled away before noon and gave our guests a lovely sunny autumnal view of this most beautiful part of England.

However, the Guild had taken on itself the responsibility of giving a free lunch to all who attended, and Sidney Henschel, now the Guild's Hon. Treasurer, had to report a deficit in our scanty finances of some £80 when the caterers' bill came to hand. But the day had been a roaring success; we scorned the idea of receiving a subsidy from the motor industry, and a whip-round among members raised most of the deficit—which Laurie Cade finally wiped out with a lordly flourish of his cheque book. Membership at that time totalled forty-eight, a big jump from the previous year, when it was only fifteen. Six of the newcomers were overseas members and another eleven were Associate members—this category accommodating artists, photographers and radio personalities who, under the original rules, had not been eligible at all for membership.

I have mentioned earlier that heaters for the inside of a saloon had not been general practice on British cars—in fact, there was no standardised fitment that could be applied to the quantity-produced type. But now that Sir Leonard Lord was head of the Austin Co., and had conceived the idea of selling British cars to North America (which seemed to most of us like sending coals to Newcastle)—and, moreover, had actually been across the Atlantic and returned with firm orders—something had to be done about fitting heaters as a regular thing.

Into the breach stepped Smiths, the motor accessory manufacturers of Cricklewood, who produced what seemed like suitable equipment. Britain is not, however, a country where winter *always* brings intense cold, and so, after developing their product here as far as they could, Smiths decided to send an expedition to the place in Europe which, they had been advised, was consistently well below freezing point in January and February. This was Tynset in Norway, a township some 150 miles north of Oslo. Frank Hurn, Smiths' managing director and in charge of the project, invited me to go along and keep a journalistic record of the testing, take photographs and come back with a story.

Towards the end of January 1949, therefore, I joined up at Newcastle-on-Tyne with a little party of about a dozen, plus six cars from different manufacturers. We went across in a quite small boat, which all but stood on its head during the journey through a very angry North Sea. It arrived safely at Oslo and, after one day there making friends with the important firm of Erik Winter, who dealt in most British makes of car, and being tipped off by his able "adjutant" Mr. Rød about the complete lack of spirituous liquors for sale anywhere in the region of our destination, we raided the Vinmonopolet and acquired a visitor's ration of gin, whisky and vermouth or wine.

As we drove north the temperature fell, until when we reached Tynset it was 20 degrees below freezing. The roads were a solid block of ice and the countryside really did look like a Christmas card. Our hotel—the one and only—was a wooden building but quite well heated, and my room had a tiny balcony on which I set out my various bottles. There was no doubt about the gin and mixed vermouth (my favourite apéritif) being adequately chilled before meals!

The latter we came to regard as a bit of a joke; first of all a dish of plain boiled potatoes would solemnly be placed on the table—never any other kind—and then, after a wait during which the potatoes became quite cold, the main dish would arrive. Usually it was fish, but now and again some unidentifiable meat was served instead, followed by cheese. No, Tynset was not a centre of gastronomy, and all one could buy to drink, apart from coffee, was weak beer.

The heater testers carried on with their job, both by night as well as by day in order to catch the very lowest temperatures, and some definite progress was made. The man in charge—Cliff Steadman—was keen to do all that could be done under the circumstances, and whenever the sun shone I badgered him to give me the chance of taking photographs. After a fortnight of this he decided that he had completed his programme, and back to Oslo we went; from there I flew with B.E.A. to Northolt, and was never more pleased to see London, damp and slushy though it might be.

My photographs were developed and luckily came out well (I had been afraid of the camera shutter freezing), and enlargements 30 by 20 inches were surprisingly clear. Smiths held a Press party at Vecchi's old Hungaria restaurant and I spoke my piece, which gained them quite a lot of publicity. There was, however, still much development work to be done plus a further testing expedition, about which more anon. I should mention the procedure which Steadman adopted, namely, to have two complete sets of test equipment for every one of the cars, and compare them over a given course at the same average speed, recording interior temperature simultaneously at fifteen different points, with the ambient temperature noted too. Never once during the whole ten days of the testing at Tynset was any car idle for longer than was necessary for the mechanics to work on it, changing the equipment.

Meanwhile, clothes rationing in Britain was abolished in February 1949, but Socialist Chancellor of the Exchequer Stafford Cripps was continually moaning about a balance of payments crisis (which was to culminate in the devaluation of sterling on September 19th). Otherwise, things seemed to be picking up slightly; the British Automobile Racing Club (my old friends the J.C.C. of pre-war) ran their second international race in Jersey, and Johnny Morgan, now General Secretary vice "Bunny" Dyer, asked me to officiate once again as Press Steward, as I had done the previous year at the same event. Bob Gerard won this time on an ERA at 77·10 m.p.h.

At the end of that year, Smiths' second heater expedition was brewing, and Frank Hurn, together with his chief assistant Dick Cave, asked me if I would once more accompany it—to North America this time. Naturally, I jumped at the chance, and on January 20th, 1950, Cliff Steadman and I sailed on the good old *Queen Mary* for New York. Here he joined up with the little fleet of cars for test, which had gone on ahead, and they all set off for Canada's Middle West, where heated British cars were in urgent demand. I stayed behind in N.Y. and started to acquaint the Press of what was afoot, with the aid of the S.M.M. & T.'s resident representative.

First I went round to all the newspaper offices and bearded the auto writers and editors in their dens, telling them what was in train—and not forgetting to put over a spiel about the Guild of Motoring Writers. Next I ran a party for them at the Waldorf Astoria and gave them an explanation of why the British auto industry wanted to sell its products in their country—how we had beggared ourselves keeping Hitler at bay while they (the Americans) dithered about coming into the war. How, too, they had forced us to fall in with their "Cash and Carry" policy to get material to fight with. Rather amazingly, a number of these Press chaps professed to know nothing about this—and certainly their films and propaganda did (and still do) make it appear that they won the war entirely off their own bat.

Promises to join the Guild I got from the auto writers of the *New York Times*, *Herald Tribune*, Associated Press and *Motor*, also the N.Y. representatives of the English *Autocar* and *Motor Cycling*. Then on to Toronto, where I went through the same routine and enrolled the Editors of *Bus and Truck Transport*, *Canadian Automotive Trade*, *Garage Operator*, *Canadian Motorist*, *Motor Magazine* and *Motor in Canada*. Their names and qualifications I duly sent over to London, and they were all elected members at the next Guild committee meeting.

Unfortunately, when it became obvious that we really had nothing to offer them in return for a subscription, most of them jibbed at our Hon. Treasurer's request to part with their good bucks, and so in due time the majority disappeared from our list of members. Rather a pity, I felt, seeing that it cost us nothing to keep them on and certainly added to the Guild's prestige.

The testing of the heater-fitted cars was done from Winnipeg, whose *Free Press* took notice of our activities by a piece on February 16th, 1950, headed "Auto Testers from England Hit Bad Weather", which went on to say we were disappointed with the mild weather. " 'British car manufacturers are determined to do everything they possibly can to meet the requirements of the Canadian market,' said Dudley Noble at the Fort Garry Hotel Wednesday. The chief problem had been to find space in the small car to install a heater large enough to cope with Canadian winter. The cars tested here are equipped with elaborate electrical recording apparatus which permits an observer to read off the exact temperature throughout the car. Findings will be incorporated in the manufacture of British cars in time for shipments to Canada next winter, Mr. Noble said."

Winnipeg has a really cold climate in February. It's a topic of conversation, and they have put up a large clock-like face in a main street to tell you just how many degrees below zero it is. If a stranger dashes at you with a handful of snow and rubs it on your nose he isn't picking a quarrel but probably saving your nasal projection from being frostbitten—a nasty thing, they told me. The evening I arrived to take up my booking at the Fort Garry Hotel I was feeling pretty frozen and asked the hall porter where the bar was. "No bars in Manitoba," he replied in a shocked voice, so that was that —the super-heating of the hotel had to do the trick.

Heater testing proceeded and eventually Smiths' men reached their target of being able to drive throughout the coldest of nights in shirtsleeves. Steadman and I did an all-night run to Dauphin and back—around 300 miles—with our jackets off, listening all the while to some broadcasting station which was pouring out lively music and commercials.

My job seemed to be done, and so I flew back with my films via Chicago and New York early in March 1950. Smiths were now getting down to large scale heater production and the British car was on the map in North America; from under 10,000 exported there in 1946 the total soared to over 54,000 in 1949, and hit 117,000 in 1950 (S.M.M. & T. figures). Len Lord's raid on the hard currency markets had paid off, and several other leading European makers now followed his example.

In May 1950 the R.A.C. organised the first really big race meeting at Silverstone, the disused airfield leased by the Club from the Air Ministry. This was the Grand Prix d'Europe, and I was asked to act as Press Steward. Since King George VI and Queen Mary were to grace the meeting by their presence, there was naturally an overwhelming demand for Press passes. The R.A.C. was pretty stingy with the number they made available and I had to dole them out with a somewhat grudging hand.

I was nearly floored by the demand put in by the B.B.C., and thought that Raymond Baxter (whom I then met for the first time) must be pulling my leg and bringing the whole staff of Broadcasting House for a day out in the country. I didn't realise on that occasion what an extensive crew is needed even for sound radio, but luckily Harry Stanley, Secretary of the meeting, came across with further supplies of passes and in the end everyone seemed satisfied—or nearly.

The meeting went off well; the weather was pretty good and there was a "matyness" in those early days about Silverstone and racing generally which has unfortunately departed since meetings, would-be racing champs and alleged

Pressmen have proliferated. The royal patrons made this first post-war Grand Prix d'Europe a notable occasion and Farina, who won it on an Alfa Romeo, was uniquely honoured by having the reigning monarch of the still existant British Empire present him with the trophy. The Guild of Motoring Writers managed to lay themselves on a mobile bar which, even if it had no royal patrons that day, at least entertained numerous notabilities of the motoring world.

A fortnight later, at Whitsun 1950, the Auto-Cycle Union's Secretary, Sam Huggett, asked me if I would undertake a similar rôle—Chief Press Steward—at the Tourist Trophy Races in the Isle of Man. My diary reminds me that I was able to fly over by B.E.A. from Northolt, such was progress, also that there was now a telephone to the mainland to save having to write out interminable Press telegrams, as we were obliged to do before the war. Again all went off well, and the *World's Press News* was kind enough to say that, "Most of the important motoring correspondents visited the Island, as well as a host of reporters from the provincial Press and news agencies, and all were very pleased with the facilities provided."

Things were now getting back to normal in the world of cars: John Black took a party of us over to Belgium to see speed trials of his new Triumph on the Jabbeke section of the Ostend–Brussels autoroute. Rovers had produced their first gas turbine-engined car and did likewise. The Guild committee asked Spencer Wilks if he would let it be demonstrated at Motor Show Test Day (for the record, he wouldn't).

Nevertheless, M.S.T.D. was again a great success in 1950 on the Sunday midway through motor show week, with large numbers of foreign journalists eager to try out the latest British cars. Once more the Guild financed everything out of its own kitty, and luckily Sidney Henschel had been able to persuade Lord Drogheda, his chief at the *Financial Times*, together with the head man of the *News Chronicle* (Charles Fothergill, the incoming Guild chairman being the *News Chronicle* motoring correspondent), that a donation would not come amiss, and they parted with fifty guineas apiece. Thus was disaster averted and the Guild enabled to enter 1951 with a credit balance of £130.

This was augmented in due course by the publication of a special Guild issue of *Milestones*, to which many of the members contributed articles and passed their fees in payment of them over to the Hon. Treasurer. At last, it seemed, the financial corner had been turned, and on a now sound foundation Sidney was able to build up a healthy balance which, when he eventually resigned the treasurership ten years later, had reached four figures.

At the A.G.M. of 1950 I, as Hon. Sec., reported that our membership had now passed the hundred mark, having gone up during the year from sixty-six to 104. Also that the Duke of Richmond and Gordon had consented to remain President, and, further, that John Cobb, then holder of the world land speed record, would be a vice-president. Harold Nockolds, *The Times*' motoring correspondent at that time, became vice-chairman and would thus be Chairman the following year, while Tom Wisdom was presented with the Harold Pemberton Memorial trophy.

Len Lord was not unnaturally cock-a-hoop at his break-in to the North American market, but he had little patience with the criticisms which the Press generally levelled at British motor manufacturers. He complained that much of what was published was written by those who knew very little, if anything, about the vexations and problems attendant upon exporters trying to find new markets.

I remember Len telling a party of motoring writers in his forthright manner, "You blighters are putting out a lot of tripe—I can't blame you because you've probably never been to America and Canada, or South Africa and Australia, and you don't understand the local conditions. So I'm going to give you the chance of doing just that." And he did.

On July 27th, 1951, therefore, a party of about twenty-five of us went over to Montreal on a plane which Austins chartered from B.O.A.C.—one of those long obsolete double-decker Stratocruisers, with a little saloon downstairs, piloted by that bearded veteran Capt. O. P. Jones. Len Lord met us at various points; one was Hamilton, Ontario, where there was a big disused wartime factory which he thought would make an assembly plant, but did not go ahead with the project. After this we went visiting the sales and service depots of such Austin distributors as there then were between Ottawa and Vancouver.

So far our journeying had been by plane, but at Vancouver we took to the road on a covey of A.40s and headed into the rising sun through typical Canadian scenery—tall pine trees and lakes gleaming like mirrors. We were three to a car, and some of the crews stopped for a wayside bathe—in the "altogether". Our trio consisted of Mrs. Kay Petre, of the now defunct *Daily Graphic*, and Ken Obank of the *Sunday Observer*, and I noticed Kay diplomatically admiring the scenery on the other side of the road whenever one of the all-male crews was glimpsed disporting itself naked and unashamed in the water or on the shore.

Three hours' driving brought us to an inn set in a forest clearing—Pine Woods Lodge, Manning Park—where a man-size breakfast was waiting, and a packed lunch was handed us as we departed. In due course exploration of this revealed that a half bottle of the wine of the country had been included ("champagne style"), and when the urge to eat came upon us we found a nice secluded lakeside clearing.

Ken Obank sampled his bottle first; with a wry face he suggested we also have a taste. One was enough, and without further ado each bottle found a watery grave. The food was pretty good, though. On, then, to a little place called

Revelstoke, where the solitary hotel—grandiloquently named the King Edward—proved to have a decided shortage of rooms, and Kay was the only one to get a sole tenancy.

Anyhow, we didn't arrive till best part of midnight and were due away at 6 a.m. for Banff, so there wasn't much time for sleep. The route was over what is now part of the Trans-Canada Highway, but then it was just an exceedingly rough track. Dust rose in clouds, and incidentally made us realise that British cars needed a lot of attention being paid to their body sealing. As I have said, this was before the days of monocoque construction or, of course, of fresh air ventilation. All one could do was try to keep well behind the car ahead.

Over the summit of the Rocky Mountains the track led us to the Great Divide, and as we descended the other side the trans-continental express was making its painful climb in a series of loops, headed by a couple of enormous locomotives belching dense clouds of smoke and steam. Then down to Lake Louise, whose water is so amazingly blue that it seems unnatural—due, I believe, to a mineral in its bed which makes it unsafe for bathing.

Banff Springs at last, where the vast hotel (nicknamed the "largest railway station in the world") swallowed up our party without disarranging any of the hundreds of guests already in residence. The only thing it seemed to lack was a bar, but luckily Sam Haynes, one of our hosts from Austins, had stocked up a suite with a nice collection of Scotch, bourbon and gin, plus suitable additives, and so we went down in good condition to appreciate a "dry" dinner.

Next day was an "easy", when we raided Banff town to acquire suitable souvenirs and the only diversion to report was an attack by bears on the way back to the hotel. They roamed freely about the trees, and evidently thought that Tom Wisdom and Harold Nockolds looked tasty dishes. Neither was devoured, but it made a good topic of

conversation in Sam Haynes' parlour before lunch, with
some on the side of the bears and others feeling that it might
perhaps be better to keep the party intact in view of hotel
and plane reservations—and, of course, the fact that they
were both so popular.

Evening saw us on the road again, bound for Calgary,
about a 2½-hour drive. En route some red-coated "Mounties"
got the impression that the Austins were exceeding the local
speed limit, but they let us off with a wigging. Eventually the
lights of Calgary spread themselves across the horizon and
one of my illusions—that this was a wooden-shed cattle town
—went west. It proved to be a real big place where, around
11 p.m., we were being right royally entertained on the
nineteenth floor of the Palliser Hotel by the distributor of
Austins for Southern Alberta, who was handing round what
tasted like real hard liquor. We reciprocated in our fashion
by visiting his showrooms—yes, and his spare parts department—soon after 6 a.m. next day, when a long run was on
the schedule.

First, both Ken Obank and I received a rocket from Kay
Petre for not having cleaned up the back compartment of
our car, in which the now decidedly rotting remains of the
fruit they had given us in Kelowna three days earlier were
not smelling exactly like Chanel No. 5. Placated at length
by our jettisoning all the garbage we could get at, harmony
descended once more and we proceeded onward to Leduc.

Looking exactly like one of those Wild West townships on
the films, Leduc was the hurriedly built centre for the
Canadian oilfields, then only just discovered. We arrived
around lunchtime and were served drinks in the local
saloon's parlour, overlooked from the board sidewalk. To
conform to Albertan law, making it illegal for a passer-by
to be depraved by the sight of boozing in actual progress, the
window shades had to be kept lowered.

Later a move was made to the oilfields themselves,

property of the Imperial Oil Co. of Canada. There wasn't much to see there, just a forest of "Christmas Trees", the name by which the complicated valve apparatus at a well-head is known—no derricks nowadays. This discovery of oil, the first commercial strike in the Dominion, was to prove immensely valuable, as the Minister of Mines and Resources made plain over dinner that evening at Edmonton.

He held forth indeed at some considerable length, and, as we had to be at the local airfield at 2 a.m., we felt we had heard enough when he finally gave over at about ten o'clock. Some had, in fact, already dozed off. The all-night flight lasted until noon next day and we dragged our weary legs around the various showrooms and spare parts departments until a coach took us out to the Granite Club, where Toronto's Scottish élite spend their evenings curling, in kilt and tammy. Then to Niagara Falls for dinner before setting off to Toronto airport to fly on to New York for the night.

Here Nature stepped in to give us a little respite, kindly laying on a thunderstorm to damage propellers and stop flights, so back to Toronto we trundled to rest briefly but comfortably at the Royal York Hotel. We made it to La Guardia airport, N.Y., in time next morning to lunch with the British Ambassador (Sir Gladwyn Jebb as he then was) at the Waldorf-Astoria. He put up a good case for English cars finding a market in North America, but I doubt if any of us realised then that it would be the sports model which would hit the buyers and not the current A.40 type of small saloon.

Austin had nothing of the sporting kind in its range until Len Lord effected a link-up with Donald Healey and the Austin Healey emerged to save the day. And very popular it became in the U.S., both as the Sprite and the big-engined 3000. Then came the amalgamation with Morris in November 1951 and the newly formed British Motor Corporation had the M.G. to offer in addition. Now sales really got moving in North America, and many foreign as well as other British car manufacturers moved in on this potentially rich field.

Len Lord was given a well deserved knighthood in 1954, and, encouraged by the successful results which derived from the fact-finding trip across the Atlantic, he had similar exploratory parties organised to South Africa in 1953 and Australia (including Tasmania) in 1955. "I want you to visit all these markets," he told us, "and see for yourselves what an out-and-out struggle every British motor manufacturer has to fight, and when you return home explain to our politicians that, for beginners, we're making a damn good job of it."

The Rootes, of course, were early in the field on the other side of the "pond", and Billy was appointed head of the Dollar Exports Corporation. In that capacity he made innumerable visits to the States, and although perhaps the products of his own factories were not sufficiently angled to North American taste, at any rate the Rootes' name became well enough known. Rovers, too, made an impact and so, later, did Triumph sports models. But the most amazing penetration of the American market was by Volkswagen, after initial setbacks, and the story of how it was eventually brought about is told in this firm's history books.*

In the first nine years after the end of World War II Volkswagens were virtually unknown in the U.S., except as weird-looking souvenirs which a handful of veterans of the U.S. Army of Occupation had brought home with them from Germany. Originally, however, Heinz Nordhoff had decided to make his first stab at selling the VW in the States, primarily to buy badly-needed American machine tools for Wolfsburg factory. He flew over to New York in late 1949 taking photographs of the "Beetle", but failed to impress a single car dealer there—not one believed it would ever sell in the States, and the Press felt the same way—so one cannot

* By Bernard Hopfinger and Walter Henry Nelson.

entirely blame the Rootes and Henry Ford II for their more or less snap judgment years before. Nordhoff returned to Wolfsburg discouraged, saying that VW would have to make its own way in the world without a source of American dollars.

The following year, nevertheless, Max Hoffmann, who dealt in imported cars in New York (he handled Jaguars at that time and built up a reputation for selling the high-class European cars then growing in popularity in America) took an interest in "the funny little German car called the VW".

Hoffman sold 330 of them in 1950, principally by forcing dealers who wanted delivery of the highly popular Jaguar (for which he was sole U.S. concessionaire) take some VWs as an inducement. This had the effect of making the dealers think there was VW business to be done; the Schmidts of Chicago, for instance, and John von Neumann of Los Angeles; Robert Fergus of Columbus, Ohio, and George Capps of Overland, Missouri, too. By the end of 1953 altogether 2,173 VWs had been sold since 1950. Herr Nordhoff realised that there was, after all, a market in America, and set out to renew his attack on it.

To head it he engaged one Will Van de Kamp, a super-salesman noted for his courtly charm and for being invariably impeccably dressed in Savile Row suit, Homburg hat and carrying a furled umbrella. He believed passionately in the VW and never doubted that it would become a great success in the United States, where he arrived in January 1954. He searched out American dealers who in the main were young, energetic and prepared to devote enthusiasm to selling the Beetle.

In one year Van de Kamp created the beginnings of a national network which formed the pattern of distribution retained even when, in 1958, Volkswagen set up its own selling organisation in the U.S. The following year, in the early autumn, Van de Kamp was killed in a crash on an

autobahn in Germany at the age of fifty. During 1958, however, 120,442 Beetles were sold in the U.S., and since then
their progress is common knowledge.

In May 1955 I received a letter from Stanley Roberts
who, as I recorded much earlier, had founded the British
School of Motoring away back before World War I. This
letter invited me to attend a luncheon at Claridges on June
16th when, following up a suggestion made by the then
Minister of Transport (The Right Hon. John Boyd-
Carpenter), Stanley felt that the time was ripe for the insti-
tution of an Advanced Driving Certificate, in the interests of
improved road safety. The object of the gathering was to
discuss in general terms the next steps to be taken.

About a dozen guests were invited, representative of the
motoring organisations, the Ministry of Transport, Police,
RoSPA, insurance interests, road and transport federations,
and of the motoring Press. Stanley Roberts was in the chair
but, having unfortunately been the victim of a stroke, he was
unable personally to address the meeting; his place was
taken by his most able assistant Miss Denise McCann. She
outlined the Minister's desire that there should be a driving
test of more searching nature than the official one for learners,
something comparable with that taken by candidates for a
master mariner's certificate.

Arising out of this function a steering committee was
formed, on which I was honoured by receiving an invitation
to sit. Meetings took place from time to time in 1955 and
gradually a hard core of enthusiasts emerged who hammered
out the Constitution of an Institute of Advanced Motorists.
Through that winter and the spring following the preliminary work proceeded until, in May 1956, the moment
was near when a public announcement could be made.

Meanwhile, at the annual general meeting of the Guild of
Motoring Writers in December 1955 I was very unexpectedly
elected its Chairman for the subsequent year. It so happened

18—MIAML

that Sidney Henschel and I had made a pact that neither of us would ever stand for Chairman but, at this A.G.M., Basil Cardew of the *Daily Express* quite out of the blue got up and made such a eulogistic spiel about me (bless his heart) that the entire meeting stood on its feet and unanimously agreed —insisted, perhaps I should say—that I accept. There was no option, but luckily Sidney took it in good part. I was now Motoring Correspondent of the *Financial Times*, of which he was a high executive, and very generously he didn't get me the sack.

A few weeks later I set out on the British Motor Corporation's visit to Australia, to which I have referred. Sir Leonard Lord personally planned the trip as Chairman of B.M.C. (Australia) Pty. Ltd., and twenty-nine of we motoring writers, accompanied by Reg Bishop, the popular general publicity manager of the Corporation (he had joined Morris Motors as Press Officer in 1934 and been transferred to B.M.C. on the amalgamation), also our old friend Sam Haynes.

This time we made a complete circle around the world, going out via New York, San Francisco, across the Pacific to Honolulu, then a brief call at tiny Canton Island to refuel, losing Friday of that week as we crossed the international date line and reaching Sydney on the afternoon of Sunday February 26th, 1956. After a short acclimatisation we made from here a thorough tour of assembly plants and distributors' premises in every one of the larger cities and towns, with visits on the side to such interesting projects as the Snowy Mountains Scheme.

Everywhere we received a right royal welcome and the best of good comradeship; incidentally I learnt that being Chairman of the Guild was no sinecure, because at the conclusion of nearly every jamboree I had to be upstanding and return thanks for our entertainment. We got a rota under way when I eventually showed signs of flagging—and dear old Sammy Davis made one of the best of all our speeches when he spoke to the West Australian distributors at Perth. Altogether it was a wonderful experience I wouldn't have missed for worlds; we spent twenty-two happy days in Australia and at the end of our journeyings were presented with the covers of our airline tickets, clipped together and opening out concertina fashion.

The homeward run took us the reverse way round the world, via Darwin, Jakarta, across the Equator and staying overnight at Singapore, where a Chinese tailor made a couple of cheongsams for my wife overnight. Calcutta and Karachi were the next day's stops, then Beirut and Zürich, to arrive at Heathrow on the afternoon of the third day. Yes, Len Lord was a great man: before we left on this trip he had told us how impressed he was by the progress of Australia and the utterly amazing potentialities of its future.

Len had lived his whole life among motors and their making; from early days at Daimler, Hotchkiss and Wolseley he rose to be managing director of Morris Motors in 1932, but had *his* inevitable "row" with W. R. M. four years later, which was when I first met up with him, at the foot of Sunrising Hill, near Banbury, spectating during the progress of a motor trial. He went back to work with Lord Nuffield in 1937, however, administering the latter's two-million-pound trust fund to aid special areas.

The following year he became works director of the Austin Co., rising to deputy chairman and joint managing director, with financial genius Ernest Payton, on Lord Austin's death in May 1941. Len took over as chairman and managing director when E. P. retired, and when the Austin/Nuffield merger was accomplished L. P. L. became its overall chief on Lord Nuffield's retirement in December 1952. His reign continued after he had been raised to the peerage and assumed the title of Lord Lambury, until he decided to retire in the early 'sixties and was succeeded by his friend and protégé, "young" George Harriman.

On my return to London I found that the Institute of Advanced Motorists had progressed to the point where the organisation was practically ready to commence operations. Our hand was forced by a front page splash in the *Sunday Express* of May 20th, 1956, when Robert Glenton let forth news of the "Super Driving Test". He wrote: "There is to be a new driving test for motorists who already hold driving licences. The standard will be high—that of police car drivers—and those who pass will form an élite of the road, with Master Drivers' certificates. The examination, for the time being, will be voluntary. The scheme is sponsored by a group of politicians and road experts and is supported by the Government."

This was, of course, a slight exaggeration; there was no political bias about the Institute, although several members of the Council were Members of Parliament belonging to both Conservative and Labour parties. Nor was the Government providing support in any financial sense, although the Minister of Transport gave the Institute his full approval and appointed a member of his Ministry to sit in at Council meetings as an observer. Later, he appointed a personal representative, Mr. Denis O'Neill, C.B., an Under-Secretary at the M. of T., who for several years gave the Council invaluable help and assistance until, regrettably, he was posted to another division of the Ministry.

The Institute's test, which candidates for membership had—and still have—to pass, was laid down as a straightforward examination without any "tricks". Routes were mapped out in different parts of the country, each containing similar characteristics and having sections of unrestricted speed together with stretches in built-up 30 m.p.h. areas. In a distance of about thirty-five miles every type of road condition and traffic characteristic was included, and the chief duty of the examiners (all of whom had to be holders of Class I—the highest—police driving certificates) was to assess the candidate's ability to handle his vehicle with Skill and Responsibility (a most apt description which was put forward by Mr. Roger Gresham Cooke, C.B.E., M.P., our Vice-Chairman, and adopted as the I.A.M.'s motto).

The Institute was extremely fortunate from the start in having as its Chairman Lord Sempill, a veteran motorist and pioneer aviator, who commanded everybody's respect and devoted a great deal of time, both in the House of Lords and at Council meetings, to the affairs of the Institute. It was also very lucky in securing the services, through the good offices of Miss McCann, of George Eyles as chief of the examining staff. He had had twenty-five years in the mobile police, and was of course holder of that coveted Class I driving certificate. He possessed exactly the right mentality for dealing with voluntary candidates for the advanced test, and also for convincing the motoring Press correspondents who were so helpful to the Institute in its early (and continuing) days. A little while after the inauguration of the I.A.M. in June 1956 another executive who was to become a pillar of the organisation joined, in the person of Robert Byron Peters, as Secretary.

Bad luck struck within a few months of the launching of the Institute: the Suez Crisis broke out in the autumn of 1956 and the consequent rationing of petrol caused a sharp drop in the number of tests conducted. This in spite of the allowance of one gallon which the Ministry of Fuel granted to those who took the test, but which concession the Institute was forbidden to publicise. Nevertheless, up to the end of that year, over 4,000 tests had been carried out in London, Birmingham, Liverpool, Manchester, Newcastle-upon-Tyne, Edinburgh, Bristol, Cardiff and Leeds. The percentages of passes for both men and women candidates were in the region of seventy in the case of the under-forties, and rather lower for the older ones.

The crisis over and petrol back to normal, the Institute

made steady progress. In May 1959, at a reception attended by The Right Hon. Harold Watkinson, then Minister of Transport (now Lord Watkinson), the 10,000th certificate of membership was presented to a lady, Mrs. Daphne Chard; Stirling Moss had been no. 9999. Enthusiastic I.A.M.-ites all over the country were now forming local groups on their own initiative, the idea having been the brainchild of member A. E. Lansdell, an optician of Nottingham, who launched No. 1 Group there in 1957. These Groups have done, and are doing, much valuable work for road safety in their areas.

Billy Rootes, who had devoted a great deal of his time to the promotion of exports to North America—not merely his own firm's productions—was created First Baron Rootes of Ramsbury in 1959. Always an ardent wooer of the Press, and much liked by them in return, it was his custom to invite members of the Guild of Motoring Writers to a cosy little lunch in Paris on the day before the annual Salon de l'Automobile opened in October. At these pleasant functions he often used to talk about his early days and how he and I had both been very minor cogs in wheels which, spinning then at lowish r.p.m., were now whizzing ever faster.

As I have recorded, he and brother Reggie were the Motoring Correspondents' Circle's very first guests in 1945 at luncheon, and now the Guild committee invited W. E. R. to become its first honorary member. He accepted, and presented the magnificent Rootes' Gold Cup, to be awarded annually at the committee's discretion for the most outstanding achievement in the field of motoring by a member of the Guild during the year. So far (to 1968) it has been won by Paul Frère (1960), Tom Wisdom (1961), Bernard Cahier (1962), Joseph Lowrey, Nick Brittan (1965) and Rico Steinemann (1967).

Sir William Lyons, Jaguar's chief, was the next to be invited to become an honorary member, and he, too, did the Guild the honour of accepting: he inaugurated a scholarship designed to find, and give practical experience to, young men desirous of adopting writing about motoring as a career. Then, too, there have been "Friends of the Guild" chosen from among members of the motor industry and others who have been specially helpful to the Press. At this present time, these are Paul Frère, Jack Croft (formerly P.R.O. of Standard-Triumph), Charles Follett, Reg Bishop (now retired from B.M.C.), A. K. Stevenson (for very many years Secretary of the Royal Scottish Automobile Club), Artur Keser of Mercedes-Benz, Robert Sicot (then of Renault and now of Fords), Sir George Harriman, also Wilfrid Andrews, Chairman of the R.A.C., who has always taken the keenest interest in the Guild's welfare, and accommodated it at the Pall Mall clubhouse, where the twenty-fifth anniversary is to take place in 1969, under the chairmanship of my good friend Courtenay Edwards.

But Time, "like an ever flowing stream" as the old hymn has it, bore away many of the men of my generation. Stanley Coryton Hugh Roberts attained three score years and eight in 1957 and passed on in September of that year. It was a far cry from his creation of the first motor driving school in 1910 to its becoming a nation-wide network with the proud title of the biggest organisation of its kind in the world. It had taught nearly two million people to drive.

Always Stanley Roberts laid stress on the absolute importance of teaching the principles of road safety, and thus it was fitting that he should be the creator of the Institute of Advanced Motorists. He also foresaw the great expansion that would take place in the motor and aircraft industries, and founded alongside the British School of Motoring the College of Automobile Engineering to provide training for students not catered for by existing colleges or universities. He always enjoyed, incidentally, the energetic and practical support of the late Lord Wakefield of Hythe, who established the now vast Castrol business after having passed his fortieth birthday.

Lord Rootes had just gone beyond his seventy years when he died on December 12th, 1964. I can add little to what I have already written about his brilliant career: however, some comments from *The Financial Times* are worth quoting. "He has been able to see our dollar earnings doubled in a decade; a good deal more than he may have expected when he pioneered the scheme at the height of the dollar crisis in 1951. He was always an enthusiast for the American way of trade—his first visit there was made in 1920, and so excited him that he made more than fifty since then. He even acquired a slight North American twang in his growling, Kentish voice.

"A genius for salesmanship and the monolithic determination which carried him through the long, agonising Acton strike (and once provoked him to knock a tooth out of an obstructive Customs man) gave him the qualities to see such jobs through. His restless energy—he could never sit still—and a straightforward patriotism sometimes jeered at gave him the drive. His marching orders were simple—'You must add two noughts to your thinking, and we must take the starch out of our stuffed shirts'."

Next of those prominent in my life to go was Lord Sempill, on December 30th, 1965. A real, natural Scottish laird, than whom no one could be more gallant and courteous, we had spent a good deal of time together after the formation of the I.A.M. He was always very reticent about his youthful exploits, but in the 1920s and early 1930s, when he was The Master of Sempill, he made the headlines time and again by his dashing flights, generally in very small aircraft. One that particularly appealed to me was his 1936 return trip Croydon–Berlin, in a B.A.C. "Drone"—the run each way cost him less than 15s. for petrol. A couple of years before this he had flown from England to Australia in a Puss Moth.

The 19th Baron Sempill, he was a representative peer for Scotland; born in 1893 he served an engineering apprenticeship at Rolls-Royce after being educated at Eton. On the outbreak of World War I he first joined the R.F.C., then transferred to the R.N.A.S. and later to the R.A.F., where he was awarded the Air Force Cross. After that he rendered special services to the Italian, Japanese and Swedish Air Forces which brought him high decorations from all the countries concerned. For seven consecutive years he competed in the King's Cup Air Race round Britain (1924–30), and he worked consistently and enthusiastically to further the flying of cheap, light aircraft. He also took an interest in airships, and once hired the Graf Zeppelin to give thirty people a demonstration cruise around England.

His interest in the I.A.M. was great, and he was always prepared as its Chairman (and later President) to go here, there and everywhere opening skidpans, supervising skilful driving events and presiding at road safety gatherings. He invariably charmed mayors and officials of localities where these duties took him by his elegant appreciation of their efforts, and could always be relied on to say exactly the right thing in front of the microphone.

I do greatly treasure the letters he wrote me from time to time, addressing me as "Dudley Mackintosh Noble of that Ilk" and signing himself "Craigievar", the name of his fine old castle in Aberdeenshire. Here one of his delights was to raise steam in the boiler of the three-wheeled vehicle made by "Postie" Lawson in the 'eighties to save his legs on his long round delivering letters. The old crock would still run if properly humoured, but how "Postie" kept it in water I just don't know; there was no condenser and he must have begged a bucketful everywhere he delivered letters. Just before Lord Sempill died the Scottish National Trust took

19—MIAML

over his castle as an outstanding example of a turreted L-plan building dating from the early 1600s.

Next, Len Lord—Lord Lambury of Northfield—President of the British Motor Corporation—passed away suddenly at his retirement home in Devon on September 14th, 1967, aged seventy-one. From what I have already written about him it will be realised that he was of the same forthright character as Billy Rootes. His successor and longtime friend, Sir George Harriman, had taken over the reins at Longbridge when Len relinquished active management in 1961. "He was my guide and mentor during the forty years we had been more or less closely associated," said Sir George: "with his natural gift of leadership he was always a man of decision—a top line man if ever there was one—who directed his team in such a way that whatever the problem or however great the project in hand, he cleared their path, dispelled their doubts and fired them with enthusiasm."

When, in 1963, Lord Sempill knew he would soon have to retire for reasons of health, he caused the I.A.M.'s Council to "place on record its profound gratitude for the skilled manner in which the Hon. Treasurer, Mr. R. K. Munday, has guided the financial policy of the Institute of Advanced Motorists. Without his wide experience and power in the world of finance, the rapid growth of the Institute would not have been possible." It seemed logical, therefore, that "R. K." should be voted into the chair at the next Council meeting, and a very worthy choice he proved.

Besides being a highly successful stockbroker with, as a colleague has said, "a computer-like brain", he is an enthusiast where motoring is concerned. From the days in the 'thirties when he and Mrs. Munday revelled in their motorcycle and sidecar combination to this present, when they peregrinate in a Rolls-Royce Silver Shadow, or a Land-Rover extensively equipped with ciné film-taking apparatus, every leisure hour is spent in motor touring.

Under R. K.'s Chairmanship the I.A.M. has continued steadily to progress, and at the time of writing is within measurable distance of reaching 100,000 members. This means that almost double that number of candidates have spontaneously come forward to take the advanced driving test, since only a proportion pass. For a purely voluntary body which has so far made its own way without subsidy from official or other sources, that is pretty good going and speaks volumes for the great amount of work put in behind the scenes by Chairman Reginald Kenneth Munday.

It is also testimony to the merits of the I.A.M.'s testing methods, its Council and staff, likewise to the efforts of the thousands of enthusiastic members up and down the country who have formed themselves into Groups and carry out much valuable work in regard to road safety generally. Many of these latter sacrifice their weekends in order to help disabled drivers learn to handle their three-wheeled invalid cars properly.

And thus today, we who have seen so much happen in the motoring world during the past half century and more are witnessing the wind of change blowing with gale force. But I could not write finis to this book without referring to one very stable organisation that exists to bring help and comfort to those former members of the motor industry who have fallen on evil days through, perhaps, illness, accident or sheer ill-fortune. A comparatively few dedicated men, conscious of the plight of the many, have carried on a work instigated as far back as 1908 and have brought to fruition ambitious schemes based on solid foundations.

Principally in this connection I would mention H. G. ("Bertie") Henly, C.B.E., founder and for many years President of the famous motor distributing firm which bears his name. Always having had a partially paralysed leg and not, therefore, being able to enjoy golfing, yachting and so on, he threw himself wholeheartedly into working for the good of the Motor and Cycle Trades Benevolent Fund. This had been started in those early years of the century by A. J. Wilson, often called "Faed" because of his inherited deafness.

When Bertie Henly was a youngster, Faed took him on as an assistant with BEN, as the fund is known for short. Sad to relate, he fired him after about eighteen months ("for bad behaviour", H. G. H. records). Bearing no ill will, however, Faed helped Bertie to obtain several jobs in the motor trade and, when the latter was discharged from the Army after the first war, he got one for him with Bayard cars. However, a kindred spirit, Frank Hough, agreed that the two of them should strike out on their own, and so Henlys Ltd. came into existence, but Frank died early on and Bertie was left to proceed alone. This, as most people know, he did with some very considerable success.

BEN continued to be a spare-time activity, but in 1935, when Lord Kenilworth, then head of Armstrong-Siddeley, was President, he insisted that H. G. H. take on the Treasurership. Invested funds stood at some £75,000, and from that time Bertie went all out to build them up, with the result that, as I write, they total very nearly one-and-a-quarter million pounds. This is a great achievement, but H. G. H. is quick to point out that it is not all his own work. He pays tribute to certain influential friends, notably Lord Evans and Claude Wallis, who was formerly head of the Iliffe motor book publishing empire.

Bertie Henly told Claude that BEN required a home for old people, and between them they discovered in 1948 a fine country house called Lynwood, standing in extensive grounds at Sunninghill, Berkshire. This they bought and opened as a home for elderly and infirm retired members of the two trades, free from rules and restrictions—and so friendly has the atmosphere proved that three marriages have taken place between residents whose average age was eighty-one!

But after a while Bertie realised that the old people were getting older and a nursing home was needed.

Our protagonists were then able to buy the one named after Lord Nuffield at Hanger Lane, Ealing, in 1955, but it soon became inadequate for the growing numbers of would-be inmates. As its site was a valuable one, the place was sold for £150,000 (showing a handsome profit) and, with £400,000 added which Bertie had cajoled out of the motor industry—he is a genius at the art of gentle persuasion—the fine new Nuffield Wing was built on to Lynwood. Opened by the Queen Mother in 1965, it raised the accommodation of the home to 120. Two blocks of flats were also built, for those retired persons who could afford to pay rent and look after themselves.

Furthermore, there are at least 400 "out-patient" bene-ficiaries of BEN who receive regular financial assistance. It would be fair to say that literally thousands have good cause to thank the many who have made all this possible. They are to be found in dozens of motor trade groups in every part of this country, who not only contribute funds but take an active interest in the organisation of outings and parties to lighten the everyday routine of Lynwood's inmates. The very existence of BEN and the active spirits behind it have made "life begin again" for many who might otherwise have been down and out after a career in cars—even if they only wrote about them!

Which leads me to the concluding thought that the year this book is published marks the twenty-fifth anniversary of the formation of the Guild of Motoring Writers. From the humble beginnings I have here recorded it is now a highly reputable and influential body, to which it is an honour to belong. I am proud to be one of its Vice Presidents.

FINIS CORONAT OPUS

Index

Saxton, Margot (see Noble, Margot)
Schmidts of Chicago, 228
Schneider Trophy Napier Lion aeroplane engine, 94
Scotsman, 199
Scott, Jack, 156
Scottish Six Days' Trial, 34
screen washer, 125
screen wiper, 125
Searle, Colonel Frank, 79, 80, 81, 88
Segrave, H. O. D. (later Sir Henry), 10, 94, 95
Selden patent holders, 40, 41
self-starter, 46
Sempill, Lord, 233, 236, 237, 238
Senior T.T., 25
Shadow Aero Engine Scheme, 154, 155, 164, 187, 191, 192, 195
Shell, 30, 134, 142, 143
Sherren, Ted, 96
Shinwell, Emanuel, 199
Shrewsbury, Earl of, 144
Sicot, Robert, 235
Siddeley-Deasy, 41, 56
Silverstone, 220
Singer, 8, 32, 41, 42, 46, 59, 91, 92
Sketch, The, 73
Skinner, James T., 150, 151
Smith, Frank, 63
Smith, Geoffrey, 131, 174, 175, 200
Smith, Harry, 22, 29, 69
Smiths' heater expedition to North America, 218, 219, 220
Smiths' heater expedition to Norway, 215, 216, 217
Smiths, motor accessory manufacturers, 215, 217, 220
S.M.M. & T., 132, 218, 220
Sopwith, T. O. M., 38
South African War, 14, 16, 39
Spyker, 4, 5, 39, 43
Sprague, R. W., 72
S.S (Standard Swallow)—see Jaguar
Standard, 41, 91, 132, 155, 197
Standard 8, 202
Standard Triumph, 235

Standard Vanguard, 195
Stanley, Harry, 211, 221
Stanley steam car, 7, 8
Starley, Hubert, 28, 91
Starley, J. K., 26, 28, 69, 72, 74, 79
Starley, Jack, 72
Starley, James, 28
Steadman, Cliff, 217, 218, 220
Steinemann, Rico, 234
Stevenson, A. K., 235
Stewart, Oliver, 174, 199
Straker-Squire, 45
Strand Magazine, 17
Stratocruiser, 223
Strode, Ronald, 199, 200
Stuart, James, 199
Sunbeam, 41, 43, 46, 50, 59, 145, 146
Sunbeam-Talbot, 146, 165, 166, 169, 179
Sunbeam-Talbot-Darracq, 144, 145
Sunday Dispatch, 199
Sunday Express, 144, 232
Sunday Pictorial, 156, 157
suspension, independent front wheel, 125
Swift, 41, 42, 63
Swiss National touring office, 149
Switzerland, tour of, 1937, 149–53
Symons, Humfrey, 126
synchromesh, 125

Talbot, 9, 12, 130, 144
Talbot Ten, 158
Tatler, The, 73, 199
taxation, 192
Temple Press Ltd., 31, 33, 62, 64, 69
"Ten Capitals in Ten Days" tour, 1937, 156, 157
Thomas, C. B., 170, 172
Thomas, Frank, 32
Thomas, Right Hon, J. H., 111
Thomas, W. M. W., (later Sir Miles), 59, 62, 69, 124, 200
Thousand Miles' Trial, 1900, 200
Throssell, George, 149, 150